AF505598

Media and the Presidentialization of Parliamentary Elections

Media and the Presidentialization of Parliamentary Elections

Anthony Mughan
Professor of Political Science
The Ohio State University
USA

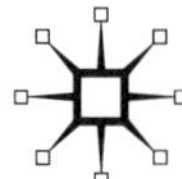

First published 2000 by
PALGRAVE
Houndmills, Basingstoke, Hampshire RG21 6XS and
175 Fifth Avenue, New York, N.Y. 10010
Companies and representatives throughout the world

PALGRAVE is the new global academic imprint of
St. Martin's Press LLC Scholarly and Reference Division and
Palgrave Publishers Ltd (formerly Macmillan Press Ltd).

ISBN 0–333–80018–4

This book is printed on paper suitable for recycling and
made from fully managed and sustained forest sources.

A catalogue record for this book is available
from the British Library.

Library of Congress Cataloging-in-Publication Data
Mughan, Anthony.
    Media and the presidentialization of parliamentary elections / Anthony
    Mughan.
        p. cm.
    Includes bibliographical references and index.
    ISBN 0–333–80018–4
    1. Elections—Great Britain. 2. Political parties—Great Britain.
    3. Political leadership—Great Britain. 4. Great Britain—Politics and
    government—1945– 5. Mass media—Political aspects—Great Britain.
    I. Title.
    JN956 .M82 2000
    324.941'0858—dc21
                                                        00–033291

10   9   8   7   6   5   4   3   2   1
09   08   07   06   05   04   03   02   01   00

Printed and bound in Great Britain by
Antony Rowe Ltd, Chippenham, Wiltshire

To Francis, Peter, Sharon and Terry
My Lifelong friends

Contents

List of Tables

List of Figures

Preface and Acknowledgements

This project was begun in the late 1980s when, on leave from University College, Cardiff, I had the great good fortune to spend a little over three years as a Senior Research Fellow in the Department of Political Science in the Research School of Social Sciences at the Australian National University. I had left a Britain where the Conservative leader, Margaret Thatcher, had been prime minister for some six years and arrived in an Australia where her Labor counterpart, Bob Hawke, seemed the same dominant political figure both within his party and in the country at large. The prevailing orthodoxy that these two leaders, like prime ministers before them, were no larger than their party because both operated in a parliamentary system of government with strong parties just did not tally with my, and many others', perception of the distribution of electoral and governmental influence and power in the two countries at the time. My first effort to untangle this puzzle was a newspaper article asking how two leaders, one of the right and one of the left and so different in personality and style, could each lead their party to its third successive election victory in 1987. Ian McAllister and I then included in the 1987 Australian Election Study that we organized a battery of leader character trait questions that had been part of the 1983 British Election Study. These two sets of questions were then used by Clive Bean and myself to publish an article in the December issue of the 1989 *American Political Science Review* entitled 'Leadership Effects in Parliamentary Elections in Australia and Great Britain'. I am most grateful to my co-author for his generous advice, encouragement and comments, as well as for the insights from his own further work on the topic of party leader effects, in the intervening period.

Once I determind to pursue the study of the presidentialization of parliamentary elections, a number of analytical obstacles soon became clear to me. First, to continue with comparative analysis would be difficult since the wealth of opinion polling, election survey and media content data over time that was available in Britain was rare, if not unique. Second, the longitudinal element of the study was crucial and could not be sacrificed to a more cross-sectional and comparative perspective. Third, in the mid-1980s presidentialization was no more than an emerging force in British electoral politics, which meant that I had to wait for more time points, or elections, to determine whether it was transient or represented a durable change in the dynamics of individual party choice and of election outcomes. This need to let time elapse is the principal reason for the book's long gestation period. Even so, its conclusions are still based on few time points and often-incomplete or inadequate survey data so that it is better regarded as a preliminary investigation into, rather than a finished statement about, the role of party leaders in shaping contemporary parliamentary election outcomes.

In doing the research for this book, I have accumulated a large number of debts to institutions and individuals without whose groundwork this project would not have been possible. Prominent among these are the Gallup polling organization and its former director, Bob Wybrow. Equally, I have drawn heavily on the British Election Studies that have been carried out by various teams (David Butler and Donald Stokes, Ivor Crewe, Bo Särlvik and James Alt, Anthony Heath, Roger Jowell and John Curtice) since 1964. Their service to students of British politics cannot be overstated. No study of this kind can fail to acknowledge its deep debt to David Butler, his various co-authors and their Nuffield election study series. Among them, I would particularly like to thank Martin Harrison for his contributions to this series since 1964. His analyses of the content of television news broadcasts are a backbone of this book; its focus on the media and leader effects would have been impossible without them. Students of the media will always be in his debt for the historical perspective that his contributions to the Nuffield series provides. Finally, the large part of the work for this project has been done at The Ohio State University. I would like to thank the Department of Political Science and the Mershon Center for providing a stimulating intellectual environment and the generous facilities and resources that made it possible, even enjoyable.

Then comes the large number of individuals who have commented on the manuscript in its various forms either in private correspondence or at conferences. Roger Scully, Clive Bean and Paul Webb are to be singled out for having read all or most of the manuscript in its various forms and drafts. While they bear no responsibility for the final product, their comments did at least sometimes stop me from going off in wrong directions or making claims that the evidence did not bear. It is my opinion that the book is stronger for their comments and for that I am grateful. A number of individuals offered helpful and insightful comments on various parts of the manuscript. Hoping that I do not offend anybody by forgetting them, these include John Bartle, Greg Caldeira, Harold Clarke, Kevin Cox, David Farrell, Michael Foley, Richard Hamilton, John Kessel, Jerry Loewenberg, Ian McAllister, Pat

Patterson, Terry Royed, Holli Semetko, Herb Weisberg and Dominic Wring. Lastly, I would like to thank the 23 former cabinet ministers from both the Conservative and Labour parties who agreed to be interviewed by me on the subject of the presidentialization of British politics. All were frank and open and discussion with them was a most informative and exhilarating experience.

My final, and greatest, debt is to family.

1
The Presidentialization Debate

This book is a study of party leaders and the role they play in shaping the conduct and outcome of parliamentary election campaigns. More specifically, it is a systematic evaluation of the widely acclaimed 'presidentialization' of parliamentary election contests. Its background is the traditional notion that parliamentary politics are party politics and, as such, are devoid of the individualistic element found in regimes where the office of president is the main political prize to be won by an individual who may be affiliated with, and supported by, a political party organization but who to a substantial degree runs for office on the basis of his own qualifications, experience, personality and promise.

The conventional view of parliamentary elections is that they are contests between parties representing cleavage groupings – middle vs working class, catholic vs protestant, clerical vs free-thinker, and so on. The personalities of those running for office, it continues, are electorally irrelevant in situations where party systems have been shaped by deep and historically rooted antagonisms that all but monopolize the battle for public office. In the famous words of Lipset and Rokkan (1967: 50): 'The party systems of the 1960s reflect, with but few significant exceptions, the cleavage structures of the 1920s.' With group loyalty and ideological exclusivism being the foundation stones of political party support, the personalities of the individual politicians competing for office were assumed to be of no importance for party choice and election outcomes. Their irrelevance is nicely conveyed by two quotations from Great Britain at the height of the class polarization of its party system in the 1950s and 1960s. The first is an academic assessment of the character of party politics in that country: 'Class is the basis of British party politics; all else is embellishment and detail' (Pulzer 1967: 98). The second comes from an ordinary voter at the time of the 1951 general election; his protestation that 'he'd vote for a pig if his party put one up' (quoted in Butler 1952: 173) vividly suggests the irrelevance of personality compared to party for the British mass public – at least at that time.

At the very time that this conventional wisdom was being propounded, however, cracks in the façade of the monolithic parliamentary party had already begun to appear. In a seminal essay, Otto Kircheimer (1966) presciently underlined the waning of the class-mass and denominational parties that had dominated the parliamentary political and electoral arenas until that time and drew attention to the emergence of the new 'catch-all' party. Compared to its predecessors, this new breed of political party displayed a syndrome of five distinctive characteristics: (i) a drastic reduction in its ideological baggage; (ii) a further strengthening of its top leadership groups; (iii) a downgrading of the role of its individual party members; (iv) a de-emphasis of its relationship with a specific social class or denominational clientele (*classe gardée*) in favour of its recruiting voters from the population at large; and (v) its securing access to a variety of interest groups (Kircheimer 1966: 190).

Kircheimer's key insight was that these changes, taken as a package, were transforming the character of parliamentary politics in the second half of the twentieth century. Other authors had drawn attention to one or other of the changes, but not to their interdependent character. For example, the German Social Democratic party's abandonment of its marxist rhetoric at Bad Godesburg in 1959 or the 'Butskellist' policy consensus shared by the British Conservative and Labour parties in the 1950s and 1960s are but two examples of the ideological depolarization of large West European political parties commonly discussed under the rubric of 'the end of ideology' (Waxman 1969). Depolarization in turn served, among other things, to enable parties in pursuit of office to cast a wider net for votes by broadening their appeal beyond their traditional *classe gardée*. It also made possible a greater differentiation between parties and their leadership as the latter, less closely tied to a party organization and a specific ideological line, came to enjoy greater autonomy in defining party policy over the wide range of issues for which democratic governments generally had assumed responsibility in their construction of the post-war mixed economy and welfare state.

There thus emerged a tendency to personalize politics so that the traditional view that running for office and making policy in government were collective enterprises built around the political party seemed increasingly inapplicable to modern parliamentary democracies. One of the earliest manifestations of personalization emerged in the early 1960s with the thesis that cabinet government in Britain had presidentialized in the sense that prime ministers were no longer primus inter pares, but had come to dominate their cabinets in much the same way that US presidents did (Crossman 1963; see also Weller 1985). Moreover, claims of personalization were not restricted to Britain or to the distribution of power within parliamentary executives. They had become common fare in commentaries on electoral politics as well. International in scope, the claim of an enhanced electoral role and impact for party leaders was rooted in the emergence worldwide of a new style of election campaigning that, to suit the presentational demands of television, pitted personality against personality at the expense of the discussion of relatively complex issues and ideas.[1]

A few examples will suffice to make the point. Take Canada. 'Pierre Elliott Trudeau initially left himself open to accusations of presidentialisation by conducting a vigorous media-oriented campaign in 1968 so effective that the public response was dubbed Trudeaumania' (Campbell 1980: 51). Similarly, 'New Zealand elections since the advent of television in the 1960s have increasingly taken on the style of American presidential campaigns in which rival leaders and their teams tour the country and vie for mass media exposure' (Cleveland 1980: 188). Finally, discussing an upcoming debate between the Labour and Liberal party leaders in the 1984 Australian federal election, a journalist observed: 'The debate will reinforce the strong and growing tendencies to presidential-style political campaigning, with its almost exclusive focus on the styles and personalities of party leaders' (Barker 1984).

Quotations like these abound. More systematic evidence of the move away from party-based campaigning to media-based personality contests comes from a specific comparison over time. In the early 1980s, a study of 21 democracies found that direct confrontations between party leaders on television had taken place in seven parliamentary regimes, Belgium, Canada, Denmark, West Germany, Ireland, Norway and Sweden, and in three presidential or semi-presidential ones, Finland, France and the United States (Smith 1981: 174–5). Such debates became more common over the course of the 1980s and 1990s, however. By the mid-1990s, to Smith's list could be added the parliamentary regimes of Australia, Japan, New Zealand, Spain and Turkey, as well as the semi-presidential Portugal (LeDuc et al. 1996: 45–8).[2]

If anything, then, the personalization of parliamentary elections would seem to have become even more pronounced in the 1980s and

1990s. This development does no more, though, than to reflect changing campaign strategies and styles in the contemporary democratic world. 'The other [that is, in addition to party image] component of a [well-conceived and well-executed campaign], leader image, is taken increasingly seriously in today's campaigns' (Bowler and Farrell 1992: 16). Thus, Helmut Kohl, chancellor of Germany for 16 consecutive years, prepared for the 1998 Bundestag election seeming to dwarf the party he hoped to have returned to office. A plethora of comparisons in the 1980s between the British prime minister Margaret Thatcher and the US president Ronald Reagan frame references to the British head of government in the same presidential way that they do the US one. Indeed, and more generally, the recent evolution of the style and substance of electoral and parliamentary politics in Britain has been described in terms of the rise of a British presidency (Foley 1993; Pryce 1997). The world over, parliamentary elections generally have the appearance less and less of contests between political parties vying for control of government and more and more presidential-style struggles between the leaders of these parties – Major vs Blair in Britain, Campbell vs Chrétien in Canada, Berlusconi vs Prodi in Italy, Jospin vs Juppé in France, Beazley vs Howard in Australia, Kohl vs Schröder in Germany, and so on.

In the face of such evidence, few would deny the claim that the style of parliamentary election campaigning in democracies generally has become more personalized in character. There is continuing disagreement, however, over whether this change in presentational style has had any consequences in substance – that is, whether it has resulted in the party leaders becoming more influential electoral forces in their own right. Certainly, the case has been strongly put that style and substance are separate so that change in the former need have no implications for the latter since the very structure of parliamentarism militates against an independent role, in elections or in government, for parliamentary party leaders. Writing at the end of the 1970s, for example, Rose (1980: 44; see also Hart 1991) insisted: 'The very high degree of institutionalisation in British government...is the most powerful determinant of what a Prime Minister can and cannot do. Personal style influences how a Prime Minister carries out the demands of office, but it does not determine what is to be done.' The same author then reiterates this argument almost a decade later, this time with respect to elections. The nature of executive authority in Britain means that prime ministers need not be a popular political figure for their party to be victorious in elections: 'Because prime ministers are not directly elected by the public, they have less need to cultivate popularity for its own sake. [A party's] success in government is considered the best guarantee of popular success' (Rose 1988: 132). The same general skepticism emerged during a personal interview I conducted with a Conservative politician who had enjoyed high cabinet office under Margaret Thatcher. 'I think I'd want to say that new forms of media have certainly quite altered the way in which the party leader is presented, but I'm not sure that they have been that significant in enhancing his role over what it has been traditionally.'[3]

A student of German politics seems to go so far as even to question whether there has been a personalization of presentational style, let alone of electoral impact, in his country:

> Available evidence for the Federal Republic of Germany reveals that in terms of personalisation of politics in the mass media systemic properties of a parliamentary democracy seem to limit the extent to which individual politicians with significant political roles (such as the candidates for the chancellorship) can come to the forefront in the media … There is no evidence now available that candidate factors are growing in importance in explaining voting choices.
>
> (Kaase 1994: 226–7)

One reason for such disagreement may be that parliamentary democracies differ considerably in their institutional structures and some types of structure may be more conducive to the personalization of presidential style and impact than others. Prime ministers, for example, may be differentially known to voters for enjoying long or short periods in office or for operating in contexts where paid political advertising is allowed on television. But more fundamentally, the disagreement may lay in the absence of a shared operational definition of presidentialism even within countries. The result can be that people talk past each other. Some adopt the minimalist position that presidentialism means simply that leaders enjoy an electoral effect above and beyond that of party. Others are maximalist and equate it with victory in the election for the party of the more popular leader; elections cannot possibly be described as presidential if parties lose elections despite having a more popular leader. In the specific case of Britain, prime ministers Wilson in 1970 and Callaghan in 1979 were the usual examples quoted by the leading Conservative and Labour politicians I interviewed. One stated explicitly, 'Take the 1979 election, for instance. Callaghan led Mrs. Thatcher on personal ratings by a very significant margin. Yet he lost the election quite decisively. Whatever was the case or not the case later, people didn't vote solely for Mrs. Thatcher in 1979. They went Conservative.'

This definitional confusion highlights the point that presidentialization is a much-remarked upon but little-investigated, let alone understood, facet of parliamentary politics. The first step in introducing some order into its discussion, therefore, must be to define the meaning of the terms presidentialism and presidentialization, a task that is undertaken in the next section of this chapter. This section is then followed by a consideration of the merits and shortcomings of the choice of Britain as a case study for systematic investigation of the presidentialization thesis.

Presidentialization defined

Defining presidentialism and presidentialization is no easy matter. Even among those giving some credence to the notion that parliamentary party leaders matter in their own right for party behaviour in both elections and government, these are notions that are all the more complex for having been used in a variety of ways and for having different meanings and connotations, positive and negative, for different people.[4] Few users of the concept have attempted to define it clearly and fewer still have concerned themselves with providing a definition that lends itself readily to empirical analysis. What follows, therefore, is an exercise in piecing together a coherent, testable meaning for the term from assertion, elliptical references and unspoken assumptions in a wide range of sources.

Most simply, presidential implies the opposite of parliamentary. The immediate problem with being any more specific is the absence of agreement on the key characteristics differentiating the two forms of government. Verney (1959: 75–7), for example, identifies no less than 11 such characteristics, whereas Epstein (1968: 149) pares the differences down to a bare minimum, defining parliamentary government as 'the form of constitutional democracy in which executive authority emerges from, and is responsible to, legislative authority'. Synthesizing the literature on this debate, Lijphart (1994) has identified three basic constitutional differences between the two forms of government. First, the president is a one-person executive, whereas prime ministers and their cabinets form a collective executive body. Second, presidential heads of government are popularly elected either directly by the people or indirectly by an electoral college. Parliamentary executives, in contrast, are selected by the legislature. Finally, except in cases of impeachment, a president cannot be forced to resign by a legislature. Heads of government and their cabinets in parliamentary systems, by contrast, are dependent on retaining the confidence of the legislature and can be dismissed, although only collectively, at any time if they lose that confidence.

Running through all three differences is the theme that parliamentary and presidential systems differ most fundamentally in the degree to which the act of governing and being held electorally accountable for it is an individual as opposed to collective responsibility. Presidential institutional arrangements encourage individualism on both counts because they make the person occupying the office of president the ultimate focus of governmental authority and accountability. The authority of the office is bestowed on the individual ensconced in it rather than on the party of which he is the ostensible head. One effect of this is that congressmen sharing the president's party affiliation can routinely deny him their vote in the legislature if individual conscience, ideological conviction, electoral self-interest, or whatever, incline them that way (Edwards 1989). The focus of governmental authority and accountability in parliamentary systems, by contrast, is the cabinet, which, being the executive committee of the legislature, is maintained in office by majority support in the legislature and can be dismissed if it loses that support. The key to winning office is to muster the support of a majority of the parliamentarians to which the cabinet is answerable and the key to retaining it is to keep that majority loyal. National elections thus become contests between parties seeking to maximize the number of parliamentary seats they win and not between individuals concerned to take control of a single office.[5]

In short, parliamentary government is first and foremost government by party and parliamentary elections contests between parties, and not even the most enthusiastic advocate of the increasing importance of personality in such elections would deny the political party its continuing primacy in them.[6] The term presidentialization therefore implies movement over time away from collective to personalized government, movement away from a pattern of governmental and electoral politics dominated by the political party towards one where the party leader becomes a more autonomous political force. It implies, in other words, convergence on the individualist American model. Importantly, however, such convergence can take several forms, all of which may be said to constitute presidentialization but not all of which conform to the meaning of the term in the specific sense in which it will be used in this book. Three such forms of presidentialization are the product of: (i) constitutional change; (ii) evolutionary change in the absence of constitutional change; and (iii) transient political circumstance.[7]

Constitutional presidentialization occurs when parliamentary constitutions are written or amended with the specific intention of empowering the party leader heading the government at the expense of the parties constituting it. The Federal Republic of Germany is an example. In an attempt to ward off the instability that helped to bring about the downfall of the Weimar Republic, the Basic Law implemented after the Second World War departs from parliamentary practice and vests an individual, the Chancellor, with a number of constitutionally entrenched powers over his cabinet. Thus, on the basis of his survey of executive leadership in Germany since 1949, Johnson (1983: 67) concludes:

> This outline of the position and powers of the Federal Chancellor has underlined the extent to which strong leadership by the head of Government has been established as an established convention and expectation in the Federal Republic…(O)n the basis of the experience of the past thirty years there is no doubt that for the purposes of classification the German type of Cabinet government deserves the epithet 'prime ministerial' or even 'presidential'.[8]

Another example of this type of presidentialization is the 1996 revision of the Israeli constitution to allow for the direct election of the prime minister. Just as with the Federal Republic of Germany, this reform was passed precisely to enhance governmental stability and efficiency by giving the chief executive greater control over smaller parties in habitually fragmented coalition governments (Lazin 1997: 217–19).

The presidential transformation of parliamentary systems of government can take a de facto as well as a de jure form. That is, the relationship between prime ministers and other political actors, even cabinet members, can be fundamentally altered to the advantage of the former without the constitution being amended. This was the essence of Crossman's (1963) claim that cabinet government in Britain had given way to prime ministerial government. Although hotly contested from the outset (see, for example, the essays in King 1985), this thesis has recently been rejuvenated in the specific context of the sources to which British prime ministers turn for advice.

Prime ministers, in a manner similar to American presidents, began (in the 1960s) casting their nets more widely for advice. They seemed less inclined to observe accepted constitutional proprieties, and more willing to undermine the traditional monopolies of Whitehall and Westminster by seeking to institutionalise alternative sources of advice. As a consequence of this, by the 1990s the cabinet was beginning to look uncomfortably like its American counterpart. It could be seen as just one among many advisory bodies orbiting the prime minister, and its members were becoming frontmen who were expected to sell the prime minister's policies to the political nation and the public.

(Pryce 1997: 4)

Lastly, there is transient presidentialization. This occurs when prime ministers come to enjoy unusually unfettered decision-making autonomy as the result of passing political circumstance. At a time of crisis, for example, the need for rapid, effective and efficient decision-making may confer on a prime minister a power and autonomy similar to that enjoyed by presidents in similar circumstances. With the crisis passed, however, the prime minister, having a more informal and fragile power base, might well find himself rejected by parliamentary colleagues unwilling to tolerate any longer than necessary the threat to their own power and autonomy that a strong leader represents. The practice of delegating executive power to the 'heroic leader' when crisis paralysed normal parliamentary processes and then ejecting him from office once it had passed in order to re-establish the supremacy of Parliament was the characteristic pattern of crisis decision-making in the Third and Fourth French Republics (Hoffmann 1992).

These three types of presidentialization illuminate the role, and relative power, of parliamentary party leaders in government. They share a perspective, however, that is different from the one guiding this book, which sees presidentialization as a personalization of electoral politics that on the one hand occurs within the parameters of an unchanging parliamentary constitution *and* on the other persists over time, albeit that the actual impact of the party leaders on mass political behaviour and election outcomes can vary in magnitude from one contest to the next. Its starting point is an ideal-type parliamentary system where party is an impersonal entity and loyalty to it fully determines the behaviour of party supporters. In contrast to an elected president, the leader of the party, no matter who it might be, has no meaningfully separate political identity in the eyes of voters so that he or she cannot act as an independent influence on their behaviour. If a parliamentary election is held to be presidential, therefore, it implies that leaders do influence behaviour. Moreover, it is a specific kind of influence. A leader is an electoral asset to her party because she attracts the support of voters who would not otherwise have cast their ballot for her party. Alternatively, of course, she may be a liability in that she costs her party votes that would otherwise have gone to it. In either case, she has had a presidential impact. The notion of presidentialism, then, implies an independent electoral impact for party leaders in a single election, whereas presidentialization implies that this impact has become stronger over a number of elections than it was in the past.

Presidentialism and presidentialization thus defined are straightforward, empirically detectable phenomena. Still, two caveats are in order if they, at least as used in this book, are to be understood properly. The first of them is that coaxing other parties' supporters into their camp or their own party's supporters into another's is not the only electoral effect party leaders can have. They can influence their party's electoral fortunes in other ways as well. They may, for example, possess an unusual ability to energize party activists or to persuade would-be abstainers from their own party ranks to turn out and remain loyal in the polling booth. In the longer term, they may even help to shape a positive image for the party in voters' minds and, in the process, reinforce their own supporters' identification with the party. A case in point is Winston Churchill. It might well be that his great success as Britain's war-time prime minister helped to form the clear and persistent perception in the electorate that, subsequent fiascos like the Suez invasion notwithstanding, the Conservatives were the party 'better able to handle foreign affairs' (Butler and Stokes 1974: 456).

The analysis undertaken in this book does not deny the possibility of alternative types of leader effects, but they are not its principal focus of investigation. Leaders have long had as one of their principal activities the boosting of morale and the reinforcement of loyalties among their own supporters. This is the logic behind the traditional view that election campaigns are meant more to mobilize existing supporters than to convert new ones (Cohan et al. 1975). Moreover, the emergence and maturation of political television may well have enhanced their mobilizational role in these regards, but it has not transformed it. Contemporary discussions of presidentialization, in sharp contrast, tend to start from the premise that the electoral role of party leaders has been transformed in that their personality can now have a positive effect in the sense of encouraging defection to their fold among identifiers with other parties or a negative one in the sense of encouraging identifiers with their own party to cast their ballot for another party. In other words, leader effects are taken to be a reality to the extent that, first, party leaders take on an identity at least partly separate from the party they lead and, second, they come to enjoy an electoral effect that accrues to them personally.

The second caveat about the understanding of the term presidentialization as used in this book is that it implies that leader effects have become stronger relative to the past, but at the same time it is agnostic on the question of the precise form, or trajectory, that this strengthening has taken. At its simplest, it could be in the form of a linear trend whereby party leaders become more potent electoral influences with each passing election. An alternative model is a monotonic one in which leader effects stay the same or get stronger, but do not decline in magnitude from one election to the next. A third model is a simple threshold model where there is a substantial increase in leader impact from one election to another, but afterwards this impact fluctuates up and down without reverting to the low levels that existed prior to the substantial increase. One aim of this analysis is to establish which, if any, of these models best depicts the nature of leader effects in contemporary British general elections.

Finally, it is worth reiterating that presidentialization has two dimensions: presentation and impact. Presentation relates to the way political parties choose to present themselves to the public. Whether it be in election campaigns or in the announcement and justification of important policy proposals, presidentialization of presentation occurs to the extent that the leader is increasingly the public face of the party. Impact, by contrast, concerns the behavioural effect party leaders have on the voting patterns of citizens. This effect may be positive, taking the form of increasing its vote share or it may be negative since party leaders are not unfailingly popular. The important point, to put it bluntly, is that leaders matter; they emerge as a political force able in their own right to help shape the outcome of elections. These two dimensions of presidentialism are, of course, related insofar as party leaders have to be known to the voter before they can be said to influence the way she behaves at the polls. But recognition is a necessary condition of electoral influence without being a sufficient one. The increased media exposure of prime ministerial candidates, for example, may well make them more familiar to the voter, but this familiarity will not necessarily breach that voter's partisanship and influence the direction of her vote.

In assessing the presidentialization thesis, therefore, two distinct, but related tasks need to be undertaken. The first involves mapping whether party leaders have indeed become more prominent in election campaigns and determining whether they are more influential electoral forces than they used to be. The second involves explaining any presidentialization of impact that has taken place. Why has it happened? This book undertakes both tasks in the specific context of postwar general elections in Britain. The choice of Britain as a research site will now be explained.

The case study: Britain

If presidentialization comprises two dimensions, presentation and impact, the first of them at least should be visible in democracies worldwide because it is a direct reflection of the tendency for political parties to campaign more and more through the mass media of political communication, and especially television, the medium that is virtually everywhere the most used, trusted and believed by voters (Gunther and Mughan 2000). A heavy focus on the party leaders follows for two related reasons. First, television is a medium that is better suited to the projection of personality than to the discussion of complex issues and ideas. As Ranney (1983: 55–6) has noted:

> Individual persons are ideal subjects for television. They are easily interviewed, taped and dramatised. Moreover, the audience feels it understands them; after all, the viewers are themselves individuals, know other individuals, and feel that they understand people…In this way, the pictorial requirements of the medium…require television news to present politics as a contest in which the main players are individuals, not groups or organisations.

Second, television producers seek out the most authoritative 'main player' – the president in the United States and government and opposition party leaders in parliamentary systems of government – to make for more compelling political coverage.

The personalization of political contestation attendant on parties' increased resort to television as an electioneering tool characterizes recent campaign practice in most parliamentary democracies (Bowler and Farrell 1992; Butler and Ranney 1992; Kaid and Holtz-Bacha 1995; Swanson and Mancini 1996; Gunther and Mughan 2000). Interestingly, though, the same need not be true of electoral impact regardless of changing patterns of media exposure. This is because a crucial variable intervening between media exposure and electoral impact is institutional structure. Advertently or inadvertently, some types of parliamentary structure would seem logically to be more conducive to electoral presidentialism than others. After the war, for example, a traditional multi-party parliamentary republic was put in place in Italy precisely to prevent the emergence of another dominating leader in the Mussolini mould. Decisions would result from collaboration and not competition between political parties united in heterogeneous governing coalitions. This design was successful, albeit at the price of high rates of governmental turnover and immobilism (Massari 1996). Italy had 19 prime ministers between 1945 and 1992, and they averaged about 28 months in office. Moreover, incumbents have tended to leave the position and come back to it in a game akin to musical chairs played out over extended periods of time. The extreme example is the Christian Democrat, Amintore Fanfani. He first became prime minister in 1954 and formed six governments in total, the last one in 1987, the one before that in 1982. This pattern of prime ministerial tenure has helped to discourage presidentialism in post-war Italian politics:

> The expected brevity of a prime minister's tenure, combined with the dual leadership that results from the prime minister/party secretary tandem, ensures that Christian Democrat (17 of 19 post-war) prime ministers can rarely create an identity in voters' minds between their own political status, and that of the party. There is thus no significant coat-tails effect. Prime ministers cannot easily take *personal* credit for government performance, translate it into personal political popularity and use it as a resource to with which to build up a position of dominance in the party.
>
> (Hine and Finocchi 1991: 87; emphasis in original)

The Italian prime minister's anonymity in the 'First Republic' was partly a function of the country's multi-party parliamentary structure and partly of the factional nature of what was long its largest party, the Christian Democrats (DC). Like the Japanese Liberal Democratic party, the DC was formally factionalized into competing groups so that the choice of prime minister involved a compromise among its factions as well as between it and other parties. One obvious consequence of this mode of prime ministerial selection was that the head of government would be a compromise candidate at least minimally acceptable to the party's factions. He was therefore usually unable to command the authority and loyalty almost automatically accorded to the leader of relatively unified, disciplined and hierarchical parties, like those found in Great Britain.[9] Ever vulnerable to the vagaries of factional politics and often having to defer to the eminences grises of other, perhaps more powerful factions, heads of government found it very difficult to build up the personal stature and pre-eminence that falls almost naturally on the normally undisputed and uncontested leaders of British parties – whose leaders generally have to fear for their position only when the party performs poorly in elections under their leadership.[10]

When coalitional and factional politics coincide, then, the emergence of 'grey', insipid prime ministers becomes almost a certainty; the position of chief executive will be filled by individuals who command no particular authority with voters or within their own party. Inevitably, this 'greyness' carries over into governmental politics. Lacking authority, prime ministers become at best one of several important players in the political game. Even if wishing to do so, they are denied the ability of, for example, a Margaret Thatcher or a Tony Blair to set the political agenda and dominate its debate. Their predicament is perfectly illustrated by the Japanese experience, which indicates that institutionalized factionalism within its single-party Liberal Democratic governments from 1945 to the mid-1990s resulted in much the same rapid cabinet turnover and limited role for the prime minister as in Italy:

> Because the prime minister is chosen mainly by a coalition of Liberal Democratic party factions, his freedom of action is restricted by the endless play and counterplay of factional politics... The vulnerability of the prime minister, and the related vulnerability of his cabinet as well, to being pushed out of office in the factional game, is sufficient to restrict considerably their freedom of choice in policy matters.
>
> (Richardson and Flanagan 1984: 337. For Italy,
> see Hine and Finocchi 1991: 79)

Nonetheless, times have changed, even in Italy and Japan. The decline of dominant parties together with all parties' increasing resort to television for campaigning and mobilizational purposes has meant that in the 1990s political personalities have become more visible to the point of being potentially worth votes to their parties. The turning point in Italy was the 1994 election when media magnate Silvio Berlusconi, under the banner of a political party that barely existed organizationally, Forza Italia, successfully used his extensive private media network to sell himself and his party and became prime minister without having held elective office before (Marletti and Roncarolo 2000). In Japan too the splitting of the dominant Liberal Democratic party (LDP) in 1993 and the growth of political television also gave opportunities for a new generation of mediagenic politicians to achieve power outside the traditional party structure. One of them was Morihiro Hosokawa, who brought the LDP's 38 years in power to an end when he formed a seven-party reformist coalition after the election (Krauss 2000).

Although of recent vintage in Italy and Japan, the personalization of politics is a relatively established phenomenon in countries like Australia, Canada and Great Britain where there is a burgeoning literature on presidentialism in the form of an independent electoral impact for major party leaders (see, for example, Graetz and McAllister 1987; Bean and Mughan 1989; Bean 1993; Johnston et al. 1992; Mughan 1993; Stewart and Clarke 1992; Jones and Hudson 1996). This is not to argue, of course, that it has always been this way, despite institutional structures in these countries having remained largely unchanged over the democratic period. The changing role of party leaders is neatly captured by the juxtaposition of two quotations, one dating from the Britain of the early 1970s and the other from that of the late 1980s. The first of them comes from an historian musing on the evolution of the British prime ministership:

> By a natural process of development the leaders personally came to symbolise the causes for which they stood. It is often alleged that this personification of politics is a new phenomenon, produced in part by exposure to the mass media. It is no doubt true that every elector nowadays knows what Mr. Heath and Mr. Wilson look like... But by the time of Gladstone and Disraeli must from cartoons and other representations have had a fair idea of the appearance of the great rivals... There is nothing new during the last hundred years in this polarisation of personalities. It depends upon the personalities.
>
> (Blake 1975: 40–1)

The second quotation comes from an expert observer of the dynamics of British general election campaigns since the early 1950s. He does not deny the validity of Blake's observation. His point is rather that it is time-bound, failing to take account of recent qualitative changes in campaign practices and in the intensity of the media exposure that party leaders receive. This presidentialization of presentation is precisely the change that underpins claims of a presidentialization of electoral impact:

> The most obvious characteristic of the last ten years has been that our elections have become more presidential... [I]n so far as viewers

receive an image of what the Conservative or Labour parties stand for, it is received through the top leader's words. Of course, Baldwin and MacDonald or Gladstone and Disraeli were the dominant figures in their party campaigns fifty or a hundred years ago, but the actual day-to-day message that the British electorate receives now comes, to a degree unknown before, through the words and the face and the character of the party leaders.

(Butler 1988: 70)

The main factor promoting presidentialization in Britain relative to other countries would seem to lie its institutional structure, more specifically in the unusually majoritarian character of its parliamentary institutions.[11] Lijphart (1984) has identified two broad classes of democracy, majoritarian (or Westminster) and consensus, which are differentiated basically by the concentration of governmental power and the clear accountability of its wielders at election time. During the period covered in this analysis, 1951–97, unitary Britain was an archetypal majoritarian system. Political power was fused in a single, sovereign chamber of the national legislature, the executive committee of that legislature, the cabinet, was the dominant policy-making body, and the first-past-the-post electoral system encouraged a two-party system and usually returned a single-party government with few constitutional restraints on its exercise of power. Governmental power, in short, was concentrated in the hands of centralized and majoritarian single-party governments and, more specifically, in the hands of single-party cabinets and the prime ministers who appointed their members. The more democracies move away from this majoritarian model in the direction of, say, federalism, proportional representation, and multi-party governments, the more governmental power is dispersed among a larger number of political actors and the more difficult it is for voters to tie political responsibility for government action or inaction to any specific one of them.

Let me elaborate this argument, starting with political unitarism. While parliamentary constitutions usually say little or nothing about the governmental role of the prime minister, the structure of the state will have clear implications for the visibility of the head of the national government. Prior to the devolution of power to Scotland and Wales in 1999, Britain was an unabashedly unitary state boasting a national media so that, the leader of the official opposition apart, the prime minister had few serious rivals for national and local media attention. There was certainly no other chief executive, even if of a sub-national government, to compete with him for the political headlines. This is not so in federal parliamentary systems like Australia, Canada and Germany where sub-national chief executives often 'grab the head-lines', especially in the local and regional media. Their sub-national governments are popularly elected, have significant powers in their own domain and, often being drawn from different political parties to the federal government, compete with it for policy influence and popular attention and approval (Patterson and Mughan 1999). The very fact that sub-national governments in federal states have constitutionally protected powers and policy jurisdictions makes it unlikely that the national chief executive will be able to hog the local and national political limelight to the same degree as his counterpart in a unitary state like Britain prior to 1999.

The pattern of tenure, rooted in the nature of the party system, is a second factor encouraging presidentialism in British electoral politics. In the period stretching from the 1945 to 1992 general elections, Britain had a total of ten different prime ministers compared to almost double that number, 19, in Italy over the same period. Moreover, with the exception of Harold Wilson, who was prime minister from 1964 to 1970 and again from March 1974 to April 1976, all Britain's post-war premiers have served unbroken terms, thereby remaining consistently in the public eye and presumably becoming better known for it.[12]

The conclusion suggested by these examples is that, other things being equal, presidentialism is more likely to the extent that government in parliamentary systems is centralized, stable and the preserve of a single, hierarchically organized and majoritarian party, three properties inhering in British governments more or less throughout the post-war period and helping to make it a prime example of majoritarian democracy. Still, while institutional structures may make it easier for British party leaders to satisfy the minimal requirement of presidentialism, that is, making themselves known to voters in the nation at large, expectations of the relative magnitude of leader effects need to be kept in perspective. Institutional structures create limits as well as opportunities and parliamentarism is no different. While majoritarian parliamentary leaders may come closer than consensual ones to US presidential candidates in their visibility and salience, they cannot hope to equal them. Parliamentary leaders are generally not popularly elected and they do not get, or indeed seek out of necessity, the same intense, unremitting media exposure. With the exception of Israel in its two most recent national elections, prime ministerial candidates, by definition, do not campaign directly for the office of chief executive; they do not even campaign against each other in a highly publicized contest in a single constituency. Rather, to a far greater degree than presidential candidates, they remain the creatures of their party. Usually ensconced in safe seats, their overriding role in the campaign remains to work for the maximization of their party's parliamentary representation through media interviews and appearances, personal campaigning, and the like. Parliamentary party leaders generally owe their first loyalty to their party, not least because they owe their position as leader to that party and not directly to voters.

This book, then, is a case study of Britain, and not a comparative study of parliamentary democracies in general. Its key assumptions, however, are two. If presidentialization has become a feature of parliamentary democracy, then it should be especially apparent, and open to investigation and explanation, in a Britain whose majoritarian democratic structure can be expected to encourage the personalization of politics rather than to be indifferent or hostile to it. Second, and relatedly, the findings and conclusions that do emerge from the study of Britain are unlikely to be unique to that country since personalization is proceeding apace even in parliamentary democracies whose relatively consensual institutional structure is less likely to promote a personal presence and electoral impact for party leaders, witness the previously discussed experience of Italy and Japan in recent elections (see, more generally, Gunther and Mughan 2000). From the point of view of testing the presidentialization thesis, in other words, Britain is a 'crucial' case study in the sense that it clearly qualifies as a 'most likely' case that ought to confirm the theory if any case can be expected to do so (Eckstein 1997: 157–60). In this context, the analysis undertaken in this book must be recognized for being deliberately stringent and conservative insofar as its focus on the leaders of the class-based Conservative and Labour parties alone sets up a high threshold that must be crossed for presidentialization to become apparent. That is, the ideological distance between these parties should make it relatively difficult for the leader of one to attract the vote of identifiers with the other compared to the vote of Liberal (later Liberal-Social Democratic Alliance and later still Liberal Democratic) partisans. Commonly perceived as a 'halfway house' between the two major parties, Liberal identifiers can be expected to be relatively easily seduced into defection by the attraction of the leader of one or other of them (Butler and Stokes 1974: 268–75).

Plan of the book

There can be no doubt that the notion of presidentialization is controversial and plays a prominent role in discussions of the contemporary electoral politics of parliamentary democracies in Europe and elsewhere.

This notion that parliamentary party leaders have come to resemble the US president in that they now enjoy a visibility and political influence that accrues to them personally and is independent of the party they steward is not the first time that European politics have been claimed to have 'Americanized'. The 1960s' 'end of ideology' debate has already been mentioned. The theme has also recently re-emerged in discussions of the political effects of the mass media (Swanson and Mancini 1996). But despite its not being without precedent, the presidentialization thesis needs to be taken seriously. It is, in fact, a singularly important thesis because it implies some reorientation of our traditional party-based understanding of the dynamics of electoral competition and government accountability in parliamentary democracies. Yet, it has received nowhere near the scholarly attention that its widespread currency and its theoretical implications would indicate that it merits. Again, take Britain as an example. Even as late as the 1987 general election, the all-conquering Margaret Thatcher's third successive victory as leader of the Conservative party, not all analysts were seized of her importance. A book purporting to 'explore the social and political sources of electoral change in Britain' between 1964 and 1987 totally ignores party leaders as one such source (Heath et al. 1991: 1). The implication of this neglect is that the two giants of post-war British politics, the Conservative party's Margaret Thatcher and Labour's Harold Wilson, might just as well not have existed for all the influence they had on voting behaviour and election outcomes during their long careers at the head of their respective parties.

Putting the presidentialization thesis to the empirical test in the context of post-war Britain, this book entertains the contrary hypothesis that leaders matter, and matter now more than they used to. A word of caution at the outset is that this is neither an easy nor a straightforward task because the notion of presidentialization itself is not a simple, unidimensional phenomenon. The distinction between its presentation and impact is one early indicator of its complexity. There are also questions about whether negative and positive leader evaluations are equally important for the vote and whether both follow the same path over time. This complexity means at a minimum that presidential change cannot be confirmed or denied by a single piece of evidence. The strategy of this book, therefore, is essentially a conservative and cumulative one. To determine whether presidentialization of presentation and/or impact have taken place, it draws not on any one piece of evidence or data source, but on different kinds of evidence drawn from different time periods and different sources in order to make its testing of the presidentialization hypothesis as rigorous as possible. In this sense, the book should be viewed not as a series of discrete chapters, but as a coherent and cumulative exploration of an allegedly durable change in British electoral politics – their presidentialization.

There are five further chapters in the book. The next one, Chapter 2, starts with the question of whether there has been a presidentialization of presentation in election campaigns. It does this by tracing the changing campaign salience of the Conservative and Labour party leaders through a variety of sources, including most prominently content analyses of the editorial pages of *The Times* newspaper since the early 1950s and of television newscasts since 1964. In both their own right and relative to their parties, the Conservative and Labour leaders are shown to have become more prominent figures in the conduct of general election campaigns. Attention then turns to the question of whether elections have also presidentialized in the sense that their greater visibility has been associated with a greater impact on the vote. Presidentialization of presentation and of impact are generally found to have moved in tandem. The initial evidence therefore supports the argument for electoral presidentialization and associates it with changing patterns of media coverage.

The question that follows naturally concerns how this presidential change is to be explained. Chapters 3 and 4 address precisely this issue. Chapter 3 evaluates a number of potential explanations culled from the existing literature on electoral change in Britain. It looks in particular at the role of partisan dealignment and the leaders as political personalities that have become more prominent and to which voters have consequently become more responsive. The evidence in this chapter indicates quite clearly that the 'great leap forward' in the magnitude of leader effects is not fortuitous. Rather, it coincides temporally with the Conservative and Labour parties' combined resort to unprecedentedly leader-centred campaign strategies and use of television as the campaigning medium of choice. Chapter 4 thus turns its attention to the role of newspapers and television, and especially the latter, in mediating the relationship between voters and party leaders and thereby explaining the presidentialism characteristic of recent British elections.

Chapter 5 switches focus a little. Starting from the observation that the cumulative evidence all points in the direction of Britain's Conservative and Labour party leaders having become more influential electoral forces than they used to be, it also observes that a sense of scale and of time is absent from the analysis in the previous chapters. Presidentialization of electoral impact there may have been, but this might mean simply that they have gone from the utterly inconsequential to the no more than marginally consequential. Equally, it is not clear whether this change represents a structural change in the dynamics of parliamentary election outcomes or a passing condition rooted in the specific circumstances of recent general elections in Britain. This chapter addresses the questions of just how important party leaders have become and just how durable is presidential change? The first of these questions is approached in two ways. On the one hand, it asks whether it makes a difference which leader a party has. More specifically, and hypothetically speaking, it poses the question: could specific election outcomes have been different had the parties had someone else at their helm? On the other hand, it asks how influential party leaders are in comparison to that more commonly studied short-term influence on the vote, campaign issues. As for the question of durability, the argument is made that presidentialism is a characteristic of British elections that is likely to persist into the foreseeable future, largely because the parties themselves are likely to be neither willing nor organizationally able to lessen their dependence on television as the campaigning medium of choice.

In the light of these conclusions, Chapter 6 observes that the discussion of electoral presidentialization in earlier chapters demonstrates it to be a phenomenon that speaks directly to fundamental issues faced by the political systems of most advanced industrial democracies. Three such issues are identified and discussed in relation to the book's findings. These concern the role of institutions in shaping opinions and behaviour, the power of prime ministers vis-à-vis their cabinet and their parliamentary party, and the implications of the personalization of politics for the rationality of voters and the accountability of governments; in short the quality of democracy. It is argued that electoral presidentialization entails very real implications for the terms of these debates and preliminary consideration is given both to what these implications might be and to the kinds of research questions to which they might give rise.

2
Presidentialization of Presentation and Impact

This chapter examines the pattern of stability and change in the role of Conservative and Labour party leaders in post-war general elections in Britain. This is an area of study that remains *terra incognita* by and large, especially relative to other influences on the vote, like social class, partisanship and issues. A good part of the reason for its neglect has been continued widespread acceptance of the unanimous conclusion of survey-based studies of the 1950s that party leaders did not matter for the vote. With the class alignment strong, the evidence suggested that people voted for their party pretty much regardless of who was at its head. Thus, party leaders were often ignored, as in the first survey-based voting study in Britain when they were mentioned only once – and that was merely in connection with the number of radio broadcasts they had made during the campaign (Benney et al. 1956). Alternatively, after consideration of any effect they might have had on the vote, they ended up being passed over as secondary, indistinguishable components of more encompassing party images and largely irrelevant to the understanding patterns of stability and change in election outcomes:

> (A) leader's real contribution to the party in the way of popular support is a great deal less than his reputation might lead one to believe … He (the leader) is not expected to transcend the party and he is not indispensable … (He) is to a large extent the embodiment of general political attitudes.
>
> (Trenaman and McQuail 1961: 60; see also
> Milne and Mackenzie 1958)[1]

Concluding that Harold Wilson was a net electoral asset for the Labour party in 1964, 1966 and 1970, Butler and Stokes (1974: 368) helped to bring this conventional wisdom into question, but at the same time perpetuated it by all but dismissing the larger importance of their findings: '(T)he pull of the leaders remains but one among the factors that determine transient shifts of party strength; it is easily outweighed by other issues and events of concern to the public, including the movements of the economy which do so much to set the climate of the party battle.' Indeed, it was not until the 1980s that a forceful argument was made that the Conservative and Labour leaders were a force to be reckoned with in understanding general election outcomes (see, for example, Bean and Mughan 1989; Graetz and McAllister 1987).

Conventional academic wisdom notwithstanding, however, the notion of presidentialization was part of British political discourse well before the publication of the revisionist research of the 1980s. Indeed, it had taken root two decades earlier when political commentators and journalists began to treat the leaders of the major parties as serious and influential players in their own right in the election game. Accordingly, this chapter has three objectives. The first is to trace the emergence and development of the notion of presidentialization in the media, partly to demonstrate that I am not alone in thinking it a phenomenon worthy of note and investigation and partly to give some clear indication of its trajectory in British political discourse. The second is to determine, through the content analysis of newspaper editorials and television news broadcasts, whether there has been a systematic growth in the tendency for the Conservative and Labour parties to project themselves through their leaders in post-war election campaigns. At issue in this exercise is whether the period has seen a detectable presidentialization of presentation. Finally, the chapter goes on to examine several pieces of survey research evidence speaking to the related question of whether there has been a presidentialization of electoral impact over much the same period.

The evolution of a concept

Dating from only the 1960s, the notion of presidentialization is of relatively recent vintage in Britain, even among non-academic political commentators. The first task of this chapter is to trace its emergence and development largely through the textual analysis of a single source, the editorial pages of *The Times* during election campaigns since the early 1950s. This dependence on a single newspaper has the advantage of offering some degree of confidence that changing patterns in journalistic resort to the concept is not an artefact of variation in, say, editorial stance in the sources being consulted.[2]

Presidentialization is a concept that seems to have first appeared in the British political lexicon in the 1964 election campaign. This is not to argue, of course, that the leaders of the Conservative and Labour parties were ignored in the campaign editorials of previous elections. To the extent they were mentioned, though, it was in their role as party spokesmen on current affairs, as individuals with certain vices or virtues, achievements or disappointments and, above all, as leaders of teams in which, in the considered opinion of the newspaper, voters should or should not vest responsibility for governing the country in the upcoming election. It is difficult to find any hint of presidentialism, any perception that the office of prime minister and the traditional practice of party-based political leadership had transmuted under Attlee, Churchill, Eden or Macmillan.

With television making its first appearance in the 1951 campaign when each of the Conservative, Labour and Liberal parties was allotted a single 15-minute televised party election broadcast, the party leaders did not emerge as an issue in the campaign; nor did their role in it attract comment for differing from what it had been in the past. But while not mentioning, or perhaps appreciating, the implications of the new medium of television for party-based electoral and governmental politics, *The Times* (10 october 1951) did give evidence of an inkling of its potentially revolutionary implications for how parties would eventually project themselves to voters: 'If what has happened in America may be taken as a guide, this is a landmark in British history…The effect of the invisible (radio) voice – so often so different from that of the speaker himself – remains an awkward hazard for those choosing their best team. Now the new hazards of television must be studied.'

The parties made more extensive use of television in the next election, in 1955, and *The Times* (23 May 1955) speculated fleetingly on the medium's tendency to personalize politics at the expense of issues: 'If a guess may be made, it is that the 1955 television broadcasts were more successful in establishing certain politicians as personalities rather than being memorable for anything said before the cameras.' There were also early signs of disquiet over television's longer-term implications for party-based parliamentary democracy in Britain. '(I)t will be an unfortunate day if it should come about that an election in this country is decided not by what either side says, but by the way they looked while saying it' (*The Times*, 23 May 1955).

Both personalization and concern over it were intensified in 1959, the first 'television election' in two important respects. In the first place, it was the first one in which the majority of British adults had access to television. The proportion in this position had jumped from 8.1 per cent in 1951, to 39.8 per cent in 1955 and to 74.4 per cent in 1959.[3] In the second place, it was the first election in which there was comprehensive television coverage of the entire campaign. Previously, television had carried only the parties' own election broadcasts. In the name of a self-imposed impartiality, all material that might be held to influence the voter had been totally excluded from its programming, even its news broadcasts. In 1959, by contrast, there was full news coverage of the campaign, as well as a number of special programs in which candidates presented their views, although there were no televised interviews with either major party leader.[4] These changes were momentous, but still the election could in no sense be described as a personality contest between the leaders of the Conservative and Labour parties. One important reason was that, beset by Labour charges of developing a 'cult of personality' around their leader, Harold Macmillan, the Conservatives had held their telegenic leader in reserve until their very last election broadcast of the campaign. Nonetheless, other aspects of the contest did serve notice that general elections had edged in the direction of becoming a personality contest.[5] *The Times* fully appreciated the implications of this shift for the practice of election campaigning and, once again, showed itself concerned for its perceived trivializing effect on the quality of political discussion in the campaign:

> The Prime Minister and the Leader of the Opposition each have one more chance to speak to the nation on television. They can yet make this election memorable for something other than scorn if they will put the technicians, the ring-masters, the clever boys and the pollsters for once in their place and address themselves, as they each can, solely to what are the real high arguments of our time.
>
> (*The Times*, 5 October 1959)

But despite television's unprecedented role in the 1959 campaign, the terms presidential and presidentialization did not appear in *The Times'* editorial columns. The thesis was taking shape, however, and the changing campaign practices with the emergence of television was not the only reason for this development. Another was governmental. Macmillan's treatment of his cabinet was qualitatively different from that of his post-war predecessors. He was a strong, assertive prime minister whose role definition went well beyond that of 'chairman of the board'. He openly sought to bend the cabinet to his will and was relatively quick to shuffle its membership or even dismiss individual cabinet ministers if it suited his purposes (Mackintosh 1968: 501–5). Indeed, his leadership style lent credence to, and may have even stimulated, a highly controversial interpretation of the changing character of government in Britain. In his introduction to the 1963 edition of Bagehot's classic work, *The English Constitution*, a senior Labour politician, Richard Crossman, argued that collective cabinet government had given way to individualistic prime ministerial government. The enormous growth in the machinery of government had combined with the prime minister's supreme central authority in the cabinet, the civil service and the party machine to place him a position where he was able to dominate his cabinet in something like the way the US president did his. In Crossman's (1963: 22–3) own words: 'If we mean by presidential government, government by an elective first magistrate then we in England have a president as truly as the Americans.'

Crossman's thesis stimulated intense debate among students of British government. It also helped to implant the notion of presidentialization firmly in the British political lexicon, with the term receiving its first mention in the editorial pages of *The Times* during the 1964 general election campaign. By this time, television had become almost ubiquitous, with about 90 per cent of the adult population having access to it. Perhaps more importantly, it had replaced newspapers as voters' primary source of political information (Harrop 1987). The Labour party welcomed political television as a way of reducing its communicational dependence on what it perceived to be a Conservative-biased printed press. It perhaps also sensed a change in the public's values and expectations when it showed no fear of the 'cult of personality' charge it had so effectively levelled against the Tories in 1959 and built its campaign to an unprecedented degree around its new leader, Harold Wilson. Wilson was a consummate television performer and his personality seemed to dominate the campaign all the more for the relative artlessness and discomfort with the new medium of the very traditional Tory leader, Sir Alec Douglas-Home (Cockerell 1988). Indeed, after the election, Home was to become the first party leader to lose office partly because of his senior colleagues' poor opinion of his television image (Gilmour 1969: 78).

Three important developments deserve special mention in the 1964 campaign. First, the presidential analogy is explicitly, if tentatively, drawn for the first time:

> One specific aspect of this campaign should not go unnoticed…
> (B)oth the Prime Minister and Mr. Wilson have in their journeys
> attracted considerable audiences which may be an indication that
> television is getting people out of their houses and into the halls. It
> may also indicate that the public is, at any rate during this election,
> tending to regard the campaign as of the presidential kind.
>
> (*The Times*, 6 October 1964)

Second, the degree of presidentialization that was seen to have taken
place was marginal and not interpreted as representing a radical break
with the past. The notion persisted that the demands of parliamentary
government are collective so that the election remains, and should
remain, a choice between the party leaders and their teams:

> The power of the executive is now too strong. It is a government that
> has to be chosen…The choice is between Sir Alec Douglas-Home,
> who has no qualifications to be a reformer, plus a strong team that
> includes some reformers, and Mr. Wilson, who is undoubtedly a
> reformer, plus hardly a team at all.
>
> (*The Times*, 14 October 1964)

Third, perhaps under the influence of Crossman, there is some recognition that, even though the choice should be between teams, the
leader's apparent indispensability to election victory for his party could
strengthen him and, in the process, undermine the integrity of the
institution of cabinet government itself:

> All would depend on Mr. Wilson himself. The weakness of his team
> could aggravate his faults. It is absurd to talk of a Presidential system
> so long as the House of Commons performs its function. But a
> Prime Minister all-powerful in his Cabinet…would be too great a
> price to pay for the kinds of reforms Mr. Wilson has to offer.
>
> (*The Times*, 14 October 1964)

The 1964 election, then, is notable for the unprecedented recognition
that the personalities of the major party leaders had become independent
forces in the country's electoral and governmental politics. This recognition in turn served to intensify concern about personality-based campaigning's implications for the quality of British democracy. An editorial
appropriately entitled 'Camera politics' bemoaned that the possibility of

a debate between the Conservative and Labour leaders had been raised:

> Mr. Wilson's challenge to Sir Alec Douglas-Home for a direct confrontation (on television)…is the *reductio ad absurdum* of current trends…What is proposed is that the leaders should engage in single combat before the eyes of the opposing armies: or to put it another way, a reversion to trial by ordeal. The criteria by which millions would be invited to make up their minds would be of the most fortuitous and superficial kind…This is not what democratic politics are about.
>
> (*The Times*, 23 September 1964)

As far as presidentialization is concerned the 1966 general election passed quietly. The 1970 election, by contrast, was characterized by a mixture of continuity and change. In terms of continuity, television's tendency to personalize politics in its focus on the party leaders appeared to have reached new heights. The 1964 notion that elections remained a choice between the leaders *and* their teams seemed to have become a thing of the past; the party leaders now dominated television coverage of the campaign almost to the exclusion of their (shadow) cabinet colleagues:

> The television authorities, who seem to have decided that Britain does, after all, have a Presidential constitution, are covering the present election as though no other parliamentary campaigns were taking place at all, and much underemphasise the two leaders' principal colleagues, except when they say something absurd.
>
> (*The Times*, 5 June 1970)

In terms of change, the 1970 election is most notable for initiating the importation of commercial, marketing-based campaigning techniques developed in US presidential contests, and it was the supposedly traditionalist Tory party that took the initiative in this regard. Previously, both major parties had used television rather passively, adapting themselves to the demands of the medium rather than seeking to manipulate it to promote the image and message they wished to impress upon voters. Their passivity was especially apparent in their televised party election broadcasts, their only opportunity to present themselves and their message to the public in a way of their own choosing since paid television advertising was, and remains, prohibited by law in Britain. From the introduction of these broadcasts in 1951, both parties had chosen mostly to work within the 'talking head' format. That is, the head and shoulders of some prominent party figure would monopolize the camera for the whole broadcast and, perhaps occasionally working with illustrative film footage, (s)he would hold forth on important issues of the day, like the economy, housing policy or defence.[6] In 1970, the Conservatives broke sharply with this format and adopted powerful visual images to attack the Labour government's record in office. One of their broadcasts, for example, attached its record on inflation by showing a £1 note being savagely attacked by a pair of scissors. Another attacked the government's record on economic growth by showing a woman holding in her hand a wage packet encased in a block of ice (Day 1982). A decisive step away from the conventional party election broadcast centring around the 'serious' discussion of issues had been taken. In the best marketing tradition, issues were presented instead as a series of contrived images.

The Conservative party's innovative use of the party political broadcast followed hard on the heels of the publication of Joe McGinniss's famous account of Richard Nixon's 1968 campaign for the US presidency, *The Selling of the President*. This book revealed that both 1968 presidential candidates, Hubert Humphrey and Richard Nixon, had made extensive use of commercial marketing experts and techniques to create a favourable image that could be 'sold' to voters 'much as had (been done) for Avis, Volkswagen and Heinz ketchup' (McGinniss 1988: xiv). *The Times* (2 June 1970) was both distraught and indignant:

> The most chilling aspect of modern elections is their impersonal quality. The elector is invited to vote not for a Member of Parliament, but for a Party; not for a Party but for its Leader; and not for its Leader but for a pre-packaged television presentation of what Market Research suggests the Leader should be. The packagers who created the Nixon manikin on American television have brothers or cousins trying their black arts over here.

In the few years since 1959, election campaigns were held to have ceased to be debates and to have become instead spectacles largely devoid of intellectual content. This change was to be especially lamented because it 'detracts both from the accountability and from the rationality of politicians' (*The Times*, 6 June 1970).

At first, marketing techniques were generally resisted by Conservative and Labour leaders, and especially the latter who were particularly uncomfortable with this new style of election campaigning. At least for the Conservatives, however, such reticence disappeared altogether with Margaret Thatcher's election as party leader in 1975.

> In (the 1979) campaign she was not the first politician to use an advertising agency, but she was the first to grasp what could be the full impact of communications across the whole spectrum of the media…She understood that striking material would be talked about in its own right. She also knew that the right man could transform her impact on the press and in television interviews.
>
> (Tyler 1987: 56)

Representing a radical break with traditional Toryism in more ways than one, Thatcher had no qualms about adapting marketing skills and expertize to her own electoral and political ends and she made extensive and innovative use of them in 1979 to propagate her blanket condemnation of socialism and to oust Labour from power. To these ends, the Conservative party hired the Saatchi and Saatchi advertising agency in 1978 to design and produce its party election broadcasts. A particularly famous one depicted life in Britain going backwards. It was also noteworthy for being the first broadcast in which the traditional 'talking head' format was completely abandoned. Tim Bell, a director of Saatchi and Saatchi in 1979, played a key role in designing the Conservative party campaign and was still a close, if informal, advisor to Mrs Thatcher two elections later in 1987. Another Tory innovation in the 1979 campaign was the 'media event'. 'The media event – that is to say, a campaign stunt performed because it will attract attention in newspapers and on television, and not because it has any connection with the issues of the campaign – became a principal element in the Thatcher campaign' (*The Guardian*, 30 April 1979). In regard to media coverage, in other words, a major party had gone on the offensive to seize the initiative from the television producers with a view to shaping their coverage of its campaign to suit its own ends.

The media's disproportionate concentration on the party leaders was by now well-established practice. What was new was the Conservative party's aggressive marketing, or 'packaging', of Mrs Thatcher in an effort to neutralize adverse popular reaction to her thorny personality and ideological radicalism. Labour strategists had throughout the campaign set her strong, firmly held and often unpopular opinions against the perceived reasonableness and moderation of the better-liked Labour leader, James Callaghan, affably known as 'Uncle Jim'. 'However passionately, some politicians may assert that this election is about issues, not about personalities, the popular assessment of the character and achievements of Mrs Thatcher will be a powerful force in deciding the outcome' (*The Daily Telegraph*, 23 April 1979). Perhaps because he felt secure for being more popular, Mr Callaghan remained faithful to tried-and-tested campaigning techniques. In his own words: 'I don't intend to end this campaign packaged like cornflakes. I shall continue to be myself' (*Time*, 23 April 1979: 40).

The Conservative victories in 1979 and 1983 helped to institutional-ize electoral presidentialism in British politics in two ways. First, they solidified Tory commitment to the use of professional marketing expertise, which the party deployed just as readily and, if anything, with greater intensity in subsequent elections held in 1987, 1992 and 1997. The Labour leadership, by contrast, retained its principled hos-tility to these techniques even in the 1983 contest and refused to play their opponents at their own game, in part because it was a style of campaigning that was particularly repugnant to the party's new leader, and one of its great traditionalists, Michael Foot. His disregard for the demands of the media is apparent in the following description of his campaign: '(His) schedule was less geared to gaining visual cov-erage, or "photo-opportunities" … His discursive style of speaking and his unwillingness actually to use the words in the speech handouts given to the media was also a handicap' (Butler and Kavanagh 1984: 271–82). The Conservative government was re-elected with a majority of more than 140 seats and the campaign was widely interpreted as a personal triumph for Mrs Thatcher and as a disaster for a Labour party out of touch with the times, divided against itself and appar-ently leaderless.

Second, Neil Kinnock replaced Michael Foot as party leader in the aftermath of Labour's disastrous general election performance. Kinnock was the first of a new, less traditionalist generation of Labour leaders and quickly and efficiently set about establishing his authority in the party organization with a view to restoring its moderate and responsi-ble image, and hence its credibility as a party of government. He led a more united party into the 1987 campaign. But more pertinently, he entered the campaign advised by a director of communications, Peter Mandelson, who had highlighted the party's changed attitude towards the media with his declaration some two years earlier that the days were long gone when a general secretary of the party could assert that Labour refused to present politicians 'as if they were breakfast food or baked beans' (*The Guardian*, 25 November 1985). Under Mandelson's guidance, the discussion of issues was unambiguously subordinated to the projection of Kinnock's personality. Labour strategists approached the campaign knowing 'they would strip the manifesto of everything contentious and build up Kinnock with a massive personality campaign, hoping to obscure the fact that they had few policies and sweep the electorate away on an American-style bandwagon' (Tyler 1987: 148). This sharp change in campaigning strategy was clearly reflected in the pattern of party expenditures.

> Though heavily outspent by the Tories, Labour invested far more in marketing and advertising in 1987 than in 1983…In all, the party spent nearly £2.2 million on advertising, while the MORI consultancy cost £148 000 and Party Election Broadcasts (PEBs) a further £143 000…In 1992 the party spent £3.3 million on media and advertising services.
>
> (Webb 1994: 131; see also Scammell 1995: 250–3)

Kinnock took to his role like a fish to water, revelling in being the undisputed centrepiece of a campaign whose tone was set by an opening party election broadcast made by a leading film director and focusing emotionally on Kinnock, his wife, their working-class backgrounds and struggles for success. This broadcast was considered so successful by Labour strategists that it was aired a second time later in the campaign. The Tories were also impressed enough by its success that they produced a similar programme about their new leader, John Major, for the 1992 campaign. Its immediate effect in 1987 was to help to propel the Labour leader to a position where early opinion in the campaign was that the Conservatives had to undermine his personal standing if they were to win the day:

> His [Kinnock's] passionate rhetoric – of a type which it was once thought had been made redundant by television – brought triumph from the hustings to the living room. In a modern, media-dominated campaign he took what passes for the high ground of politics. The Tories were left with the job of knocking him off.
>
> (*The Times*, 10 June 1987)

The Conservative party likewise built its campaign unambiguously around Mrs Thatcher, so much so that one account describes the party's presidential-style campaign strategy in terms of the 'selling of the prime minister' (Tyler 1987).

The 1987 election, then, 'marked the full migration of American political packaging techniques to Britain' (O'Shaugnessy 1990: 218). In the words of a seasoned observer of the media's campaign role: 'Never before had the parties tailored their efforts so single-mindedly to capturing the cameras' attention…Every party, from the largest to the Greens and the nationalists made television their first priority, and the broadcasters responded to scale' (Butler and Kavanagh 1988: 139). This concentration on television helped to make the 1987 election the most personalized contest in British political history to that point. Conservative and Labour unabashedly centered their campaigns around their leaders in the most intensive and sustained interaction between political personalities and the people through the media ever. The consensus was that Mr Kinnock performed best as the party's 'front man', though not well enough to deny Mrs Thatcher her third victory in a row. 'Even though the Prime Minister looks set to win her third successive victory, the perceived wisdom that it was Mr Kinnock who "won" the campaign can bring no comfort to the campaigners on the Tory side' (*The Times*, 10 June 1987).

In 1987, Labour reached a new peak in terms of campaign management by 'experts in opinion polling, advertising and public relations…', just as the Conservatives had done in 1979 (Butler and Kavanagh 1992: 77). As such, and in direct consequence, a new status quo in the style of election campaigning seems to have been established, with one of its defining characteristics being presidentialism of presentation. Moreover, journalistic comment on, and often taking the form of disapproval of, the tendency for the Conservative and Labour parties to project themselves more and more through their leader all but disappeared, with this new style of campaigning apparently having come to be accepted as the norm. Thus, comment, approving or disapproving, on the role of the party leaders all but disappeared from the editorial pages of *The Times*, even though the presidential flavour of the campaign was amply evident in the titles of individual editorials, e.g., 'Major v. Kinnock' (14 March 1992), 'Paddy's (the Liberal Democrat leader, Paddy Ashdown) Blackmail' (6 April 1992) and 'Major's First Test' (8 April 1992). *The Times* having succumbed to this presidentialization of presentation, it was left to *The Economist* (22 February 1992: 54), to deplore the highly personalistic direction that the upcoming campaign looked set to take:

> It will be, the nation is informed, the most 'presidential' election in British history. Aeroplanes with silly names like Blue Leader have been

hired. Conservative Central Office has copied the 1987 Labour campaign's broadcast about the Kinnocks by commissioning an arty film about the Majors. Spin doctors and policy-surgeons on both sides concur that the personalities of John Major and Neil Kinnock will be an – even the – issue ... [But election-watchers] should reject the notion that Mr Major and Mr Kinnock are the two most significant points in the coming campaign. Their leading cabinet and shadow-cabinet members are, collectively, just as important – and the party policies on education, tax and industry will matter far more than either.

But such resistance notwithstanding, the mould had been set and the major party leaders continued to be the centrepieces of the their parties' campaigns for office in the 1992 and 1997 elections. Moreover, journalists seemed inured to the prime ministerial candidates' new-found electioneering primacy in the traditionally party-based British parliamentary system. Some even seemed to welcome it. In stark contrast to its earlier opposition to the personalization of election campaigns, for example, *The Times* did a complete U-turn and early in the campaign came out strongly in favour of televised debates between the Tory and Labour leaders. With this reversal of opinion on the desirability of leader debates came the pronunciation:

> The purpose of debates is to allow the electorate to take stock of their prospective masters. The rules are only significant insofar as they impact on that objective. A simple but formal format would allow the best comparison between the two contenders. The central function of democracy has always been to let the people speak. In this election that process would be helped if debates let the people see and listen.
>
> (*The Times*, 25 March 1997)

As it turned out, agreement between the parties could not be reached, but this did not stop *The Times* trying to revive the idea halfway through the campaign on the ground that a debate 'would play a powerful role in concentrating the voters' minds on the men who want to lead them. It would allow voters to see their candidates under pressure from each other, without the intrusions of advertisers, strategists and TV interviewers (*The Times*, 11 April 1997). Implying a direct communion between voters and candidates for the position of prime minister, the wheel had turned full circle. The politics of personality, once a threat to voter rationality and government accountability in parliamentary democracy, had come to be seen as the essence of both as voters were invited to choose not between parties and the issues that separated them, but between candidates for the position of chief executive British-style.

This textual analysis of the emergence and development of the notion of presidentialization in British politics suggests three broad conclusions. The first is that there can be no doubting the popularity, at least in journalistic circles, of the presidentialization theme over the last three decades. The second is that its becoming part of British political discourse coincides with the coming-of-age of political television around 1960 and, perhaps still more importantly, with the changing campaigning usages to which both the Conservative and Labour parties later put this medium. Finally, a strong normative stance has conventionally been taken on television's personalization of politics, equating it with a trivialization of parliamentary democracy. That is, the medium's emphasis on the manipulable image of the prime ministerial candidates has tended to be seen as going hand in hand with the debasement of voting choice among gullible voters without strong partisan anchors and prey to skilled advertising executives and market researchers more concerned with winning the election than with the health and quality of democracy.

Having established the prima facie plausibility of the electoral presidentialization thesis, the task now is to put it to the rigorous empirical test. The complexity of this thesis, however, cautions that no one piece of evidence can be taken to be sufficient to confirm or refute it. Instead, the cumulation of systematic evidence presented over this and the next chapter of this book has to be weighed before arriving at a final decision. The next section of this chapter makes a start on tackling this evidence. Charting the pattern of the attention both newspapers and television pay to the Conservative and Labour party leaders election by election, it speaks to the question of the form that the presidentialization of presentation has taken in post-war campaigns.[7] This is followed by a matching treatment of the pattern of the leaders' electoral impact.

Presidentialization of presentation

Party leaders, of course, have always figured prominently in British election campaigns; one has only to look back to the era of Disraeli and Gladstone. A presidential-style increase in media prominence, however, can involve leaders becoming more prominent in their own right or at the expense of other significant governmental actors. The important question in the analysis of patterns of media presentation, therefore, is not only whether party leaders come to receive more attention than they used to, but also whether they get more of it relative to other, potentially relevant electoral actors as well. Two such actors are explicitly considered here, their political party and their (shadow) cabinet colleagues.

The pattern of leader presentation is established by tracing the attention given to Conservative and Labour party leaders over time in two different media, newspapers and television. The printed press is used for two reasons. One, it allows the coverage of the party leaders to be documented as far back as the immediate post-Second World War years. Two, account can be taken not only of the party leaders, but also of their senior party colleagues and of their party itself. By contrast, the analysis of television news content on which I draw was carried out by others and does not include party as a coding category. Television coverage is presented nonetheless since this medium is the most important, trusted and credible source of political information for most British voters (Gunter and McLaughlin 1992: 37–41; Negrine 1989: 1–3).

Take newspapers first. The methodology employed in determining coverage patterns is the straightforward one of counting the number of references to relevant political actors in campaign editorials whose focus is British domestic politics. Given the earlier textual analysis, as well as for reasons of simplicity of presentation and comprehension, this exercise focuses on *The Times* (excluding *The Sunday Times*), with analogous results from *The Guardian* occasionally being reported in footnotes. The 1979 election is not included because industrial action led to *The Times* not being published during the campaign. The campaign is defined as a period of 21 days up to and including the day of the election.[8] To be included in the total, each mention had to have a specific target so that collective references to, say, 'all parties' or 'all party leaders' were ignored since their referent was not always clear, sometimes seeming to refer to the leaders of minority parties as well.

Charting the number of times the two major party leaders were mentioned over the course of the campaign for each election (except 1979) since 1951, Figure 2.1 presents an initial look at the evidence for there having been a presidentialization of presentation in post-war British elections. The number of mentions is aggregated over the entire

Figure 2.1 Absolute Number of Newspaper Mentions of Prime Minister and Opposition Leader (per 10 000 editorial words)

campaign period and standardized by total number of editorial words to allow for the considerable variation in length from editorial to editorial and from election to election. The results are presented graphically to allow for their easier interpretation and at the end of each line in the graph is a summary measure of the relationship between time and media prominence. More specifically, the figure presented is the zero-order correlation between year of the election and number of mentions. Varying in value between -1 and $+1$, a positive coefficient suggests presidentialization of presentation.

The immediately striking feature of Figure 2.1 is the upward trend in the media prominence of both the prime minister and the leader of the opposition, and especially the former.[9] Presidentialization trend there is, then, and the figure also indicates that it is non-linear in form. More explicitly, the number of mentions of both the prime minister and the leader of the opposition are substantially higher on average in the three elections since 1987 than they were in the preceding ones, although it must also be said that 1997 sees a substantial dip in the number of prime ministerial mentions relative to the immediately preceding contest in 1992.

These observations are clearly pertinent to the question of presidential change and its explanation, but they are also best taken as preliminary. This is because the figures in the table are absolute values, whereas, as was pointed out earlier, presidentialization also entails a relative dimension as well; party leaders become more prominent at the expense of other political actors. Figure 2.2 presents the number of party leader mentions as a ratio of, first, mentions of their party and, second, mentions of their senior colleagues in the (shadow) cabinet.[10] Thus, for example, a figure of, say, 0.33 in 1951 in the case of a comparison of the prime minister and his party indicates that *The Times* made an average of 33 mentions of the sitting prime minister, Clement Attlee, for every 100 mentions of his party, Labour. It follows that a score greater than unity means that the party leader receives more mentions than her party or (shadow) cabinet.

Figure 2.2 presents strong evidence that a presidentialization of presentation has taken place in the way that British newspapers cover election campaigns, and especially in the attention they bestow on prime ministers. The correlation coefficients confirm that over the period as a whole, *The Times* significantly increased the attention it paid to sitting prime ministers relative to their party and did likewise, albeit more mutedly, for opposition leaders relative to theirs.[11] As with Figure 2.1, the figure also strongly suggests that presidentialization has not been a linear phenomenon, but that attention to prime ministers relative to their party in particular jumped sharply in 1983 and continued to increase with each subsequent election. Finally, there is substantial evidence that newspaper coverage came as well to favour prime ministers relative to their senior party colleagues, and, again, especially in elections held in the 1980s and 1990s.

Taken as a whole, then, the major party leaders have not benefitted equally from the presidentialization of presentation trend evident in Figures 2.1 and 2.2. Newspapers have increasingly and disproportionately focused their attention on prime ministers at the expense of their party on the one hand and, to a lesser degree, of their cabinets on the other. These trends have built up gradually over the post-war period, but they underwent a surge in the 1980s and 1990s. Given the small number of observations involved, of course, it might be countered that Figures 2.1 and 2.2 reveal less an underlying trend and more the idiosyncratic circumstances of particular election campaigns. Three considerations make this argument less than convincing, however. First, newspaper attention to the prime minister relative to senior party colleagues in periods of 'normal' politics – that is, outside election campaigns – follows a similar

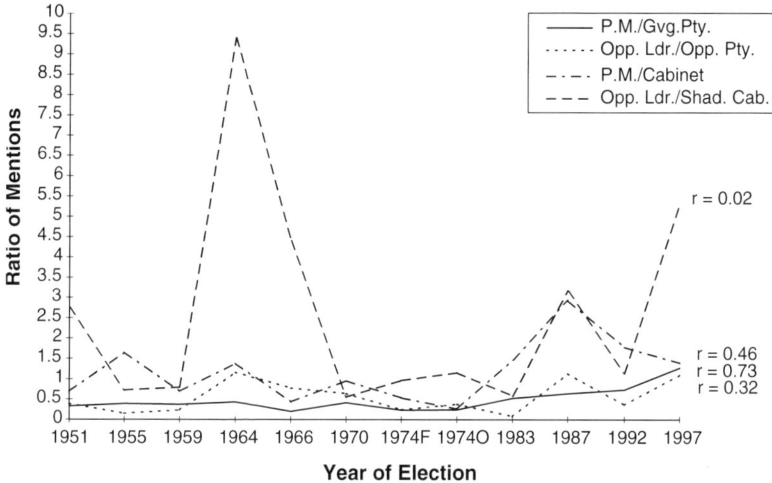

Figure 2.2   Ratio of Newspaper Party Leader Mentions to Party and (Shadow) Cabinet Mentions (per 10 000 words)

residential trajectory over the course of the 1980s (Foley 1993: 123–5). Second, the disproportionate increase in newspaper attention to the major party leaders coincides not with the emergence of political television in 1959 and 1964, but largely with purposive campaign management 'reach(ing) a new peak for the Conservatives in 1979 and for Labour in 1987' (Butler and Kavanagh 1992: 518). Third, as mentioned earlier in the chapter, newspaper coverage is a conservative test of the presidentialization of presentation thesis. Account must also be taken of television partly because it is watched more than newspapers are read by the majority of voters and partly because its visual nature means that it personalizes politics more than other media do.

Figure 2.3 documents television's attention to the major party leaders since 1964. Coming from studies carried out by Martin Harrison and reported in the Nuffield studies of David Butler and his various co-authors, the number constituting it reflect the number of times the leaders and their senior colleagues were quoted in BBC and ITN nightly campaign news broadcasts.[12] While this broadcast medium shows an even sharper increase in the attention paid to prime ministerial candidates than do newspapers, the presidential pattern of coverage in the two media is remarkably similar in two important respects. First, the correlation coefficients bear witness to a clear presidentialization of presentation trend, with both prime ministerial candidates coming to figure more prominently in the country's nightly television news broadcasts and at much the same rate of increase. Second, for both of them, there is a sharp break with the past in 1983, increased prominence in 1987 and, in the case of the prime minister at least, a further increase in prominence in 1992. Television attention to the leader of the opposition remains static in 1992 and then, just as with the prime minister, it dips somewhat in 1997.[13] Overall, though, both leaders are vastly more prominent in television news broadcasts of the 1980s and 1990s than previously.

The series on which Figure 2.3 is based does not contain matching data on party mentions in news broadcasts so it is impossible to say whether the greater prominence of the leaders has come at the expense of their parties. If it is the case, though, that television simply exaggerates trends apparent in the newspapers (Semetko et al. 1991: 87–114), it likely did. What is more certain is that television's heavier focus on the party leaders did not come unduly at the expense of their senior party colleagues. As with newspapers in Figure 2.2, there is some slight evidence of greater relative prominence in television news broadcasts for the prime minister in this regard, but none at all for the opposition leader.

Overall, then, Figures 2.1, 2.2 and 2.3 collectively suggest three conclusions. One, there has indeed been a presidentialization of the presentation of campaign news in newspapers and on television. This is especially true in regard to attention paid to leaders in their own right as opposed to in relation to their party or senior colleagues. Two, the rate of increase in attention to party leaders has proceeded unevenly over the post-war period, being at its strongest on average in the 1980s and 1990s. Finally, presidentialization is somewhat more pronounced for prime ministers both in their own right and relative to their parties and senior colleagues. Opposition leaders differ slightly in that there is strong evidence for their greater media prominence in their own right and relative to their parties, but not relative to their senior colleagues. However, patterns of electoral influence cannot be inferred from patterns of media coverage. Their greater prominence in the media may have made prime ministerial candidates more visible to voters, but this implies no necessary impact on the choice these same voters make in the polling booth. A promising beginning has been made, but the question of electoral impact must also be considered if a full evaluation of the validity of the presidentialization thesis is to be made.

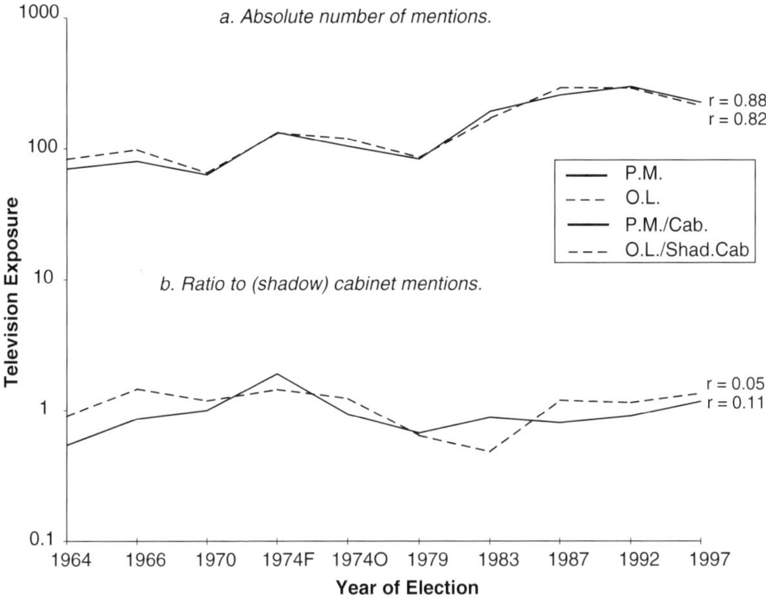

Figure 2.3   Television News Broadcast Exposure of Party Leaders

Presidentialization of impact

Change in the influence of party leaders on the vote lies at the heart of the presidentialization debate. A large part of the recent interest in the adaptation of personality-centred marketing techniques to the demands of election campaigning originates in a normative concern with the consequences of the 'packaging' of politics for the criteria individuals use in arriving at their voting decision (see, for example, Franklin 1994: 203–26). But this change in campaigning techniques does not mean that the case for British party leaders having become more significant in their electoral impact can be considered proven. The argument continues to be made that party leaders remain no more than secondary components of more encompassing party images so that it makes little sense to treat them electoral forces in their own right (Rose and McAllister 1990: 134–7). More pragmatically, a longitudinal study speaking to precisely the issue of the leader effects since 1964 concludes that there is no evidence for the presidentialization of their electoral impact with the passage of time (Crewe and King 1993).[14] At the same time, however, evidence that party leaders matter for voters in the 1980s and 1990s continues to mount. This is true whether party support in opinion polls or general election outcomes is at issue. A recent, highly sophisticated study of government support in monthly Gallup opinion polls between 1979 and 1992 concludes that 'evaluations of prime ministerial performance have sizable short-run and long-run effects on Conservative support' (Clarke and Stewart 1995: 160). Similarly, a larger number of cross-sectional studies of individual elections, and especially recent ones, all claim to detect an independent effect on the vote for party leaders (see, for example Bean and Mughan 1989; Miller et al. 1990; and Stewart and Clarke 1992).

The question of the pattern of leader effects over time can be addressed using two separate time series. Neither is perfect for our purposes since both were collected for journalistic rather than academic purposes. Nonetheless, each has merits that make it invaluable to the longitudinal aspirations of this analysis. The first series comprises the campaign surveys that Gallup conducted from the 1964 to 1992 elections inclusive (apart from 1966), but then abandoned after 1992.[15] The advantage of these surveys is their time span; they are unique in using the same closed-ended questions to gauge voters' evaluations of the individual parties, party leaders and their leadership teams over almost three decades.[16] Their main weakness is that they do not include a measure of long-term party affiliation, or party identification, that can be used as a baseline from which defection can be established. As with all correlations of views of parties and their leaders, they also probably misrepresent the magnitude of leader effects because of rationalization on the part of respondents. That is, voters' prime ministerial preference can influence their vote, but equally their voting decision, made on other grounds, can influence their preference for prime minister. Both influences are conflated in the estimates in Figure 2.4 and Table 2.3, and the surveys allow no way of disentangling them.

The problem is more apparent than real, however. The purpose of the present exercise is not to arrive at a precise estimate of the magnitude of leader effects in individual elections, but to determine whether they have become stronger over time. In this regard, the rationalization problem can be assumed to apply equally to all the surveys so that its biasing effect on the coefficient estimates can be taken to be constant throughout the period covered by the table. Put more simply, the pertinent feature of Figure 2.4 and, later, Tables 2.1 and 2.3 is not the absolute or relative magnitude of leader effects, but the pattern in their variation over time. Moreover, in regard to the interpretation of this pattern, it is worth emphasizing here that large shifts in the magnitude of these effects should not be anticipated. As argued in Chapter 1, institutional differences mean the candidates for the position of chief executive in party-dominated parliamentary elections will always have a substantially more muted electoral role and impact than their counterparts in presidential elections.

Figure 2.4 graphs the values election-by-election of the unstandardized, partial regression estimating the impact of preference for prime minister between the Conservative and Labour party leaders, as well as of other variables.[17] Before turning to its interpretation, a few observations need to be made about the procedure giving rise to these estimates. First, the model is parsimonious in that the addition of potentially relevant sociodemographic variables like occupation, education, trade union membership and home ownership did little or nothing to change the results. Second, both dependent and independent variables are dichotomies scored '0' for Labour and '1' for Conservative. This means that the independent variables can be interpreted as the percentage difference (ignoring the decimal point) in the probability of voting for a party between those preferring and not preferring, its leader for prime minister, controlling for the other variables in the equation.[18] Third, the series excludes the 1966 and 1997 contest because Gallup did not collect comparable data for these elections.

The sharpest change in Figure 2.4 involves not the prime ministerial preference variable, but the drop in the explanatory power of the policies variable in 1992 and the concomitant rise in that of the problems variable. This change is consistent with the argument that exasperated voters opted for the Conservative party in 1992 because it was the lesser of two evils. The election was held during an especially deep recession – despite Thatcherite economic policies that had promised to deliver the country from the economic woes visited on it by Keynesianism. The Labour party, however, did not offer a particularly attractive alternative. Holding out the prospect of higher taxation in the campaign, it failed to dent the Conservative party's image as being the more competent manager of the economy. Labour's 'image problem' would seem to have kept voters in the Conservative camp despite their misgivings about its policies (Sanders 1993).

In regard more specifically to the presidentialization thesis, the correlation of prime ministerial preference with time points to an upward trend in leader effects over the period as a whole. This trend would be stronger, of course, were it not for the considerable importance of leader effects in the 1964 election. This is a puzzle. The 1964 coefficient may well represent accurately the impact enjoyed by the contrasting personalities of the Conservative party's Sir Alec Douglas-Home and Labour's Harold Wilson in this contest; the Labour leader certainly attracted phenomenal media attention, in his own right as well as relative to both his party and senior colleagues, in this contest (see Figures 2.1 and 2.2). But the high 1964 value should not be interpreted as proof positive that elections have become no more presidential since then. For a start, there is still a modest upward presidential trend despite the 1964 anomaly. Indeed, the correlation coefficient of 0.22 in Figure 2.4 becomes 0.67 if the 1964 election is excluded from the series. In addition, the value of the prime ministerial preference coefficient drops to its lowest value of all in the 1970 election, whereas the distinctive characteristic of the 1987 and 1992 contests is that the importance of party leaders is more or less sustained from one to the other. Finally, the case for party leaders playing a more autonomous, or presidential, role in later elections is strengthened by voters' preference for a leadership team becoming less influential at the same time that their preference for prime minister becomes more so.

A final observation on Figure 2.4 concerns similarities and differences between the pattern of the party leaders' electoral impact and the pattern of media attention to them discussed earlier. First, the general upward trend over the period as a whole in Figure 2.4 matches that found in media attention to the party leaders (see Figures 2.2 and 2.3). Second, there is, however, some evidence of divergence in the 1990s, with the impact of the leaders declining in 1992 at the same time that newspaper and television attention to them continues to increase. The same divergence is apparent in the next Gallup time series, which has the advantage of including the 1997 election.

The second series of surveys speaking to the presidentialization issue again comes from the Gallup organization. Relative to the series on which Figure 2.4 is based, however, it has one disadvantage and, more importantly, two advantages. The disadvantage is that it does not cover the same extended time span. By way of advantages, however, the series does go beyond 1992 to include the 1997 contest. Additionally, the surveys used in the table include an explicit party identification, or partisanship, variable so that in the event of prime ministerial preference and party identification being in conflict, the success of the former in encouraging voting defection from the latter can be

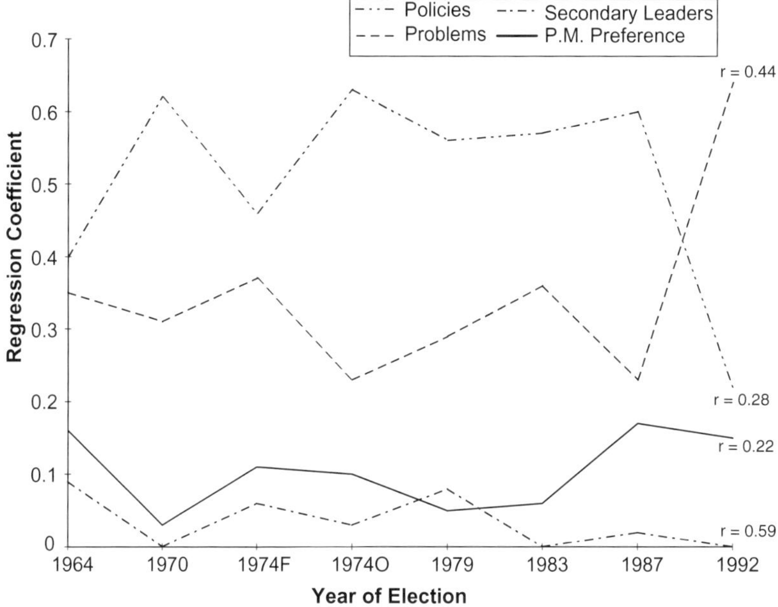

Figure 2.4   Electoral Impact of the Major Party Leader, 1964–92

estimated.[19] The availability of this question allows the adoption of a proportional-reduction-in-error (PRE) approach, which generates estimates of the magnitude of leader effects that have the advantage of being readily interpretable by a wide audience. They are also reliable in that they lead to conclusions about the relative magnitude of election-by-election estimates of leader effects that are the same as when more sophisticated, multivariate statistical techniques are used.

Table 2.1 presents the fruits of the PRE analysis. Its first row contains bivariate coefficients of determination (R^2 values), which indicate the proportion of the variation in the dependent variable, in this case the two-party vote, determined by the independent variable, in this case party identification. Thus, in 1979, other things being equal, 85 per cent of Conservative and Labour partisans voted for the party with which they identified. But when other things are not equal and account is taken of prime ministerial preference, this figure drops by 32 per cent. Partisans of both parties, in other words, were substantially more likely to defect when they thought the leader of the other party would make a better prime minister than the leader of their own party. It follows that the larger the reduction in the value of the R^2 coefficient, the more powerful the electoral impact of the leaders. The pattern of leader effects in Table 2.1 bears a striking resemblance to that found in Figure 2.4 in two key respects. First, neither time series indicates that a linear, or even a monotonic, presidentialization of impact has taken place, although both indicate that leader effects are stronger on average in the post-1983 period than previously. Second, both time series show the impact of the party leaders to decline after reaching their highest point of all in 1987. The leaders' prominence in the media, by contrast, followed a somewhat different trajectory in that it continued to climb in 1992 and at worst stabilized at this peak in 1997 (see Figures 2.2 and 2.3). It would seem, therefore, that the electoral impact of the party leaders is not a simple function of the volume of media coverage that they receive. I shall return to this important observation when considering explanations of leader effects in the next chapter.

A potential criticism of the PRE approach adopted in Table 2.1, of course, is that it is potentially misleading for not taking account of other long- and short-term influences on the vote. People's behaviour at the polls may be rooted in sociodemographic characteristics like age, gender and class as well their habitual party loyalty. It may also be susceptible to short-term forces other than the prime ministerial candidates. A Labour partisan, for example, could prefer the Conservative party leader while at the same time preferring her own party on the campaign issues important to her. Under these circumstances, it is an empirical question as to which, if any, of these contradictory short-term forces influences her vote. Reliable estimation of leader effects requires that other potential influences on the vote be controlled, and principally issues.

To maintain continuity with Table 2.1, the same Gallup surveys are used to measure issue preferences as well as prime ministerial preference. Specifically, each of the surveys presents respondents with a number of issues and then poses the question 'When you decided which way to vote, which TWO issues did you personally consider most important?' Respondents are then free to choose none, one or two issue items from the list presented to them.[20] Table 2.2 presents the distributions of responses by year on this issue question. In 1979, for example, 12.9 per cent of voters declared none of the specified issues had been important to their voting decision, 31.2 per cent thought one issue had been important and fully 56.0 per cent felt that two issues had been influential in their choice of party.

The results presented in Table 2.2 would seem to hold out great potential for the electoral effect of issues. In none of the four elections do fewer than 85 per cent of respondents claim not to have been influenced in their voting decision by at least one issue and always more than a majority deemed themselves to have been swayed by two of them. Importance may not be enough for a net electoral effect, however. Party preference also has to be taken into account. A respondent may, for example, feel that two issues were important to her vote, but thought that the Tories were the party better able to handle one of them and Labour better able to handle the other. Taken together, these conflicting assessments of party competence would serve to cancel the person's issue preferences out so that they would have no net effect on her choice of party (Butler and Stokes 1974: 290–5). Fortunately, the 1979, 1983, 1987 and 1992 Gallup surveys allow party preference to be incorporated into a measure of issue voting through their inclusion of a separate question that, referring back to the same issues, presents them as 'problems facing the country' and asks respondents 'which party (they) personally think would handle the problem best?'. The issue importance and party preference questions can thus be combined by creating two new variables, one tapping a net Conservative preference on issues of importance and the other a Labour preference. Simply put, if a respondent deems an issue to have been influential in his voting choice *and* he prefers the Tories on that issue, then his Conservative preference variable is given a score of 1 and his Labour preference variable is scored 0. If Labour is his preferred party on it, the scoring is reversed. This procedure is repeated for the second important issue and the scores on his Conservative and Labour preference variables are then summed separately, with each

Table 2.1 Prime Ministerial Preference and Voting Defection from Partisanship, 1979–97

	1979	*1983*	*1987*	*1992*	*1997*
Party identification ×					
Vote	0.85	0.81	0.86	0.84	0.84
R² reduction controlling for:					
Best PM	0.32	0.27	0.39	0.32	0.34

Sources: 1979–87, BBC-Gallup Exit Polls; 1992, Gallup Post-Election Survey; 1997, Gallup, Final Pre-Election Study.

Table 2.2   Distribution of Number of Issues Important to Party Choice, 1979–92

	1979 %	*1983* %	*1987* %	*1992* %
None	12.9	9.5	10.4	15.0
One	31.2	32.7	33.6	34.4
Two	56.0	57.9	55.9	50.6

being able to range in value between 0 and 2. Finally, to match the scoring of a pro-Conservative response on the 'Who would make the best prime minister?' variable, a pro-Conservative stance on the issues is measured by subtracting the Labour from the Conservative issue preference score.

We are now in a position to determine two things. The first is whether the prime ministerial candidates remain a significant influence the vote after that other short-term force, issues, has been controlled. The second is whether leader effects follow the same general pattern once issues are controlled. Table 2.3 speaks to both of these questions. It includes as predictor variables party identification, prime ministerial preference, issue preference and a range of sociodemographic predictors common to all four surveys.[21] Dummy variables for the most part, these predictors are: married vs single/divorced; employed vs unemployed/retired; male vs female; white vs non-white; and membership of a household in which one or both spouses belongs to a union vs being part of a non-union household. The age variable groups respondents into categories ranging from 18 to 22 years old to more than 70 and the social class measure is the standard occupational scale ranging from 'A' (higher managerial or professional) to 'E' (residual, on pension or state benefit) (Butler and Stokes 1974: 69–83). The multivariate results are presented in the form of unstandardized partial regression coefficients since these have the property of being directly comparable across equations. This means that the pattern of leader effects can be charted across the four elections. A disadvantage of unstandardized coefficients is that their magnitudes cannot be compared to determine their impact relative to each other within equations. However, the question of which is the more powerful electoral force, issues or leaders, is addressed explicitly in Chapter 5 of the book.

For this analysis of the presidentialization thesis, the pertinent conclusion to be drawn from Table 2.3 is that even when the issue and

Table 2.3   Candidates, Issues and Conservative Party Choice, 1979–92

	1979	1983	1987	1992
Con. party identification	0.60***	0.55***	0.56***	0.59***
Con. best PM	0.26***	0.30***	0.33***	0.17***
Con. best issues	0.05***	0.05***	0.05***	0.08***
Age	−0.01	−0.00	0.00	0.00
Middle-class	0.02*	0.00	0.01**	0.00
Male	0.02*	0.00	0.00	0.02
Union household	−0.01	0.00	−0.00	−0.01
Employed	0.02	0.01	0.02*	−0.01
White	0.03	0.03	0.06**	−0.02
Married	0.01	0.02	0.01	−0.02
R^2	0.89	0.87	0.90	0.87

$*p < 0.05$; $**p < 0.01$; $***p < 0.001$ (one-tailed test).

sociodemographic variables are taken into account, the Conservative and Labour leaders remain highly significant electoral forces. Moreover, the pattern of leader effects follow much the same broad presidential trajectory as uncovered in Figure 2.4, which is based on different data sets and different questions, and Table 2.1. They increased in magnitude in the 1980s, and especially in 1987, but then receded from this high point in the 1990s. There is variation, in other words, but it does not take the form of a linear trend. Nor does there seem to be a substantial trade-off between issue and leader effects. Issue preferences are fairly stable in their impact, whereas prime ministerial preference is substantially more variable. It is only in 1992 that issues become more influential relative to previous elections at the same time that the party leaders become relatively less influential. Thus, some kind of trade-off with issues cannot be invoked to explain the variation in leader effects between 1979 and 1992.

In sum, then, party leaders matter, and they generally matter more now than in the 1960s and 1970s. But even if at a generally higher level, their impact on the vote still varies up and down from election-to-election. It is clear that this variation is not a function of leader effects being inversely related to that other well-known and short-term electoral force, issue effects. The unanswered question, therefore, is what makes them matter sometimes more and sometimes less. This question is addressed in the next chapter.

Conclusion

This chapter has sought to trace the emergence and development of both the theory and the practice of presidentialization in British politics. It has been a complex story and it is now time to take stock. At one level, it is difficult to deny the presidentialization thesis. There is widespread agreement that British electoral politics have experienced a qualitative change in that, to a degree unprecedented in the past, party leaders now matter for the way parties present themselves to voters between and during campaigns, as well as for the way elections turn out. The turning point seems to have been 1964. In the absence of survey data that can be used to estimate leader effects prior to this election, we cannot be certain that this was the transitional contest. It is the case, though, that the small number of voting studies undertaken in the 1950s concurred in attributing to party leaders no independent influence on election outcomes; they were simply overshadowed by their party in an era of strong partisan loyalties. But whether one looks at the evidence presented in this chapter or in Butler and Stokes' (1974) seminal study, the same absence of influence did not characterize their role in the 1964 election. In addition, the textual analysis of editorials in *The Times* identifies 1964 as the election in which the notion of presidentialization makes its first appearance in serious political discussion (see also Pryce 1997).

The emergence at this time of a concept alien to the traditional, party-based characterization of the British political process is apparently not coincidental. The editorial pages of *The Times* suggest two key reasons for it. The first is television's displacement of the printed press as political parties' pre-eminent campaigning medium and voters' principal, most trusted and most credible media source for political information. The assumption seems to have taken hold that voters could not help but fall prey to the visual image and the unprecedented personalization of politics inevitably associated with this revolutionary medium. The second stimulus is Richard Crossman's a provocative and controversial introduction to the 1963 edition of Bagehot's *The English Constitution* in which he argued that cabinet government had given way to prime ministerial government. Coming hard on the heels of Macmillan's forceful, domineering style of cabinet leadership, this argument struck a more receptive chord than it probably would have done with earlier, more collegial post-war prime ministers.

The story of leader effects since 1964 is another matter. More systematic Gallup survey evidence has been brought to bear on the question of whether electoral politics have presidentialized since then. Not purpose-designed for rigorous testing of the presidentialization thesis, however, the evidence these surveys generate is not always entirely satisfactory. For this reason, attention in evaluating their results has focused on broad areas of agreement rather than precise values of statistical coefficients in individual analyses. In this regard, the media and survey analyses concur in indicating that elections have become more presidential since 1964, and especially in the 1980s and 1990s. The presidentialization of electoral impact that has taken place should not be overstated, however. Even in recent elections, leader effects have turned out not to be fixed and have gone down as well as up from one contest to the next. Little else could reasonably be expected in parliamentary elections where the leaders' contribution to election outcomes will be more marginal than decisive, except in closely fought contests where a relatively popular leader may make the difference between victory and defeat for her party (Bean and Mughan 1989). Nonetheless, leader effects remain important even after a host of other factors, including issues, have been controlled so that the conclusion that party leaders cannot be ignored in the study of the dynamics of contemporary parliamentary election outcomes is inescapable. But equally, their impact cannot be taken for granted; it is a variable and the next chapter addresses the question of what it is that accounts for this variability.

3
Explaining Leader Effects

The cumulative evidence presented in the previous chapter demonstrated that British general elections have not presidentialized in the sense of the Conservative and Labour party leaders coming to enjoy a stronger electoral impact with each passing election. Rather, leader effects inched upwards in fits and starts between 1964 and 1983, jumped sharply in 1987 – the first election in which both major parties fully embraced leader-centred campaigning strategies – fell back, although not to the 1983 level, in 1992 and then moved a little upwards again in 1997. The absence of a secular trend notwithstanding, election contests were concluded to have presidentialized in the more limited sense of having become more leader-centred after 1983 in terms of both presentation and impact than their post-war predecessors. Presidential change there has been, then, and the logical next question is: how do we account for the actual pattern of leader effects that has transpired? The problem with a question of this type, of course, is that it is difficult to provide a simple answer to it since complex change is, by its nature, unlikely to be susceptible to univariate explanation.

The strategy adopted in this chapter, therefore, is to explore several plausible explanations of the pattern of leader effects separately and to bring the results together in a concluding section. Carrying on from the last chapter, this one begins with a specific focus on the media. The specific potential explanation considered is a simple agenda-setting hypothesis that the magnitude of leader effects is a direct function of the prominence of the party leaders in the mass media of communication. Insofar as their prominence is generally greatest during the period, 1987–1997, when their electoral impact is at its strongest, this hypothesis is found to afford some explanatory leverage, but at the same time to leave important aspects of the relationship unresolved.

The chapter moves on, therefore, to test potential complementary, and in some cases overlapping, explanations of the pattern of leader effects. These are: (i) partisan dealignment; (ii) the popularity gap hypothesis; (iii) the personalities of the party leaders; and (iv) negative vs positive voting.

Media agenda-setting

For a considerable period of time the media's political effects at election time were interpreted as being direct in nature – that is, making themselves felt in line with a simple stimulus–response model whereby citizens exposed to a medium whose partisan messages were at odds with their own voting preference were persuaded to change their preference to match that of the medium (Mughan and Gunther 2000). Eventually, media theorizing became more sophisticated and it came to be acknowledged that effects could be indirect as well as direct. The agenda-setting hypothesis represents the first recognition of the possibility of systematic indirect effects.[1] In the words of one its earliest advocates:

> The press is significantly more than a purveyor of information and opinions. It may not be successful much of the time in telling people what to think, but it is stunningly successful in telling its readers what to think *about*…The editor may believe he is only printing the things that people want to read, but he is thereby putting a claim on their attention, powerfully determining what they will think about, and talk about, until the next wave laps their shore.
>
> (Cohen 1963: 13; emphasis in original)

This hypothesis is a natural starting point for efforts to understand the pattern of leaders effects since Chapter 2's tracing of both the media prominence of the Conservative and Labour party leaders and their electoral impact clearly implies, in the agenda-setting tradition, some relationship between the two. Indeed, the way in which both move sharply upwards in 1987 would itself seem to be good reason for the expectation of such a relationship since this was the first election in which *both* the Conservative and Labour parties unambiguously embraced leader-centred campaigning through television for the first time. Albeit tentative for spanning only a short time period – 1964 to 1997 – one way of establishing at least the plausibility of the agenda-setting hypothesis is to determine the extent to which media coverage and electoral impact move in tandem. If the relationship is weak to non-existent, then the media would have to be concluded as playing little or no role in shaping the pattern of leader effects. Table 3.1 presents the zero-order correlations between various aggregated measures of the leaders' prominence in the media on the one hand and their impact on the vote on the other. Thus, for example, the newspaper mentions measure referred to in it is simply the sum of the absolute number of mentions of the prime minister and the opposition leader in Figure 2.1.

The next chapter will examine in more detail what it is about the media that promotes leader effects. Suffice it for the moment to restrict attention to the question of whether there is a relationship between the volume of media coverage of the party leaders and the magnitude of their electoral impact. In this regard, the immediately striking feature of Table 3.1 is that the correlation coefficients in it are always positive and generally non-trivial in magnitude, which lends some considerable credence to the agenda-setting hypothesis. At the same time, however, the positive and substantial nature of the relationship also throws into sharp relief the explanatory limitations of this same hypothesis and cautions against any simple stimulus–response model of media effects in the explanation of electoral presidentialism. Specifically, it will be recalled from Chapter 2 that the presentation and impact of the Conservative and Labour leaders took divergent paths after the 1987 elections, with media attention to them continuing its upward trajectory and their effect on the two-party vote taking a downwards one. This divergence means that media coverage of the

Table 3.1   Zero-Order Correlations between Leader Effects and Aggregated Media Prominence Measures[a]

	r
Newspaper mentions	
Leaders	0.68
Leaders/party	0.61
Leaders/Cabinet	0.67
Television mentions	
Leaders	0.58
Leaders/Cabinet	0.12

[a] The newspaper correlations coefficients are based on the years 1964–92, excluding 1979 since *The Times* was not published during that campaign. The television figures are based on 1964–92 inclusive. The measure of leaders effects is taken from Figure 2.4.

party leaders cannot be the sole determinant of the electoral impact they enjoy. This is not to conclude, of course, that the media are unimportant; the correlation coefficients in Table 3.1 are sufficient in themselves to advise against such a conclusion. Nonetheless, it is clear that newspapers and television may lavish unprecedented attention on the party leaders; however, this is no guarantee that this will lead to an equally unprecedented electoral impact. It is necessary, in other words, to acknowledge the apparently important agenda-setting role played by changing amounts of media coverage, but account must also be taken of other, potentially complementary explanations of leader effects.

A variety of such explanations exist and prominent among them stand party identification and the party leaders themselves. These will now be examined and their explanatory potential for understanding the changing pattern of leader effects in the 1980s and 1990s evaluated. Party identification comes first.

Partisan dealignment

There are two ways in which party identification, or partisanship, can have implications for the magnitude of leader effects in one or more elections. The first involves its relationship to prime ministerial preference and the second its pattern of waxing and waning.

The first possibility is that the impact of prime ministerial preference fell from its 1987 electoral peak in 1992 and 1997 because the nature of its relationship to partisanship transmuted. To be more precise, perhaps having crossed some psychological threshold, prime ministerial preference changed from being the product of party identification to becoming one of the forces shaping that identification. The party leaders moved, in other words, from the status of epiphenomenon, or product of party identification, to being one of its structuring forces. One effect of such a transmutation would be that prime ministerial preference exercises less of a moderating effect on the relationship between partisanship and the vote because some part of the leader's importance for voters would already have been incorporated into their long-term sense of identification with the Conservative or Labour parties. Should there have been such a transmutation after the high point of leader effects in the 1987 general election, it means, empirically speaking, that partisanship's relationship to prime ministerial preference can minimally be expected to be stronger in the two subsequent elections, 1992 and 1997. But this does not turn out to be the case; at 0.86, 0.84 and 0.84 respectively, the simple correlation between the two dichotomized variables turns out in fact to have been at best a little higher in 1987 than in 1992 and 1997.

The second way in which party identification may explain the pattern of leader effects is through the weakening of popular identification with the Conservative and Labour parties. Post-1970 partisan dealignment, it has been argued, has made voters more volatile in their behaviour at the polls and more susceptible to short-term influences, such as campaign-specific issues and candidates for the position of chief executive.[2] A succinct statement of this thesis is:

> As partisan and class ardour cooled, however, considerations other than habitual party and class loyalties began to influence the voting decision of more and more electors. In particular, campaign-specific factors – the outgoing government's record, the major issues of the day, *the party leaders' personal qualities*, specific and perhaps quite trivial incidents – took on a greater significance…The committed electorate has begun to make way for the hesitant electorate.
>
> (Crewe 1984: 203–4; emphasis added)

Stated thus, dealignment might be taken to entail an automatically enhanced impact for party leaders, the logic being that as the long-term force of party identification gets weaker, short-term forces cannot help but get stronger as they rush in to fill the vacuum left by the weakened commitment to the Conservative and Labour parties. However, there are three reasons to doubt that the electoral fortunes of prime ministerial candidates necessarily wax and wane in direct proportion to the weakness of long-term Conservative and Labour partisan loyalties. First, it is not logically necessary that prime ministerial candidates must become more influential as partisanship gets weaker. The increased volatility resulting from weakened party loyalties might simply lead to other short-term factors, like issues, being more consequential for the way voters cast their ballot.[3] Second, empirical investigation has failed to provide much support for the hypothesis of a presidentialization of electoral impact moving in tandem with the decline in party identification. For example, in a detailed study addressing itself explicitly to the phenomenon of partisan dealignment in the 1970s, Särlvik and Crewe (1983: 132–3) find no evidence that this phenomenon has been associated with stronger leader effects. Rather, echoing Butler and Stokes with regard to the elections of 1964, 1966 and 1970, they conclude that leader images continue to have

Table 3.2   Presidentialization in British Elections: a Comparison of the 1964–70, 1974–83 and 1987–92 Election Groupings

	1964–70	*1974–83*	t-*value*	*1974–83*	*1987–92*	t-*value*
Policies	0.56	0.55	0.42	0.55	0.56	0.55
Problems	0.34	0.32	1.95	0.32	0.26	6.93
Secondary leaders	0.01	0.03	1.58	0.03	0.01	1.58
PM preference	0.07	0.08	1.90	0.08	0.18	8.70
R^2	0.89	0.90		0.90	0.93	

minor effects at best on election outcomes. Third, the evidence in Figure 2.4 and Table 2.2 in the previous chapter indicates that the jump in the electoral impact of party leaders did not coincide with the dealignment of the mid-1970s, but came something like a decade later.

The disjuncture between the onset of dealignment on the one hand and the heightened electoral presidentialism of 1987 and after on the other is particularly evident in Table 3.2, which presents a pooled analysis of the same Gallup campaign polls that figure in Figure 2.4 in the last chapter.[4] The *t*-values reported in the table are a measure of the size of the change in strength of each variable's impact on the vote from one election grouping to the other. Statistical (and substantive) significance at the 5 per cent level can be assumed when the *t*-values for the variables are 1.65 or higher.

It is immediately obvious from these *t*-values that, at least from the perspective of leader effects, the 1964–92 period is best treated in trichotomous rather than dichotomous terms. Dealignment may have got underway in the mid-1970s and it may also have resulted in a somewhat increased electoral impact for party leaders in the subsequent 1979 and 1983 elections, but the difference is not startling. The 1987 and 1992 contests, by contrast, are a different story altogether. The null hypothesis of no difference in the magnitude of leader effects between the 1974–83 and 1987–92 election groupings can be seen to be resoundingly rejected by the evidence. The simple fact of the matter is that presidentialization has not progressed at an even rate over the period of dealignment, never mind over the three decades from 1964 to 1992. Rather, leader effects are not strikingly stronger in the dealigned period stretching from 1974 to 1983 compared to the more strongly aligned years 1964–70. This finding is consistent with the conclusion reached elsewhere that the Conservative and Labour leaders initially remained a minimal influence on the vote despite the weakening of party identification (see, for example, Särlvik and Crewe 1983). In the 1987 and 1992 contests, by contrast, presidentialism can be seen to have taken take a steep upward turn relative even to the immediately preceding dealigned elections.

Of course, merely to point to the distinctiveness of the most recent election contests does not preclude dealignment as a sufficient explanation of their more distinctly presidential character. It might well be that the impact of the prime ministerial candidates was so high in these most recent contests precisely because there was a commensurate acceleration in the weakening of party identification in them. Again, however, this proves not to be the case. As with the agenda-setting hypothesis tested earlier, the link between the strength of partisanship and magnitude of leader effects proves more complex than single-factor explanations would imply. This is readily apparent from Table 3.3, which uses British Election Study data to track the pattern of partisan dealignment from 1964 to 1997. Two findings in this table merit special comment. First, insofar as it shows partisan dealignment, like the leaders' media prominence, to be at its peak in the 1980s and 1990s, the electoral presidentialism of this same period cannot be fully understood without taking account of this decline in psychological attachment to the Conservative and Labour parties. Second, dealignment may be a necessary condition of such presidentialism, but it is not a sufficient one. Changes in the number of weak identifiers and in the magnitude of leader effects do travel together, not least insofar as both reach and sustain their respective high points in the 1980s and 1990s. Nonetheless, it is also the case that they do not move faithfully in tandem. For example, the proportion of weak identifiers changed little between 1983 and 1987, yet analysis of different data sets has shown that the magnitude of leader effects to have jumped substantially from the first to the second of these contests (see Table 3.3). Similarly, the proportion of weak identifiers is clearly at its highest in 1997, but the impact of party leaders still falls considerably below its 1987 value.

The conclusion, therefore, is that, as with media agenda-setting, the search for an explanation of electoral presidentialization must be nested in the phenomenon of partisan dealignment, but at the same time go beyond it. Moreover, in view of the considerable up-and-down movement in the pattern of leader effects in the relatively heavily dealigned 1980s and 1990s, whatever it is that complements media

Table 3.3   Weak Partisanship and Leader Effects by Election

	% Weak Identifiers[a]	*Job Approval (see Figure 2.4)*	*Best PM (see Table 2.2)*
1964	11.5	0.16	n.a.
1966	12.9	n.a.	n.a.
1970	12.4	0.03	n.a.
1974F	21.2	0.11	n.a.
1974O	20.9	0.10	n.a.
1979	25.7	0.05	0.32
1983	31.0	0.06	0.27
1987	30.5	0.17	0.39
1992	27.4	0.15	0.32
1997	33.5	n.a.	0.34

[a] The figure in this row is the percentage of Conservative and Labour partisans combined who identify 'not very strongly' with their party.

agenda-setting and partisan dealignment in explaining this pattern cannot be assumed to be constant from one election to the next. Rather, it is more likely an entity to which voters react differently in different circumstances. The logical candidate to fill this explanatory gap is the party leaders themselves either in relation to each other or in their own right. This line of reasoning suggests two hypotheses centred around the leaders as individual stimuli, hypotheses that complement the wider media and partisan context in which they find themselves. The first of these is commonly known as the popularity gap hypothesis, while the second treats party leaders as individuals in their own right with personal qualities that voters do or do not value in a chief executive at a particular point in time.

The popularity gap hypothesis

Butler and Stokes (1974) were the first analysts to take seriously the possibility of an electoral role for the leaders of Britain's Conservative and Labour parties. Two reasons probably go some way to explaining why their 1960s study was unusually sensitive to the possibility of a changed electoral role for these hitherto ignored political actors. First, it was around this time that television emerged as a political force, replacing newspapers as voters' primary information source. Second, the Labour leader in the 1964 election, Harold Wilson, was the centre of his party's new, media-based presentational initiative designed to modernize the party's image with the public at large (Wring 1996).[5] The circumstances were right, in short, for a re-evaluation of the 1950s conventional wisdom that, being indistinguishable from their party, the candidates for the position of prime minister did not matter for the way individuals voted and elections turned out.

On the basis of their analysis of the 1964, 1966 and 1970 elections, Butler and Stokes came to two conclusions about the impact of party leaders, one firm and the other more tentative. Notwithstanding the enhanced electoral impact that party leaders have come to enjoy, their major conclusion is as valid today as it was then: '[I]t is clear that attitudes towards the parties were a better guide to voting behaviour than attitudes towards the leaders' (Butler and Stokes 1974: 363). Still very apposite today, this observation serves as a healthy reminder of the inherent limits to presidentialism in party-centred parliamentary elections. Their second conclusion is more impressionistic, if only for being based on the study of no more than three elections. It is that 'party leaders have enough hold on the public's consciousness...for popular feeling towards them to have demonstrable effects on the party balance when it becomes preponderantly positive or negative' (Butler and Stokes 1974: 367–8). Leader effects, in other words, are seen as conditional, as an artefact of circumstance. Moreover, the circumstance that matters is how prime ministerial candidates stand relative to each other in public opinion – the wider the popularity gap between them, the greater their impact on both individual choice and on the inter-party distribution of the vote.

Despite its tenuous empirical foundations, this intuitively plausible hypothesis has achieved the status of received wisdom. Denver (1989: 90), for example, opines: 'The conclusion reached by Butler and Stokes is judicious. They say that if there is a marked imbalance in the public's estimation of party leaders, if one is clearly preferred or more disliked than another, then that will have some impact on voting choice.' Similarly, King has held that one condition for party leaders to matter in British elections is that the gap between them must be wide (*The Economist*, 14 March 1992: 22). This being the case, and given the pattern of leader effects uncovered in the last chapter, the gap between the two leaders can, broadly speaking, be expected to be greater in the 1980s and 1990s than in the 1960s and 1970s. More specifically still, it should be at its widest in 1987 and narrower in subsequent contests.

The discrepancy between expectation and reality, though, is only too apparent in Table 3.4, which uses two different measures of the leaders'

Table 3.4   The Popularity Gap and the Impact of Party Leaders

	1964	1970	1974F	1974O	1979	1983	1987	1992	1997
Job Approval									
% difference[a]	11.0	23.0	1.0	12.0	0.0	32.0	14.0	15.0	37.0
Leader effects (see Figure 2.4)	0.16	0.03	0.11	0.10	0.05	0.06	0.17	0.15	n.a.
Best PM									
% difference[b]	n.a.	n.a.	n.a.	n.a.	12.2	53.8	21.8	24.4	22.5
Leader effects (see Table 2.2)	n.a.	n.a.	n.a.	n.a.	0.32	0.27	0.39	0.32	0.34

[a] This figure is the percentage difference between those approving the prime minister and the leader of the opposition. It comes from Gallup polling figures in the month before the election. See Butler and Butler (1994: 247–59).
[b] Looking only at those thinking one or other of the major party leaders would make the best prime minister, this figure is the percentage difference between them.

standing relative to each other to put the popularity gap hypothesis to the stringent test. The first of them is a simple job approval measure, with the figure reported being the percentage difference in approval of the two party leaders in the Gallup poll conducted the month before the election. The second asks voters to make a direct choice as to who would make the best prime minister and the figure reported is the percentage difference between those choosing the Labour leader and those choosing his Conservative counterpart.[6] Each measure is then paired with the corresponding estimate in Chapter 2 of the party leaders' impact on the vote in the particular general election.

In a nutshell, Table 3.4 provides no support at all for the popularity gap hypothesis. Whether the leadership differential is measured by job approval or by preference for the position of prime minister, even the most cursory glance at the table shows there to be no systematic relationship between it and the magnitude of leader effects. Take the best prime minister measure. Leader effects can be seen to be at their highest (in 1987) when the divergence of opinion over who would make the best prime minister is at its next to lowest point in the five-election series. The same goes for job approval-based popularity. In 1970, leader effects were at their low point, but the approval difference between the Conservative and Labour leaders was among the highest for any election. Indeed, the simple correlation between the job approval measure and electoral impact from 1964 to 1992 is negative at a value of -0.23. Statistically insignificant, it is a coefficient that is probably best interpreted conservatively, i.e., not as being in the opposite direction to that predicted by the popularity gap hypothesis, but as indicating the absence of a relationship. Equally, there is no sign that the popularity gap is at its highest in 1987 and declines thereafter. Indeed, the gap between the two popularity measures widens, and especially for job approval.

Thus, variation in the size of the popularity gap between the Conservative and Labour leaders bears no relation to the magnitude of leader effects in recent British elections. Taken together with the findings that the leaders have become more prominent in the media and that partisan dealignment is also at its highest point in the 1980s and 1990s, the failure of the popularity gap hypothesis raises the possibility of an explanation of leader effects rooted not in the prime ministerial candidates relative to each other, but in their being unprecedentedly salient individuals whose personalities have become a more powerful stimulus for the voter.

Character traits

It has long been accepted that candidates are the strongest force for change in the distribution of the vote from one US presidential election to another. This is because, casting their ballot for the president directly, American voters are able to react to the candidates as individual personalities as well as party representatives. Long-term partisanship is thus not necessarily the primary cue on which they base their presidential choice. Rather, voters often approach the election with a well-defined mental image, or schema, of what a president should be like and evaluate the candidates on offer to them against this schema, commonly voting in contradiction to their partisanship if their candidate preference predisposes them that way. There is also considerable agreement that 'competence' and 'caringness' are among the personality traits that are most valued by voters and are consequently the traits with the greatest impact on their choice for president (Kinder et al. 1980; Miller et al. 1986).

The dominant influence on individual choice in parliamentary elections, by contrast, is the political party, which means that the relevance of personality-based voting models to them has been, and remains, a matter of dispute. As shown in Chapter 1, the argument is made that in parliamentary systems, like Britain and Germany, where party loyalties are still relatively strong and the political culture adversarial, the study of the personalities of prime ministerial candidates adds little or nothing to our understanding of election outcomes (Kaase 1994; Rose and McAllister 1986; 1990). Stated more fully, this argument holds that, in view of their strong tendency to see leaders through the lens of their partisanship, voters show an instinctive preference for their own party's leader and a matching aversion to the other's so that Conservative and Labour leaders are seen by and large in zero-sum terms. For identifiers to perceive their party leader as being, say, caring serves to preclude them from attributing the same quality to the other party leader with the result that their loyalty in the polling booth is reinforced.

This is the traditional view of the British political process. Pitted against it is a mounting body of evidence indicating that in a dealigned party system the personalities of the party leaders have come to matter more than they used to for the way people vote. More specifically, studies of recent election contests suggest that British voters react to candidates for the position of chief executive on the basis of a similar structure of preferred character traits as the one found among American voters. Bean and Mughan (1989: 1176), for example, conclude their comparison of Australia and Britain with the observation that 'prime ministerial candidates are judged against some kind of well-defined schema in the public mind and … they will have a positive electoral impact to the extent that they conform to this mental image of what a leader should be like'. In line with US findings, they also identify 'effectiveness' and 'caringness' as the pre-eminent character traits defining this schema. In a separate analysis of the 1987 British general election, Stewart and Clarke (1992: 455; see also Jones and Hudson 1996: 238–9) bolster this general line of argument with their demonstration that 'competence' and 'responsiveness' structured voters' images of both Thatcher and Kinnock in 1987, with 'caring' being the strongest constituent element of leader responsiveness.

If it is the character traits of party leaders that are responsible for the presidentialism evident especially in recent British elections, then three consequences should follow. First, these traits should be apparent to voters independently of their partisanship. Second, these same traits should have an influence on the vote that is independent of partisanship. Third, the trajectory of this influence should resemble the one found in Figure 2.4 and Table 2.2 – that is, trait-based leader effects should not only be stronger in later than in earlier elections, but also they should decline, albeit not to their prior level, after hitting their peak in 1987.

Table 3.5 speaks to the first of these consequences, the independent place of party leaders in the public mind. Character trait questions appeared in the British Election Study for the first time in 1983. In 1987, a major revision of the questionnaire occurred and only the 'effectiveness' and 'caring' trait questions from 1983 were asked again. Then the 'effectiveness' question was itself dropped in the 1992 study.[7] This meant that 'caring' has been the only trait question asked across all four elections since 1983.[8] Within the constraints set by such changes in questionnaire content, Table 3.5 details how voters perceive the personalities of the Conservative and Labour party leaders in the 1983, 1987, 1992 and 1997 elections. The argument that leaders are pale reflections of their party for voters is seriously undermined in two respects. The first is the distribution of the personality traits of effectiveness and caringness. There is simply too much variation in their distributions to allow them to be dismissed as artefacts of partisanship. For example, a full 90 per cent of major party identifiers see the Conservative leader, Mrs Thatcher, as effective in 1983 and 1987, while no more than 37 per cent of the electorate identified with her party in either of these two elections (Heath et al. 1991: 12). Moreover, the attribution of a trait to the same leader can change substantially from one election to the next

Table 3.5 The Distribution and Inter-Correlation of Character Traits by Election, 1983–92

	1983	1987	1992	1997
Distribution (%)				
PM Effective	90	90	n.a.	n.a.
PM Caring	18	57	75	64
OL Effective	31	47	n.a.	n.a.
OL Caring	47	80	78	82
Zero-Order Correlations				
PM × OL: Effective	−0.22	−0.13	n.a.	n.a.
PM × OL: Caring	−0.11	−0.16	−0.16	−0.06
PM Effective × Party Identification	0.38	0.32	n.a.	n.a.
PM Caring × Party Identification	0.31	0.71	0.59	0.47
OL Effective × Party Identification	0.50	0.48	n.a.	n.a.
OL Caring × Party Identification	0.32	0.30	0.32	0.25

despite the distribution of party identification remaining relatively stable. The large increase from 1983 to 1987 in the proportion seeing Mrs Thatcher as caring is a particularly vivid example.

The second respect in which Table 3.5 indicates that the Conservative and Labour leaders are not pale reflections of their party is apparent in how voters perceive them relative to each other. Little indication is given that voters are slaves to their party identification in the sense of their perceptions of the prime minister and leader of the opposition being zero-sum. If such were the case, the correlations between perceptions of the two leaders on the same personality trait would not only be negative, but would approach unity. But in fact they can be seen to be far from perfect, averaging only −0.18 for effectiveness and −0.12 for caring. Voters would appear generally to be about as able to attribute desirable traits to one party leader as the other and, as such, are not irredeemably partisan in their reaction to prime ministerial candidates. In the same vein, the correlations between party identification and personality traits demonstrate that partisans fall short of instinctively attributing desirable qualities only to their own party leader. The fact that the correlations are positive and not trivial in magnitude indicates that, as is only to be expected, there is some tendency to do so, but at the same time the relationship is far from deterministic.

Table 3.5 belies any suspicion that leaders are simply the creatures of their party in the public eye. How, if at all, these same leaders influence the behaviour of voters, though, is another question altogether. A voter may perceive the rival party leader, and not her own, to be effective, but this does not necessarily mean that she will ignore her long-standing party loyalties and change her vote to accommodate her leader preference. Thus, the question of leader effects has to be addressed separately from that of the perception of character traits.

If it is true, first, that leader preferences are substantially independent of party identification, second, that leaders have been the focal point in the media of recent election campaigns more than in the past, and, third, that Labour became as leader-centred as the Conservatives only when Neil Kinnock took his place at its helm in time for the 1987 contest, then it follows that the electoral impact of leaders' personalities should be measurably stronger in this contest than previously. Given the findings in Chapter 2, it further follows that if it is the personalities of the leaders themselves that account for variation in the pattern of leader effects, then the impact of their character traits should drop in 1992 after having peaked in 1987 and then rebound somewhat in 1997.

In light of the often-demonstrated importance of the leadership traits of effectiveness and caringness for both British and US voters, any change there may have been in the electoral potency of party leaders should be reflected in the impact of these two traits on voting choice.[9] Table 3.6 details this relationship for each of these traits separately, although an incomplete series is all that is possible for effectiveness. Two features of the table merit special mention. First, and most important, the pattern of trait effects closely mirrors that of the larger pattern of leader effects (estimated by means of the prime ministerial preference question) uncovered in the last chapter. Moreover, this observation holds, albeit more tentatively in the case of effectiveness, for both traits. Controlling for the perceived effectiveness of the opposition leader, for example, results in a three percentage points weakening in the strength of the 1983 relationship between partisanship and the vote. The matching figure for 1987 is a little higher at four percentage points. Moreover, repeating this exercise for caringness leads to the same general conclusion. The R^2 drop is only one percentage point for the prime minister in 1983, but it is 14, six and seven points in 1987,

Table 3.6   The Effect of Leader Traits on Party Identification's Relationship to the Vote, 1983–97

	1983	*1987*	*1992*	*1997*
Party Identification × Vote	0.89	0.86	0.89	0.87
R^2 *reduction controlling for:*				
PM Effective	0.01	0.02	n.a.	n.a.
OL Effective	0.03	0.04	n.a.	n.a.
PM Caring	0.01	0.14	0.06	0.07
OL Caring	0.00	0.02	0.01	0.02

1992 and 1997 respectively. If, in other words, 1983 is taken as the norm in a dealigned party system, the relatively presidential character of the three subsequent contests can hardly be doubted.

The second noteworthy feature of the table is its suggestion that while voters may judge prime ministerial candidates against some kind of well-defined schema, they would nonetheless seem to weigh the component elements of this schema differently according to the specific circumstances of individual elections. This suggestion is at its strongest in the behaviour of the caring variable, a personality trait that had mattered little for either party leader in the 1983 election. In 1987, by sharp contrast, the perception of whether or not Mrs Thatcher in particular was caring was highly consequential for the way Conservative and Labour partisans voted. In 1992 and 1997, its effect weakened for both the prime minister and the leader of the opposition, but still remained stronger than it had been in 1983.

Of course, not too much should be made of change in the impact of a single variable over a small number of elections even if its importance for leader influence in elections has been widely demonstrated. Still, it is pertinent to note that the large jump in the both the distribution and impact of the caring variable coincided with Mrs Thatcher's conscious efforts to moderate her public image so as to appear less strident, more understanding and more sympathetic. This involved her paying close attention to her looks, makeup and dress, but it also led her to take voice lessons to lower her natural pitch level and moderate what Young (1991: 429) describes as a 'grating, relentless monotone that drove half the nation into paroxysms of irritation'. Insofar, then, as there was growing concern among voters in 1987 over some of the undesirable social consequences, such as persistently high levels of unemployment, of Thatcherite economic policies, the sharp increase in the proportion of voters seeing her as caring (up to 57 per cent from 18 per cent in 1983), brought electoral dividends from the prime minister that her party would not otherwise have enjoyed.

In sum, character trait analysis indicates that the pattern of leader effects in recent British general elections can be convincingly explained, at least in part, by voters responding directly to the personalities of the candidates for the position of prime minister, with different character traits enjoying greater influence on their party choice at different points in time. At the same time there is little reason to believe that this change in the stimuli to which voters responded was coincidental. Partisan dealignment, the unprecedented packaging of leaders by party campaign strategists and unusually leader-centred media coverage of the campaign probably all contributed to it. Indeed, this combination of developments probably made the greater presidentialism of the last three general elections inevitable.

Maintaining its focus on what it is about party leaders that influences voters, the next section of this chapter asks whether it is the negative or positive side of their personality that has the greater influence on the choice made in the polling booth.

Negative voting

A counter-intuitive feature of the presidentialization of electoral impact in Britain is that it has gone hand in hand with another change that would seem to contradict it, namely, declining public satisfaction with the performance of the prime minister and leader of the opposition, and especially the former. Since 1945, the Gallup organization has regularly asked Britons whether they are satisfied with the sitting prime minister and leader of the opposition.[10] Table 3.7 breaks down the pattern of responses to these questions by the election groupings identified in this chapter's earlier discussion of partisan dealignment. The results are surprising. Party leaders may have come to enjoy a somewhat greater role in shaping the outcome of elections, but at the same time the public's level of dissatisfaction with them, and especially with the prime minister, has increased or at best remained static. Indeed, in some respects the table understates the starkness of these contradictory trends. For example, in the run-up to what was apparently the most presidential of all post-war elections, 1987, Margaret

Table 3.7   Percentage Satisfied with the Prime Minister and the Leader of the Opposition

	Prime Minister	*Leader of the Opposition*
1945–64	50.4	49.0
1964–74F	42.3	40.3
1974F–83	43.2	36.6
1983–87	39.4	38.9
1987–97	34.0	45.2

Thatcher was the second most *unpopular* prime minister of the post-war period to that point. It was only in the case of Edward Heath during his 1970–74 tenure of the premiership that satisfaction ratings were lower. His averaged out at 37 per cent compared to Thatcher's 39.4 per cent between 1983 and 1987. Thatcher's opponent in 1987, Neil Kinnock, performed no better; satisfaction with him over the 1983–87 period averaged out slightly lower, at 38.9 per cent.

Initially it may seem illogical that party leaders should become more influential as public dissatisfaction with them remains more or less static at best and, in the case of prime ministers, goes sharply into reverse at worst. Most people would intuitively expect the reverse. The solution to this paradox may be, however, that voters are moved by the negative more than by the positive and party leaders are becoming more influential precisely because voters have become particularly influenced by negative perceptions of them. In the specific context of Britain, this hypothesis is especially plausible for two reasons. First, it could well be the fruit of the widespread disillusion stemming from the failure of successive governments and prime ministers of both parties to halt, never mind reverse, the country's post-war economic decline (Gamble 1994). Partisan dealignment could be seen as another manifestation of this disillusion. Second, the conventional wisdom is that voters are more receptive to negative stimuli than to positive ones. In Kernell's (1977: 51, 53) words: '[R]ecent research in social psychology largely complements the view that negative opinions exercise disproportionate influence in political behavior … To the degree that negative evaluations are more determinative than positive ones, even a popular president may prove to be a net liability to his party.' This notion of the primacy of the negative derives mainly from the study of US elections, but it has successfully crossed the Atlantic. 'There is complete agreement among advertising people (in Britain) that political advertising is more effective when it is negative rather than positive' (Crewe and Harrop 1989: xv).

In reality, though, the case is not as open and shut as it might seem. The argument has been made just as convincingly for the primacy of the positive. Rose and McAllister (1986: 156) note that British 'voters endorse more positive than negative statements about parties'. For them, the evidence suggests that voting for a party is more a positive than a negative act. 'An individual's vote is not an exclusive endorsement of one party; it is cast with the recognition that other parties have good points too' (see also Norris et al. 1999; ch. 9). Rose and McAllister, of course, are talking about political parties, but their observations can be expected to apply just as much to their leaders. Indeed, the primacy of the positive in regard to leaders is explicitly defended in a recent longitudinal study of the ever greater importance of candidates to the outcome of US presidential elections. Analysing the responses to open-ended questions on what voters like and dislike about the candidates in presidential elections from 1952 to 1988, the author concludes: 'Contrary to the popular wisdom, the like/dislike data provide excellent evidence for the conclusion that American voters cast their ballots with a focus more on the positive than the negative' (Wattenberg 1991: 150).

Given the substantial leader effects in the 1987, 1992 and 1997 British general elections, these contests would seem to offer a particularly good opportunity to test whether it is the positive or negative in party leaders that moves voters more. It is fortunate that the British Election Studies for these three contests include a series of questions that allow us to tackle this question head-on. Common to all three surveys is a battery of three items asking respondents whether they saw each party leader as extreme or moderate, capable or incapable of strong leadership and looking after one class or all classes.[11]

There are two issues in the positive vs negative voting debate. The first is whether voters tend to see party leaders in negative rather than positive terms and the second is the relative importance of the two types of evaluation for party choice in the voting booth. Table 3.8 speaks to the first of them in the specific context of the 1987, 1992 and 1997 elections. Summing each respondent's perceptions on the positive and negative trait items separately, it presents the mean value of both types of response to the Conservative and Labour leaders. Its striking feature is that no support is given to the argument for the primacy of the negative. Rather, insofar as their positive scores are in all cases higher, and often substantially so, than their matching negative

Table 3.8   Mean Summed Positive and Negative Personality Traits by Party Leader

	1987	*1992*	*1997*
Positive			
Prime Minister	1.70	2.12	1.53
Opposition Leader	1.53	1.42	2.42
Negative			
Prime Minister	1.16	0.76	1.36
Opposition Leader	1.25	1.39	0.37

ones, prime ministerial candidates, like the parties they lead, clearly constitute more of a positive than negative pole of attraction for Conservative and Labour supporters.

Once again, though, common sense dictates against overinterpreting findings based on a small number of elections. Fortunately, however, the 1964, 1966 and 1970 British Election Studies contain open-ended questions ascertaining respondents' likes and dislikes of the prime ministers and leaders of the opposition of the time. Allowing each respondent to volunteer up to four likes and four dislikes for each of the major party leaders enables the exercise summarized in Table 3.8 to be replicated, albeit with open-ended rather than closed-ended questions, for these earlier contests.[12] Doing so suggests that neither the negative nor the positive consistently predominates in the way the public responds to the major party leaders. While Harold Wilson, the Labour leader in these three elections, was always more liked than disliked, negative responses to the Conservative leaders, Alec Douglas-Home and Edward Heath, outnumbered positive ones in both 1964 and 1966. By 1970, however, Heath had become a little more popular than he was unpopular and, at the same time, the popular response to Wilson had moderated to become more heavily tinged with negativism.[13]

Thus, the conclusion suggested in the previous section of this chapter is buttressed. The way voters respond to prime ministerial candidates is dictated less by some unchanging mindset rooted deeply in negativism and/or long-standing party loyalties, and more by a contemporaneous assessment of party leaders' suitability for the position of chief executive, including their perceived ability to get things done, their caringness, the performance of the sitting prime minister and the potential of his opponent.

The second issue in the positive vs negative attraction debate concerns whether voters respond asymmetrically to the two types of character trait in the polling booth. It may well be that the public is more prone to view leaders in positive terms than negative ones, but this does not necessarily mean that positive evaluations are as powerful a stimulus as their negative counterparts when it comes to party choice. As is widely believed, negative responses could well arouse stronger emotions, thereby making partisans more likely to defect when their reaction to their own party's leader is negative rather than positive.

Table 3.9 speaks to this aspect of the positive vs negative voting debate. It details separately the effect of positive and negative leader evaluations on the relationship between partisanship and the vote. Looking at the first row in 1987, for example, we see that the larger the number of positive traits Labour identifiers saw in the prime minister at the time, Margaret Thatcher, the more likely they were to vote Conservative. The second row tells us that Mr Kinnock had a similar, if slightly less powerful, effect on Tory partisans favouring him. This exercise is then repeated to estimate the relative impact of negative evaluations of the leaders of the two parties.[14]

What is clear from the table is that, whether it be positive or negative traits that are in question, prime ministers are always a more potent electoral stimulus than opposition leaders, probably because they are better known for having been more unremittingly in the public eye during their period in office. Beyond this observation, however, there is little uniformity. In particular, the hypothesis of the primacy of the negative fails once again to be supported by the evidence. Rather, positive trait perceptions are always the more powerful in the case of the opposition leader, whereas the story is more chequered with the

Table 3.9   The Effect of Positive and Negative Leader Traits on the Partisanship–Vote Relationship

	1987	*1992*	*1997*
Party Identification × Vote (R^2)	0.86	0.89	0.81
R^2 *reduction controlling for:*			
PM Positive	0.10	0.10	0.15
OL Positive	0.09	0.05	0.03
PM Negative	0.12	0.09	0.15
OL Negative	0.07	0.04	0.01

prime minister, with negative traits being more powerful in one election (1987), positive ones more powerful in another (1992) and the two being even in the remaining one (1997). The evidence, in other words, suggests that there is no hard and fast rule as to which type of evaluation is the more potent influence on the vote.[15] Moreover, this conclusion is reinforced when the party leader like/dislike questions in the 1964, 1966 and 1970 British Election Studies are used to project the analysis undertaken in Table 3.9 backwards. Positive evaluations enjoy a somewhat greater impact than negative ones in 1964, about the same impact in 1966 and, again, a somewhat larger impact in 1970.[16] Thus, while there is a slight tendency overall to favour the argument for the primacy of the positive, it is the variable importance of the two types of evaluation that is the more striking finding.

In light of these results, it is difficult to avoid the conclusion that voter response to prime ministerial candidates is sensitive to personality and evaluational criteria shaped by the circumstances prevailing in specific elections. Thus, a likely part of the explanation for the greater importance of negative evaluations of the prime minister in 1987, for example, is that Thatcher elicited a strong and polarized response from voters uneasy with the social consequences, especially high and unremitting unemployment, of the prime minister's past radicalism and wary of her promise that more was to come. A further term for her as premier promised more confrontation and another bout of government without a great deal of social conscience. Kinnock's image also had a strong tinge of the negative, albeit a different kind of negativism. He persisted in holding to policies, most spectacularly unilateral nuclear disarmament, that were unpopular with the general public and his stance on which he failed to justify to its satisfaction. In addition, he presided over, and appeared not to be able to control, open policy disagreements at the very highest levels of the Labour party leadership (Butler and Kavanagh 1988). All this contributed to an image of his being weak, indecisive and ill-equipped to run the country.

By 1992, the leadership of the two parties had changed markedly. Thatcher had been replaced by the relatively conciliatory and consensual John Major and, conveying an altogether more moderate and reasonable image, he downplayed the socially divisive aspects of Thatcherite radicalism. Kinnock too had matured substantially. While the question of his prime ministerial calibre continued to bedevil him and provide damaging ammunition for the Conservative campaign artillery, he had brought official Labour policy, on important issues such as nuclear disarmament, into line with public opinion and he had the party more firmly under his personal control. Both parties, in other words, went to considerable lengths to invite voters to evaluate their leader in the positive terms of a harmonious present rather than the negative terms of a divided past (Butler and Kavanagh 1993).[17] The perhaps surprising feature of the 1997 contest is that, contrary to much of the publicity surrounding the highly mediagenic creator and leader of 'New Labour', Tony Blair, the much higher leader effects for the prime minister in Table 3.9 suggest that the election was a referendum on the Conservative party's John Major rather than on the opposition leader who led his party to a stunning 179-seat majority in the House of Commons in his first election as leader.

Conclusion

Starting from Chapter 2's demonstration that British general elections have presidentialized, this chapter has sought both to confirm the heightened leader effects in most recent contests and to throw some light on the explanation of this development. It suggests that presidential change needs to be seen as being nested in a broader context defined by other important changes in British electoral politics over the period. Prominent among these contextual changes is partisan dealignment. The widespread weakening of party loyalties in the British electorate, reaching new heights in the 1980s and 1990s, has undoubtedly contributed to party leaders having become a somewhat greater influence on election outcomes. It is not an adequate explanation of this development in and of itself, however, since leader effects did not increase substantially until 1987, some 13 years and five elections after the onset of dealignment. Rather, what seems to have happened is that unequalled levels of dealignment interacted in the 1980s and 1990s with unprecedented media coverage of the party leaders.

In this larger context, two major conclusions flow from this chapter. First, while party leaders may traditionally have had minimal consequences for the outcome of elections in Britain, the higher media profile they assumed in the 1987, 1992 and 1997 campaigns seems to have paved the way for their personalities to become more salient stimuli for voters and to weigh more heavily in their decisional calculus than in the past. This rebalancing of electoral forces is evident in the greater impact of the effectiveness and caring character traits.

Second, the relationship between leader personality and the vote is dynamic and cannot be reduced to a simple formula. Even if voters do have internalized images, or schema, sketching the qualities of the prime minister they would prefer, the influence these qualities have on the vote can vary with the political circumstances of individual elections. With the removal in 1990 of the dogmatically anti-collectivist, anti-welfare Thatcher as leader of the Conservative party, for example, the question of the caringness of the prime ministerial candidates mattered far less for choosing between the Conservative and Labour parties in 1992 than it had in 1987. Similarly, positive evaluations of the party leaders do not always carry the day over negative ones, or vice versa. The primacy of one type of evaluation over the other seems to be related to the nature of the choices offered to voters in the circumstances of particular elections. In 1987, the contest between Kinnock and Thatcher contained strong elements of a choice between the lesser of two evils, the former caring but of questionable effectiveness as a leader and the latter of undoubted effectiveness but widely perceived as uncaring. By 1992, the choice for prime minister was much less heavily tinged with negativism. The Conservatives had acquired a new leader, John Major, who was widely seen as being more socially concerned than his immediate predecessor and Labour's Neil Kinnock was more in command of his party and was more consistent and authoritative in the articulation of what he and it stood for.

Leader effects, then, can not only be substantial in magnitude, but they can also differ in subtle detail when individual character traits are examined. This variation serves immediately to raise the question of whether the presidential change evident in the 1980s and 1990s was not itself a function of particularistic circumstance. Does the presidentialism characteristic of these contests represent a short-term blip in the dynamics of British election outcomes or does it point to a more durable change in the balance of forces in them? In one sense, of course, this question is difficult to answer with any degree of confidence since at issue is a development characteristic of only a small number of elections, and this makes extrapolation hazardous. But it does not necessarily make it premature to address the question. The crucial consideration is less the number of observation points and more the reasons suggested for the phenomenon observed. In other words, the source of the presidential change should have greater bearing on the question of its permanence than the number of elections over the course of which it is observed to have taken place. If leader effects are greater because of the presence of one or two unusually charismatic figures on the political stage, then this should have fewer implications for how election outcomes are routinely determined than if these effects are the results of longer-term structural or institutional change.

In this regard, the media presentational analyses in Chapter 2 constitute good reason to believe that the change in question is structural rather than ephemeral. A striking feature of recent British general election contests was shown to be the deliberate personalization of party campaign strategies and, as a result, the unprecedented attention paid to the party leaders by both newspapers and television. Interacting with unprecedentedly high levels of partisan detachment from the Conservative and Labour parties, the emergence and maturation of political television, together with the changing campaigning usage to which the major parties have put the medium, would seem to be central to the explanation of the pattern of leader effects in recent contests. Being on the one hand the principal, most trusted and most credible source of political information for a dealigned and volatile electorate and, on the other, a vehicle enabling parties to communicate directly with unprecedented numbers of voters, the medium of television has transformed election campaign strategy and practise. Once the political parties decided to exploit television for their own political ends, however, they had to accommodate themselves to one of its basic features, which is that, being primarily a visual medium of communication, it is better suited to the projection of personalities than to the discussion of complex issues (Ranney 1983; Franklin 1994; Kavanagh 1995; Scammell 1995; and Rosenbaum 1997). As a result, leaders inevitably came to figure more prominently in television-driven election campaigns and, almost equally inevitably it seems, the balance of electoral forces shifted in their direction.

All the evidence, then, indicates that leader effects are a mediated function of dealigned voters' evaluations of the personalities of the prime ministerial candidates in an era in which the leader is more than in the past the public image of the party, the vehicle through which it projects itself to mobilize its own supporters and convert those of other parties. But while this argument offers a seductively simple explanation of the more presidential character of recent election contests, it must be remembered that a great deal of myth, bluster and unsubstantiated hyperbole suffuses discussion of the political role of television. In truth, much remains shrouded in mystery. 'The state of research on media effects is one of the most notable embarassments of modern social science...[T]he scholarly literature has been much better at refuting, qualifying, and circumscribing the thesis of media impact than supporting it' (Bartels 1993: 267). Chapter 4, therefore, explores the relationship between media exposure and leader effects with a particular view to determining what it is about the media and exposure to them that explains their political influence.

4
Media and Leader Effects

The analyses in Chapters 2 and 3 have suggested two clear conclusions. The first is that the mass media, specifically newspapers and television, have sharply increased the attention they pay to the Conservative and Labour party leaders in the course of their coverage of recent election campaigns as compared to previous ones. The second is that at the same time that the party leaders have become more prominent in the media, they have come to enjoy a stronger influence on the choice of party that voters make. In other words, the presidentialization of presentation that has come to characterize British newspapers and television seem to have some association with a presidentialization of electoral impact. Arguing that, for television at least, this association is not coincidental, the purpose of this chapter is to specify the nature of the linkage between presentation and impact.

Before setting about this task, however, two important characteristics of the structure of the newspaper and television media in Britain need to be spelled out. The first is that, like politics itself in a unitary state, their structure is overwhelmingly national. The majority of Britons read at least one of the dozen or so national newspapers edited in London and available on the same day across the whole country. Scotland and Wales, and especially the former, may have their own editions of these newspapers, but their content is similar enough and their circulation small enough so as not to put much of a dent in the image of a predominantly national press. Similarly, television is national. The television audience has long been, and remains largely the preserve of two major networks, the British Broadcasting Corporation (BBC) and Independent Television (ITV). For the most part, the programmes of both networks are broadcast at the same time across the country and, in the case of both, their major news programmes are produced in London. Their television monopoly may have eroded since the arrival of satellite television in 1989, but even in the 1997 election, the main satellite news broadcaster, Sky News, still enjoyed access to no more than 'roughly 25 per cent of TV reception points' (Boulton 1998: 197). Moreover, the character and content of its election newscasts were not substantially different from those of the BBC and ITV (Goddard et al. 1998).

The second important characteristic to note is that newspapers and television are subject to very different regulatory regimes. Neither medium is completely free to gather and disseminate information as it sees fit. Both operate under a set of formal and informal constraints, such as the Official Secrets Act, libel and contempt laws, D-Notices and parliamentary privilege (May and Rowan 1982). At the same time, however, there are significant regulatory differences between the two media. In particular, the printed press is able to be openly partisan in its political coverage and editorial opinion. This has generally translated in practice into the national press being largely and openly pro-Conservative in its political sympathies. The exception was 1997 when a number of usually pro-Tory newspapers, including most prominently the high-circulation *Sun*, endorsed Labour as their choice to form the next government. Television, by contrast, is obliged by law to be impartial in its coverage of politics. In general elections, and indeed at all other times, it must treat the major competing political parties equally and fairly. This obligation manifests itself in a number of ways. The most obvious is with respect to the distribution of party election broadcasts (PEBs), which provide the political parties with free air time and are broadcast on all television channels – simultaneously until 1979. Impartiality and equity have also been the informal norm with broadcasters. One practice is called 'stopwatching' and it involves going to lengths to ensure that the time allocated to the political parties in news broadcasts approaches equality.[1] '[O]ther criteria of impartiality are also applied by producers; for example, even-handedness in the relative position of parties in the running order and equivalence of tone in reporting campaign events. Leader is matched against leader, issue against issue, and press conference against press conference' (Norris et al. 1999: 31).

The picture that emerges, then, is one of a largely biased (in a partisan sense) newspaper sector and a largely unbiased (again in a partisan sense) broadcasting one. It might reasonably be expected under these circumstances that partisan coverage of the party leaders in newspapers will translate into an advantage for one or other party at the polls, whereas neutral coverage of them on television will not. This expectation, however, runs counter to the conventional wisdom of voting studies in Britain, which is that neither medium has implications for election outcomes. The question these studies generally ask of newspapers is whether readers favour a party because it is supported by their preferred newspaper or, rather, do they choose a newspaper in the first place because it shares their partisan convictions (for example, Butler and Stokes 1974: 115–19).[2] The legal requirement for television to remain impartial in its political broadcasting has meant, by contrast, that its political effects have tended to be conceptualized, and investigated, in terms of setting the voter's political agenda. The medium may not try to bring viewers around to a particular view on important issues of the day, but perhaps its coverage of some campaign issues to the neglect of others determines the issues that voters come to think most important (Miller et al. 1990: ch. 6; Miller 1991: 137–40).

The largely unanimous conclusion of research addressing these questions has been that neither newspapers nor television changes political attitudes or behaviour. Rather, their only effect worthy of note is that they reinforce political predispositions that already exist. A recent study of newspaper readership, for example, concludes: 'There is no evidence in our panel that there was any relationship between vote switching during the election campaign and the partisanship of a voter's newspaper' (Curtice and Semetko 1994: 55; see also Norris et al. 1999: ch. 10).[3] Similarly, the issue agenda of voters seems barely susceptible to television influence. 'The ebb and flow of controversy in television news items did *not* produce any corresponding trends in public interest and discussion … In the short span of a four- or five-week election campaign our conclusion must be that television failed to set the public agenda … ' (Miller et al. 1990: 231–2; emphasis in original).[4]

There are at least three good reasons, however, why it is time to reassess this widely shared 'minimal effects' conclusion. First, experimental evidence from a 1997 election study shows that, contrary to what may have been believed in the past, 'exposure (to television news) affects perceptions' (Norris et al. 1999: 150). Second, the notion of minimal effects is inconsistent with the findings of this book to this point since it denies any future to an explanation of presidential change that is founded on increased media attention to the party leaders. The problem is that more frequent newspaper and television coverage of the prime ministerial candidates will be irrelevant to election outcomes if the messages communicated by these media fail to influence what voters take into account when choosing between the parties on the day of the election. Moreover, if most voters do not get their information about, and impressions of, the party leaders from the mass media, then where do they get them from? What else can be responsible for the enhanced leader effects apparent in recent election contests? Few citizens meet the prime minister or opposition leader personally or see them during campaign appearances, political rallies, and the like. The majority of voters in fact depend for their political cues on the images, information and analysis provided by the mass media and not on, say, talking to people (Negrine 1989: 1–3). Finally, a dealigned electorate's exposure to the party leaders in the media can be expected to be influential since, as Table 3.5 makes clear, evaluations of these individuals are only weakly rooted in voters' long-standing party loyalties.

Questioning the continued validity of the minimal effects thesis, this chapter examines closely the role of newspaper and television media in explaining the greater electoral impact that the leaders of the Conservative and Labour parties have come to enjoy. In particular, it asks whether the coverage of party leaders in the two media translates into the same electoral influence for them. The necessary starting point of this exercise, however, is specification of how this translation might take place. After all, if newspapers effectively do no more than preach to the converted, if paid political advertising is not allowed on television, and if television newscasts are impartial and balanced in their coverage of the leaders, the question inevitably arises: where do the informational cues that promote leader effects come from? The answer is that these cues are not direct; partisans do not come to prefer the leader of the other party because of, say, a sympathetic portrayal of her on the television news the previous evening. Rather, the influence of television is indirect and one of the forms it can take is known in media theory as *priming* (Iyengar and Kinder 1987).

The case for priming

British media research has traditionally adopted a very stringent and demanding definition of what constitutes a media effect in electoral politics. To have influence, newspapers and television are required to change individuals' voting preference or issue agenda in the short term. Newspaper effects, for example, occur when a change of newspaper readership leads the reader to switch his vote to bring it into line with the partisanship of his new information source in the printed press. Put otherwise, the media must convert voters if they are to be credited with political influence. A major problem with sticking to this definition of a media effect, however, is that there is mounting evidence of a more subtle, indirect and in many ways no less consequential effect for the media on political attitudes and behaviour. That is, media research in the United States and Canada has shown that television can have substantial influence on voters by 'priming' them to react in certain ways to political stimuli. Put briefly, priming is a process whereby people do indeed change their opinions as a result of media exposure. They do so, however, not because the media bludgeon them through partisan propaganda into changing their beliefs or evaluations of an object, but because exposure to the media leads them to alter the relative weights they give to the component elements of their evaluation of that object (Iyengar and Kinder 1987; Johnston et al. 1992).

More fully, the starting point of the theory of priming is that people are 'satisficers'. When faced with the need to make a choice or judgment, they do not seek out all relevant information and considerations, weigh up the 'pros and cons' and then come to a decision. Rather, they make the decision on the basis of the information that is readily accessible to them. The media are crucial in this process since they play a substantial, if not the leading, gatekeeping role in shaping the flow of political information to the large majority of citizens. Thus, by emphasizing some newsworthy facets of, say, performance rather than others in the course of what may be balanced and self-consciously non-partisan news coverage, the media help to shape the criteria that citizens bring to bear on the evaluation of political objects. Take prime ministers as an example. There is some evidence that they are held as personally accountable for national economic performance as US presidents are (Mughan 1995). Poor performance in their management of the economy, though, need not harm their personal popularity as long as newspapers and/or television pay more attention in their political coverage to policy areas in which the prime minister has performed relatively well – for example, foreign policy. By concentrating its coverage on the flattering, in other words, the media can prime citizens to respond positively to the prime minister's performance in office, thereby boosting his public standing, which in turn is likely to help his party by keeping its identifiers loyal at the polls.

The way the media cover political actors, then, can be important even if that coverage is ostensibly non-partisan in character. Media images leave impressions of the party leaders in the public mind and these impressions can have electoral consequences. Whether they do or not, however, is a separate matter, and one to which the analysis now turns.[5] It starts with newspapers.

The evidence: newspapers

A problem common to all non-experimental research is that there will always remain room for doubt as to whether an association that has been identified between phenomena can be taken to signal a direct causal connection between them; correlation cannot always be interpreted to signify causation. This problem is particularly marked in the area of media effects research. Take newspapers. These are simply one of multiple and wide-ranging potential influences on the mass public's political attitudes and behaviour. Voters' evaluations of a party leader may be shaped, for example, not only by the leader's personality, but also by their own family, friends, partisanship, policy preferences and, perhaps, their reaction to the leader's idiosyncratic characteristics – gender, social class, national origin, and the like. Margaret Thatcher's status as Britain's first ever female prime minister probably affected, for better or worse, some voters' personal reaction to her. Equally, Neil Kinnock's being derogatorily nicknamed 'the Welsh Windbag' in the popular press may well have hurt his standing with some voters.

This multiplicity of forces shaping popular evaluations of the party leaders makes it very difficult to isolate the independent role, if any, of newspapers in this process. Reading the pro-Conservative *Daily Mail*, for example, will virtually always be associated with a highly positive evaluation of the Tory leader. It could well be, however, that, being rooted in the reader's prior identification with the Conservative party and/or a range of socioeconomic characteristics that predispose her towards a particular ideology, this positive image of the Tory leader was firmly established in her mind before she picked up the newspaper so that reading it only served to reinforce pre-existing assessments. If such were the case, it would be very difficult to argue that newspaper readership was directly responsible for the reader's evaluation of the party leaders or for any impact this evaluation might have on her choice of party in the polling booth.

A way around this causal inference problem becomes available if a newspaper reverses its position on a leader or party from election to the next. Such a U-turn allows a determination of if, and how, the people reading this newspaper before and after its partisan reversal evaluate that leader. If the newspaper does prime successfully, there should be a substantial difference between the pattern of change in the leader evaluations of its readers on the one hand and, on the other, those of non-newspaper readers or readers of newspapers consistent in their partisan preference over the two elections. If the newspaper that reverses its partisan preference in question has no priming effect, by contrast, the leader evaluations of its readers should have changed no more or less than those of non-readers or of readers of newspapers consistent in their partisan message from one election to the next. Fortunately, precisely such a rare, quasi-experimental situation arose between the 1992 and 1997 general elections as the result of the *Sun's* switching its allegiance from Conservative to Labour. Doubly fortunate in this reversal is that, as a tabloid newspaper, the *Sun* tends, more than its up-market, or 'quality,' counterparts, to focus on the personalities of leading politicians. 'The media – especially the popular media – intensify the personalization of government, viewing Prime Ministerial activities in short catchy phrases' (Rose 1980: 22). If newspapers do prime, in other words, it should manifest itself in a disproportionately negative reaction to John Major among people who read the inconsistent *Sun* in both the 1992 and 1997 campaigns.

The *Sun's* readers can hardly have avoided the newspaper's different treatment of the Conservative leader in 1997 as compared to 1992. In 1992, the newspaper had systematically lauded the Conservative leader, John Major, and derogated his Labour counterpart, Neil Kinnock. '[*The Sun*] lost no opportunity to pour scorn on Kinnock's credibility and it waged a sustained campaign contrasting "untrustworthy" Kinnock to "honest" John Major' (Butler and Kavanagh 1983: 182). In 1997, however, the tables were turned as the newspaper swung its support to Labour (a good general analysis of newspaper content is Seymour-Ure 1997). 'Although it had enthusiastically supported Major against Kinnock in the (1992) general election, the press now turned savagely against him. With the Eurosceptic *Sun* in the vanguard, Major was portrayed as a weak and indecisive muddler, and he never regained even lukewarm support…' (Denver 1998: 20). The change in Mr Major's image, of course, was not wholly of the making of any single newspaper. Rather, it was founded on his generally being seen as having performed poorly as prime minister after his party's surprising re-election in 1992. His slide was all but inevitable after a number of episodes that sapped his authority within his party and dramatically weakened his own and his government's public standing. Prominent among these episodes was Britain's ignominious ejection from the European Exchange Rate Mechanism (ERM) only five months after the 1992 Conservative party's manifesto had declared 'membership of the ERM (to be) central to our counter-inflation discipline' (quoted in Denver 1998: 19). Major's image took other knocks as well. Among them was his launch of a 'Back to Basics' campaign lauding family values and his party's support for them, only for the public to discover in a series of sensational disclosures that several members of the Tory parliamentary party, boasting mistresses and illegitimate children, took these values more seriously in theory than in practice (see more fully Norton 1998; Whiteley 1997).

This record would predict a general decline in popular evaluations of John Major from the 1992 to 1997 general elections. If newspapers do prime evaluations of the party leaders, however, this decline can be expected to be especially pronounced among consistent readers of a *Sun* newspaper that had turned on its erstwhile favourite. Following the same logic, the decline should be less pronounced in two groups not subjected to the negativism and personality attacks characteristic of this newly converted, pro-Labour newspaper. These are non-readers of newspapers in general and readers of consistently Tory tabloids, namely the *Daily Express* and the *Daily Mail*. To be sure, the general decline in support for Major should be apparent in all these groups, but the important point is that it should be greater in magnitude among *Sun* readers little accustomed to the hostile coverage that their newspaper gave the sitting prime minister and his Conservative party during the 1997 campaign. These expectations of change in the pattern of positive and negative evaluations of John Major between 1992 and 1997 are put to the empirical test in Table 4.1, which draws on the 1992–97 British Election Study Campaign Panel to compare and contrast the leader evaluations of respondents who read the *Sun*, *Daily Express* or *Daily Mail* at both time points, as well as those respondents who read no newspaper in either campaign. The measure of change in the final column is obtained simply by subtracting the 1992 evaluation figure from its 1997 counterpart.[6]

Table 4.1   Changing Evaluations of John Major by Newspaper Readership, 1992–97

	1992	*1997*	*Change 92–97*
Positive evaluation			
No newspaper read	2.18	1.49	−0.69
Sun	2.09	1.27	−0.82
Daily Express	2.76	2.17	−0.59
Daily Mail	2.79	2.00	0.79
Negative evaluation			
No newspaper read	0.73	1.45	0.72
Sun	0.89	1.67	0.78
Daily Express	0.23	0.77	0.54
Daily Mail	0.18	0.91	0.73

Two findings in the table stand out clearly. First, positive evaluations of the sitting prime minister decrease sharply and negative evaluations of him increase sharply in all four readership groups. In the general public's eyes at least, Mr Major was not the laudable prime minister in 1997 that he had been in 1992. Second, directly contrary to expectations, his fall from grace was not markedly more precipitous among *Sun* readers despite that newspaper's conversion to the Labour party between the two elections. Indeed, the fall in his popularity was of almost the same magnitude among consistent readers of the steadfastly Tory *Daily Mail* and the swing against him was much the same among readers of this same newspaper as well as among non-readers. This failure of the *Sun*'s conversion to Labour in 1997 to have a significantly disproportionate impact on its readers' evaluations of John Major would tend to confirm the traditional view of newspapers as being a conservatizing force; their priming potential notwithstanding, they reinforce rather than change (Klapper 1960). But while this conclusion may be appropriate by and large to the pattern of findings in Table 4.1, it also remains the case that *Sun* readers, no matter how small the difference, do show a bigger drop in positive evaluations and a bigger increase in negative evaluations than the other three groups. Albeit only marginally, in other words, the possibility remains that newspapers encourage leader effects by priming evaluations of the prime ministerial candidates.

It stands to reason that if greater newspaper attention to the party leaders does indeed bear some responsibility for electoral presidentialization in Britain, then leader effects should be more pronounced among 'tabloid' readers because this type of newspaper personalizes politics more than do its 'quality' counterparts (Rose 1980: 22). Moreover, it also stands to reason that the pattern of leader effects among tabloid readers should follow the presidential trajectory uncovered time and again in Chapters 2 and 3 – namely, their magnitude should decline in 1992 and rebound in 1997 but without hitting their 1987 peak. Table 4.2 charts the pattern of leader effects among readers of the two types of newspaper over the course of these three elections.

This table is interesting for confirming a number of earlier conclusions, as well as for speaking directly to the issue of whether or not tabloid readers are the more susceptible to presidentialism in their voting behaviour. It shows once again, for example, that neither the negative nor the positive in party leaders is consistently more attractive to voters. But more pertinent from the point of view of the newspaper priming issue, the table lends no support to the hypothesis that readership of

Table 4.2   Leader Effects among Readers of 'Tabloid' (T) and 'Quality' (Q) Newspapers

	1987		1992		1997	
	T	Q	T	Q	T	Q
Party Identification × Vote (R^2)	0.84	0.93	0.90	0.84	0.89	0.71
R^2 reduction controlling for:						
PM and OL Positive	0.19	0.08	0.14	0.15	0.11	0.22
PM and OL Negative	0.19	0.09	0.12	0.17	0.11	0.19

tabloid rather than quality newspapers moves in tandem with the pattern of electoral presidentialization in Britain.[7] On the one hand, leader effects are not consistently higher among tabloid readers; they may be so in 1987 but are not in either 1992 or 1997. On the other hand, and more to the point, the pattern of leader effects in neither readership group conforms to the presidentialization trajectory described earlier. To be sure, the impact of the leaders drops in 1992 relative to 1987 among tabloid readers, but then it drops again in 1997 instead of rebounding. As for quality newspaper readers, leader effects are at their lowest, not highest, point in 1987 and they go up in each subsequent election.[8]

In sum, no compelling evidence has been presented that newspaper type systematically primes readers' perceptions of the Conservative and Labour party leaders and is thereby responsible for the presidential character of recent British general elections. Importantly, this is not to argue that no newspaper or type of newspaper primes under any circumstances. The case of the *Sun* between 1992 and 1997 offers some limited evidence otherwise. Rather, the more modest conclusions suggested by this analysis are, first, that partisan coverage in the printed press does more to reinforce evaluations of the party leaders than to change them and, second, that there is nothing about reading newspapers in general or types of newspaper in particular that goes hand in hand with the pattern of presidentialization uncovered in earlier chapters of this book. Thus, when account is also taken of the steady downward trend in newspaper circulation (Norris et al. 1999: 24), there is little reason to conclude that newspaper readership of any kind has a significant and systematic role to play in accounting for the greater electoral impact of the Conservative and Labour leaders in the 1980s and 1990s. This leaves television.

The evidence: television

Television holds out the potential of being a different story to newspapers when it comes to accounting for the stronger leader effects characteristic of more recent general election contests. Not only has the attention it paid to the two prime ministerial candidates increased more sharply than did that of newspapers over this period (see Chapter 2), but also this change in the character of its campaign coverage is more likely to have had electoral consequences for at least three reasons.

First, television is a political medium upon which parties and voters alike depend increasingly heavily and from which each draws substantial benefit at low cost. For parties, it is preferable to more traditional campaigning methods, like church hall meetings and door-to-door canvassing, because it is a cheap and efficient means of reaching unprecedented numbers of actual and potential supporters. Moreover, it allows voters to be reached in the privacy and comfort of their own homes when their resistance to discordant messages is likely to be relatively low. Thus, especially when, as in contemporary Britain, instinctive partisan loyalties have weakened, television offers political parties unequalled opportunity not only to reach and mobilize their own supporters, but also to convert the opposition's. Voters, for their part, generally spend long hours in front of the television set and the medium is, and increasingly so, their most important, credible and trusted source of political news and information (Negrine 1989: 1–2; Gunter and McLaughlin 1992: 37–41). At the very least, therefore, the preconditions for a television effect would seem to be there.

Second, and relatedly, politicians themselves generally credit television with a new-found importance in the politics of election campaigning. The former cabinet ministers I interviewed virtually all agreed it to be a medium that had fundamentally altered the role party leaders play in modern campaigns and election outcomes. With phrases like 'it obviously has,' 'it has been a crucially important force in elections', 'I think that the personality of the leader has become very important largely because of the media, and particularly of television' and 'I think they (party leaders) have become more important, because of television, you know', Conservative and Labour politicians alike endorsed the view that television had altered the role of party leaders and introduced an unprecedented personalized element into modern parliamentary election contests.

Third, some evidence of an increased voter dependence on television for electoral cues can already be found for the 1980s. In the 1979, 1983 and 1987 BBC/Gallup post-election surveys (there were none for 1992 and 1997), respondents were asked whether Conservative, Labour or Liberal broadcasts on television counted among the reasons they had finally decided to vote the way they did. The percentage replying positively in 1979 was 11 per cent, in 1983 it was 14 per cent and in 1987 it was 15 per cent (see also Negrine 1989: 182–91).[9]

For these reasons television must be taken seriously as a potential explanation of the presidentialization of parliamentary electoral politics. In the specific case of Britain, the opportunity for systematic exploration of the interaction between voters' exposure to political programming on television, their evaluation of the personalities of the party leaders and their choice of party became available for the first and only time with the 1992 British Election Study.[10]

The television context

The legal and broadcasting context in which television operates defines the opportunities available to party leaders to present themselves to, and seek to influence, voters during the election campaign. That television is a national medium and that it is highly regulated are points that have already been made. Unlike in the United States and some other democracies, part of this regulatory framework is that paid political advertising is not allowed on British television. Nor have televised debates between the party leaders ever been a feature of election campaigns. This means that campaign strategists have three vehicles over which they have some greater or lesser degree of control in bringing the leader of their party to the attention of the viewing public; they are party election broadcasts (PEBs), leader interviews and daily news broadcasts.

The first television opportunity involves the leader appearing in one or more PEBs. These are television programmes, no more than ten minutes in length, broadcast over the course of the campaign, air time for them is free and the parties, with the technical assistance of the television authorities, determine their content and take full editorial responsibility for them. The number to which each party is entitled is allocated on the basis of their vote share and determined by a body made up of representatives of the broadcasting institutions and the political parties. All PEBs are broadcast on all television channels (Negrine 1989: 199–201). They have traditionally been seen as instruments used primarily not to 'sell' the party or its leader, but to rally the faithful, convince the wavering and provide committed supporters with ammunition and information they can use to argue the party's case during the campaign. But as Chapter 2 mentions, presidential-style change reared its head in 1987 when Labour allotted the whole of one of its five PEBs to the life, struggles and successes of its self-made leader from humble origins, Neil Kinnock. This PEB was considered so successful by Labour strategists that the party re-ran it in preference to one of its remaining PEBs towards the end of the campaign. Moreover, as part of a larger post-Thatcher Conservative party effort to promote a more caring and compassionate image, the Tories mimicked the Labour PEB in the 1992 election with one centred just as much around John Major, their own upwardly mobile leader. Then, in 1997, came 'Tony: The Home Video'. In this party broadcast,

> Tony Blair was seen with his family, playing tennis, fooling about with kids on a soccer pitch, and talking about his background, why he was in politics, his hopes and ideals…(T)he aim was chiefly to convey an impression of Tony Blair as Mr Nice Guy – a youngish, well-intentioned family man, who had known difficult times, had come through and would make a good neighbour.
>
> (Butler and Kavanagh 1997: 153)

The second publicity channel open to party leaders is the televised interview with popular commentators and journalists. In practice, these meetings vary in character from being polite conversations between like-minded people to being near-gladiatorial contests involving thrust and counter-thrust. Almost by definition, though, they touch on divisive, partisan issues so that voters are likely to be seated in front of the television set watching them with their partisan loyalties aroused and their judgments already made. Thus, where Labour supporters will see an interviewer as being deferential to the Tory leader and hostile to their own, Conservatives will lean towards the opposite perception of the encounter. Moreover, even if party identifiers can bring themselves to accept that their leader did not do well in an interview or that the other party's leader was impressive, such deviations from the expected can, as with newspapers, be ignored or rationalized away. The interviewer can be dismissed as having been biased, her questions unfair, their man was tired after a long day's campaigning, and the like. Aroused partisanship together with the ever-present potential for rationalization should mean that television interviews do little or nothing to foster an independent electoral impact for party leaders.[11]

Finally, there are the news broadcasts that each television channel offers one or more times per day. As mentioned earlier, these broadcasts are under the strict control of television authorities whose guiding principle is impartiality. Nonetheless, unlike with interviews, party strategists can exercise some indirect influence over their content, and thus, they hope, over viewers, by staging, specifically for television consumption, newsworthy events with the leader as their centrepiece. These include making policy pronouncements on the campaign trail in highly staged settings (for example, denouncing Conservative National Health Service policy in a run-down hospital surrounded by tired, dispirited doctors, nurses and ancillary workers), daily press conferences, 'photo-opportunities', the unveiling of campaign posters, walkabouts, and the like. A second important and relevant feature of news broadcasts is that voters on the whole do not view them as being biased so that they should less readily trigger rationalization and partisan defences (Miller 1991: ch. 6). When taken together with the fact that it is precisely in news programmes that the Conservative and Labour leaders have become more prominent in recent elections (see Figure 2.3), such 'partisan disarming' should leave viewers relatively susceptible to the discordant influence of the party leaders and more likely to defect at the polls.

Because it contains questions measuring Conservative and Labour supporters' exposure to all three publicity channels – PEBs, interviews with the leaders and news programmes – the 1992 British Election Study allows a uniquely in-depth analysis of how exposure to different types of political programming mediates any impact the personalities of the party leaders may have on voting behaviour. To simplify the presentation of this analysis, attention focuses first on PEBs and leader interviews and then turns to the communications channel at the heart of the presidentialization of presentation demonstrated in Chapter 2, the television evening news.

PEBs and leader interviews

A good place to start the empirical analysis is with the reiteration that the general expectation is for neither PEBs nor leader interviews to be systematically related to evaluations of the party leaders and their effect on the vote. These are television programmes that tend to reach the voter with her political awareness mobilized and partisan defences raised so that the potential for them to change her choice of party should be low.

Table 4.3 presents the pattern of leader effects associated with viewership of PEBs and leader interviews separately.[12] A mixture of similarity and difference is apparent in the findings. The two types of programme

Table 4.3 Leader Effects by Differing Levels of Exposure to PEBs and Leader Interviews

	PEBs Seen				Interviews Seen			
	0	*1*	*2*	*2+*	*0*	*1*	*2*	*2+*
Party Identification $\times$ Vote (R^2)	0.92	0.79	0.84	0.92	0.90	0.86	0.86	0.90
R^2 reduction controlling for:								
PM Positive	0.09	0.17	0.15	0.07	0.10	0.10	0.12	0.10
OL Positive	0.03	0.07	0.07	0.04	0.03	0.06	0.05	0.05
PM Negative	0.08	0.14	0.15	0.07	0.07	0.11	0.12	0.09
OL Negative	0.02	0.07	0.06	0.03	0.03	0.04	0.06	0.04

are similar in that each shows viewers with middle levels of exposure to manifest the strongest susceptibility to the party leaders at the ballot box; this finding coincides with similar conclusions on media effects in the United States (Zaller 1992). Not being exposed to the leaders at all understandably lessens their impact on individual party preferences, but so too, and perhaps less understandably, does maximum exposure to them. Remembering the earlier discussion of self-selection into newspaper readership, the interesting question is whether the weaker leader effects at high levels of exposure is the result of self-selection or simply of repeated exposure. The self-selection explanation would imply that the partisanship–vote relationship is not weakened by leader effects because it is the strongest identifiers who choose to watch more political programming. The repeated exposure explanation, by contrast, would predict that those in the high exposure group would be no stronger in their partisan identification because it is high levels of exposure that ties partisans closer to their party and neutralizes the appeal of the opposing party leader. As it turns out, self-selection is the more plausible explanation since those with the highest levels of exposure to the two types of political programme are also the strongest identifiers on average.[13]

There is a striking difference between the two types of broadcast, however, and it is that the negative relationship between exposure to one or more broadcasts and magnitude of leader effects is considerably stronger for PEBs, and especially when it comes to positive evaluations of the prime minister, John Major. This finding is puzzling since it seems counter-intuitive that middling levels of exposure to PEBs is associated with higher-than-average leader effects. If anything, direct and sustained exposure to the party leaders in interview settings might more logically be expected to influence viewers' reactions – positive or negative – to them. The solution to the puzzle may be, however, that the different patterns of leader effects in Table 4.3 reflect less a structural difference in the impact of the two types of political programme and more the specific circumstances of the 1992 campaign.

Leader effects have been shown time and again to be stronger for prime ministers than opposition leaders. This being the case, the fact that Prime Minister Major might well have been particularly influential among consumers of one or two PEBs could well be a function of the combinbation of the specific PEBs seen in 1992 and the general tone of the Conservative party's re-election campaign. After Thatcher's dismissal as party leader in 1990, the 'Conservatives opted not just for a new leader but for new policies and a new image. In place of Thatcher's reputation for harsh, even ruthless domination, the party felt the need to create a softer and more caring style' (Newton 1993: 133). Moreover, this image was well conveyed through the persona of the party's new leader, John Major. 'It is ironic that Kinnock's strongest point, his power as an orator who could move large audiences, was largely irrelevant to the media electioneering techniques of 1992, whereas Major's nice, caring, likeable and reasonable features shone through best on television' (Newton 1993: 151). It may well be that these were precisely the qualities that attracted Labour defectors after three successive elections in which Margaret Thatcher had been the Conservative prime ministerial candidate.

In the absence of information on which PEBs survey respondents actually saw in 1992, an interpretation of Table 4.3 based on their having seen particular PEBs cannot be tested directly and so must remain inferential and speculative. What is certain, though, is that a plausible competing interpretation can be discounted, namely that the relationship between leader effects and PEB exposure is spurious. That is, this argument starts, viewers who expose themselves to only one or two PEBs do so because they are little interested and involved in politics. As such, it continues, they are unusually vulnerable to the ephemeral and the highly visible in the campaign, in this instance, its central figures, the leaders of the Conservative and Labour parties. Thus, it concludes, the leader effects in the table have little or nothing to do with television exposure, but are actually a surrogate for voters' marginality to the mainstream political process and, hence, their susceptibility to the short term in election campaigns.

This argument is plausible, but is less so to the extent that two conditions are satisfied. First, if it is exposure to John Major himself that is directly responsible for the pattern of results in Table 4.3, then, being less diluted, the perception of him as being caring should be more influential among voters who saw only a small number of PEBs than among voters who saw none at all or a relatively large number of them.[14] Likewise, moderate PEB consumers should be more likely to defect from their partisanship when they see Major as caring than when they see the same trait in a Labour opponent for whom pains were taken to promote an image of authority and effective leadership rather than caringness. Second, if it is not PEB exposure but weak partisanship and marginality to the political process that leave voters vulnerable to the appeal of the party leaders, then variables like political efficacy, knowledge, interest and involvement should discriminate cleanly between the low, moderate and high PEB exposure groups. Conversely,

Table 4.4   The Differential Impact of Caringness Among PEB Viewers

	PEBs Seen			
	0	*1*	*2*	*2 +*
Party identification × Vote (R^2)	0.92	0.79	0.84	0.92
R^2 reduction controlling for:				
PM Caring	0.04	0.09	0.10	0.04
OL Caring	0.01	0.03	0.01	0.01

to the extent that they fail to do so, the negative relationship between number of PEBs seen and leader effects is arguably better explained by viewers having been primed as the result of direct exposure to Mr Major in the one Conservative party PEB centred around him.

Table 4.4 speaks to the first of these conditions, the impact of the perception of Major as caring in different exposure groups. Two findings stand out clearly. First, while all four groups are more responsive in their voting behaviour to perceiving the prime minister rather than the opposition leader as caring, the former's advantage is especially marked among those with middling levels of PEB exposure. For moderate consumers, in other words, there would seem to be a Major effect on the caring trait that, while part of a generalized party leader effect, also transcends it. Of course, it cannot be established beyond doubt that this 'extra' impact for Major's caringness is attributable to PEB exposure being restricted solely or almost solely to the one of which he was the subject, but it is a plausible interpretation of the findings.[15]

It is also an interpretation that is still more plausible when attention turns to the alternative explanation of the relationship between PEB exposure and leader effects, which is basically that it is spurious. That is, leader effects are not a function of television exposure, but of the possession of certain social and political characteristics that leave moderate PEB consumers open to the influence of ephemeral decisional criteria, like the personalities of the prime ministerial candidates spearheading their parties' campaigns. Put differently, getting their cues from their political marginality rather than directly from the prime ministerial candidates, this highly susceptible group of voters would have shown the same relatively high leader effects even if they had seen no PEBs. On reflection, though, there are two reasons to doubt this argument. First, voters may respond to prime ministerial candidates, but there is little evidence that their response is to the trivial and the superficial in them. Rather, recent research findings indicate that presidentialism results from voters in Britain and other parliamentary democracies knowing what they want in a prime minister and what they want are qualities few would deny are desirable in any leader – competence, reasonableness, a commitment to principle and caringness (Bean and Mughan 1989; see also Stewart and Clarke 1992). Second, if this 'surrogate' logic applies to PEBs, it should apply equally to leader interviews. Leader effects should be stronger among voters seeing few of them (that is, the politically marginal) and weaker among those seeing more of them (that is, the politically interested and involved), but Table 4.3 clearly shows there not to be the same systematic relationship as for PEBs between the number of leader interviews seen and the size of leader effects.

Table 4.5 examines the impact of a battery of political interest and involvement variables on the number of PEBs seen.[16] To minimize potential bias in the estimates, the analysis includes a range of sociodemographic characteristics that could well influence television viewing patterns independently of voters' political interest and involvement. Elderly people, for example, spend more time at home and probably watch more television as a result. Equally, better educated people are more likely to take the initiative and seek out political information from television during the campaign. The crucial point to remember in interpreting the table is that leader effects are negatively related to

Table 4.5 The Influence of Political Interest and Involvement on the Number of PEBs Seen on Television

	PEBs Seen
Strength of partisanship	0.04
Sex	0.03
Age (in years)	0.01[***]
Education	0.00
Objective social class	0.01
Newspaper reader	0.01
Cared a good deal which party won	0.16[***]
Talk regularly about politics	0.11[**]
Read election leaflet	0.17[***]
Hear candidate meeting	0.00
Extent of political knowledge	0.01
No say in government actions	−0.02
Don't care what I think	−0.01
Adjusted R^2	0.04

*$p < 0.05$; **$p < 0.01$; ***$p < 0.001$ (one-tailed test).

number of PEBs so that interpreting how the political interest and involvement variables are related to leader effects requires the reversal of the signs in the table. Thus, for example, while age may be positively related to PEB viewership, it is negatively so to leader effects. Having made this point, two features of the table stand out. First, there is some evidence that the politically interested and involved are less likely to be swayed in their voting decision by the party leaders. Second, this observation notwithstanding, the evidence in question is weak at best. The R^2 value is a measure of the percentage of the variance in the dependent variable explained by the battery of independent variables included in the equation and its value can range between zero and one. A value of 0.04, therefore, is low and leaves open the very real possibility that interest and involvement's relationship to leader effects is more apparent than real, being the product of circumstances unique to the 1992 campaign. Specifically, the strong leader effects among moderate PEB consumers would appear to be less an inherent property of this type of political broadcast and more the product of a single, leader-centred Tory PEB. Had it not been aired, PEBs as a type of political programme would probably have generated no more systematic a presidential response than leader interviews did (see Table 4.3).

In sum, while this analysis provides some evidence that PEB exposure encouraged leader effects in 1992, this evidence is no more than indirect and conclusions drawn from it speculative. The number of times leader interviews are watched, by contrast, is unrelated to leader effects. In the absence of compelling evidence to the contrary, therefore, the appropriate conclusion would seem to be the tentative one that neither type of television programme in itself plays much of a role in explaining the presidentialization of election outcomes in Britain. The likely reason is that, as mentioned above people tune into and watch these programmes with their partisan defences raised so that exposure to them reinforces political attitudes and behaviour more than it changes them. But can the same be said of news broadcasts, a form of political programming that Chapter 2 has shown to be characterized by a sharp presidentialization of presentation in the 1980s and 1990s?

Television news broadcasts

To this point, then, the evidence on PEBs and leader interviews lends substantial support to the 'minimal effects' view of television's short-term impact on political attitudes and behaviour. It would be short-sighted to stop at this point, however. The argument has been made that PEBs and leader interviews act largely as agents of reinforcement because voters will generally watch them with their partisan defences raised, but the same is not necessarily true of televison news broadcasts. These are commonly perceived to be trustworthy, credible and unbiased sources of political news and information, and therefore not threatening in their political coverage. They are central to the presidentialization issue in two other important respects as well. First, they air much more frequently than the other types of political broadcast and have a wider audience. In 1992, the year of this media analysis, the two major channels each had one early and one late evening national news programme of about half an hour in length, and Channel 4 had a similar broadcast in the evening only.[17] Thus, while 17.3 per cent of 1992 British Election Study respondents saw no PEBs and 17.8 per cent saw no leader interviews, only 3.2 per cent saw no BBC1, ITV or Channel 4 evening news programmes. Second, and relatedly, a strong presidentialization of presentation characterizes the evening news' coverage of the campaign over the course of the last three or four British general elections (see Figure 2.3). Thus, if television has helped to make British voters more presidential in their voting habits, its influence should be apparent in their reaction to television newscasts.

An important characteristic of television news broadcasts is that, even at the height of an election campaign, they are not the wholly political and election-oriented broadcasts that PEBs and leader interviews are. They are relatively lengthy and, even in the white heat of the campaign, they touch on a variety of subjects. The election itself may well be the most heavily covered item, but a broadcast will also typically feature other domestic stories, foreign affairs and overseas news, sports and human interest stories.[18] This diversity makes it important to recognize that all viewers do not watch news broadcasts for the same reasons. Political 'junkies' will tune in for election coverage, sports fans for up-to-date results and reports, and so on. The determinants of frequency of watching the news, therefore, are unlikely to be the same as those of paying attention to particular segments of it since there is no reason to expect that different interests (sports, say, as opposed to politics) will systematically shape how often people will tune into the news. What these interests should predict to, however, is the segment of the news broadcast that commands viewers' interest and attention. The important point being made here is that a rigorous test of television's responsibility for electoral presidentialism must go beyond establishing a simple association between exposure to news

Table 4.6 Leader Effects by Different Types of Exposure to Television News Programs

	Times per Week News Watched				Attention to Political Content			
	0	*<1*	*2–3*	*4+*	*None*	*A Little*	*Some*	*A Lot*
Party Identification × Vote (R^2)	0.82	0.85	0.89	0.91	0.84	0.94	0.85	0.89
R2 reduction controlling for:								
PM and OL Positive	0.17	0.16	0.15	0.13	0.15	0.08	0.15	0.19
PM and OL Negative	0.16	0.16	0.13	0.11	0.15	0.07	0.13	0.17

broadcasts and leader effects. If people are watching the news for non-political reasons, any such association that might emerge would be spurious. Confidence in the reality of the impact of the party leaders is better grounded if this impact is related systematically to attentiveness to the programme's political content.

As expected, the frequency of watching the news and the amount of attention paid to its political content are distinct activities, as is indicated by their having a zero-order correlation of only 0.16.[19] More to the point, however, Table 4.6 shows them to be behaviours engagement in which produces different patterns of leader effects. In the case of frequency of watching the news, there is a modest linear and negative relationship; leader effects decline slightly as voters tune into the news more often. When it comes to attentiveness to political content, however, leader effects are more positive in direction and stronger in magnitude insofar as the absolute difference between the lowest and highest values of the reduction coefficient are 0.05 in the case of viewership and 0.11 in that of political attentiveness. As speculated, the reason for this difference would seem to be that viewers have multiple reasons for tuning into the news and specifically political ones may, but need not always, be prominent among them. This is apparent in Table 4.7, which shows clearly that political interest and involvement do not predict strongly to frequency of viewership of the news. Variables like concern over which party won the elections and reading an election leaflet may have a significant impact, but their overall impact, as measured by the R^2 value, is not great. Furthermore, political knowledge's contribution to the equation's explanatory power is ambiguous since its impact could just as well be a function of watching the news as a reason for deciding to do so in the first place. Paying attention to the content of the television news, by contrast, is a markedly more specifically political act. Albeit again that political knowledge may be as much a product of attentiveness as a cause of it, all five interest/involvement variables in Table 4.7 predict highly significantly to viewers' degree of political attentiveness and, hence, to leader effects.

This finding provides strong support for a television-based explanation of presidential change in recent British elections. The jump in the magnitude of leader effects apparent in the late 1980s and the 1990s coincides more or less exactly with a sharp increase in the attention television news broadcasts lavished on the major party leaders. Assuming that variation in levels of political attentiveness have remained more or less stable over these same election contests, it

Table 4.7 Determinants of Exposure and Attentiveness to the Television News

	Times per Week News Watched	Attention to Political Content
Strength of partisanship	0.02	0.05**
Female	0.09*	−0.07
Age (in years)	0.00	−0.00
Education	−0.00	0.03
Middle-class occupation	0.05**	0.01
Newspaper reader	0.07	0.04
Cared a good deal which party won	0.23***	0.45***
Talk regularly about politics	0.05	0.23***
Read election leaflet	0.17**	0.73
Hear candidate meeting	0.20*	0.47***
Extent of political knowledge	0.05***	0.03**
No say in government actions	−0.03	0.02
Don't care what I think	−0.04*	−0.01**
Adjusted R^2	0.07	0.15

*$p < 0.05$; **$p < 0.01$; ***$p < 0.001$ (one-tailed test).

stands to reason that an important source of electoral presidentialization has been the more frequent appearance of the party leaders on television news programmes.

Table 4.7, then, suggests that leader effects are stronger among the more attentive. This is not the whole story, though, since Table 4.6, indicates at the same time that leader effects are at their strongest when political attention is relatively high *and* viewership relatively infrequent. In other words, leader effects need to be conceptualized as an interactive function of attentiveness and viewership. But even here, there are competing hypotheses. The argument might be made, for example, that party leaders can be expected to be at their most influential when both viewership and attentiveness are high since this scenario maximizes their exposure even if it does not guarantee public responsiveness. Equally, there is a 'couch potato' hypothesis, implicit in the *Times* editorials analyzed in Chapter 2, that it is the politically uninterested and uninvolved (i.e., the infrequent and lowly attentive viewer) who are in fact the more susceptible to the lure of personality. Clearly, understanding the presidentialization of British electoral politics requires choosing between these competing hypotheses, i.e., clarifying the circumstances under which viewership and attentiveness interact to translate most effectively into an impact for the party leaders.

The clarification strategy adopted is to estimate the magnitude of leader effects in each of the nine cells of a 3×3 table with attentiveness to political content on the vertical axis and frequency of viewership on the horizontal one. The R^2 reduction coefficients in the individual cells can then be compared directly to determine which combinations of attentiveness and exposure are most strongly associated with leader effects.[20] This is done in Table 4.8 and its very important message is that viewership and attentiveness in combination substantially influence the susceptibility of voters to the party leaders, but in neither a linear nor straightforward fashion. Least susceptible to the lure of the party leaders are those who are both the least attentive politically and the least regular news watchers. Medium-level leader effects are found among moderate (2–3) and regular (4+) news watchers regardless of their level of attention to the political content of the news they watch. Finally, the impact of the party leaders is greatest among the third group of voters, namely those watch the news least but have moderate (some) and high (a lot) levels of political attentiveness.

The pattern of media influence depicted in Table 4.8 is both complex and consistent with the findings of similar public opinion research. In his seminal work on the dynamics of public opinion in America, for example, Zaller (1992: 267) writes: 'Sometimes the least aware people are susceptible to influence…and sometimes the most aware are most open to influence…These differences across types of persuasion situation depend on differences in what people have been and are being exposed to…and not on differences in individual psychology in different political contexts.' In a similar vein, a recent study of how political interest moderated television's influence on popular affect for President Bush during the Gulf War concluded, as I have done, 'substantially, but not straightforwardly (so)'. When viewed linearly, 'high levels of

Table 4.8 Magnitude of Leader Effects by Different Combinations of Attentiveness and Viewership of Television News

| | | *Times per Week News Watched* | | |
		<1	*2–3*	*4+*
Attention to Political Content	*A Little*	0.05[a]	0.11	0.12
	Some	0.19	0.17	0.10
	A Lot	0.27	0.12	0.14

[a] These coefficients are R^2 reduction estimates for each group when the partisanship–vote relationship is controlled for the summed positive personality traits of the prime minister and opposition leader combined.

exposure and interest reduced priming (i.e., Bush's poll rating), although the coupling of exposure and interest was associated with slightly increased priming' (Krosnick and Brannon 1993: 972).

It is one thing, of course, to note the complexity of media effects, but another to make sense of them. If it is not simply how often the news is watched or how much attention is paid to its political content that accounts for variation in susceptibility to the party leaders, what is it? One way of answering this question is to go beyond the media variables and look at the kinds of people who fall into the low, moderate and high leader effects groupings in Table 4.8. What variables distinguish them systematically and how might these variables improve our understanding of variation in the magnitude of the electoral impact that the prime ministerial candidates enjoy? Table 4.8 defines the leader effects groupings for us. With an effects coefficient of 0.05, the low effects grouping is clearly to be found in a single cell, the little attentive and least regular viewers of the news. Equally clearly, the high effects grouping is concentrated in the two cells in the table with the distinctly highest effects estimates, 0.19 and 0.27.[21] Between these two extremes is the medium grouping and its membership is distributed over the majority of the cells in the table, ranging in value from 0.10 to 0.17. Thus identified, the three groupings can now be compared.

Table 4.9 Magnitude of Leader Effects by Political Interest and Involvement: One-Way ANOVAs

	Leader Effects Groupings			
	Low	*Medium*	*High*	*F-value*
Strength of partisanship	1.82	2.03	2.02	5.02[**]
Female	0.54	0.54	0.48	1.04
Age (in years)	43.53	47.17	45.46	3.02[*]
Education	3.24	3.50	3.41	0.96
Objective social class	3.19	3.68	3.48	8.92[**]
Newspaper reader	0.70	0.71	0.71	0.00
Cared which party won	0.76	0.88	0.90	7.21[***]
Talk regularly about politics	0.67	0.52	0.58	3.60[**]
Read election leaflet	0.67	0.87	0.93	22.63[***]
Hear candidate meeting	0.01	0.05	0.03	2.44[*]
Extent of political knowledge	4.74	5.68	5.43	11.24[***]
No say in government actions	3.41	3.06	3.18	6.97[***]
Don't care what I think	3.34	2.96	3.12	6.23[***]

$*p < 0.05$; $**p < 0.01$; $***p < 0.001$ (one-tailed test).

Using one-way analysis of variance, Table 4.9 compares the mean scores of the three effects groupings on each of the explanatory variables used earlier in Tables 4.5 and 4.7. The F-value presented in the final column is generated by a one-way analysis of variance and indicates whether the three group means are significantly different from each other in a statistical sense. Overall, it can be seen that the sociodemographic variables – like age, level of education and gender – do not predict well to the magnitude of leader effects. Their interest and involvement counterparts, however, are another matter. Of them, only caring which party won and reading an election leaflet are linear in the sense that leader effects increase in value from the low to medium to high effects categories, but the others nonetheless discriminate powerfully between the low effects grouping on the one hand and the medium and high groupings on the other. Moreover, with the sole exception of talking regularly about politics, the direction of increase in value is generally from the low to the medium and high groupings, which means that, contrary to much conventional wisdom painting voters influenced by leaders as mindless couch potatoes, it is the middle class, the politically sophisticated and those integrated into the mainstream of political life that are the more likely to fall under the sway of the prime ministerial candidates. Moreover, they do so despite their having a somewhat stronger party identification on the average.

The overwhelming conclusion to be drawn from Table 4.9, then, is that leader effects are not a function of viewership of, and attentiveness to, political news or even strength of partisanship alone. Voters' socioeconomic and political characteristics mediate television's influence. Moreover, the characteristics that do so are usually positively associated with leader effects and would generally be seen as desirable in democratic voters – for example, caring about the election outcome. The striking exception to this obseevation is the talking about politics (political discussion) variable. In direct contrast to the other interest and involvement variables in the table, it scores highest in the low effects grouping and explaining its deviant status promises to throw more light on the dynamics of television effects.

The simple, if often neglected, answer to this puzzle lies in the recognition that television's effect on attitudes and behaviour is socially mediated and is not the autonomous process that is implied by experimental studies in which participants are all but exclusively dependent for their political information and cues on contrived television news broadcasts. Indeed, focusing attention on the political discussion variable, Table 4.10 highlights the degree to which this is the case. It details three

Table 4.10   Magnitude of Leader Effects by Frequency of Political Discussion and Discussion with Fellow Partisans: One-Way ANOVAs

| | Leader Effects Groupings | | | |
	Low	Medium	High	F-value
Political Discussion				
How often see 1st discussant	2.42	2.84	2.83	12.44[***]
How often see 2nd discussant	2.40	2.67	2.67	5.44[**]
How often see 3rd discussant	2.55	2.68	2.78	0.34
% Talking with Fellow Partisan				
1st discussant fellow partisan	88.7	90.4	88.8	0.20
2nd discussant fellow partisan	85.3	85.3	81.5	0.42
3rd discussant fellow partisan	82.5	73.3	71.9	0.42
Disagree in Political Discussion				
How often disagree 1st discussant	2.45	2.59	2.46	1.98[*]
How often disagree 2nd discussant	2.38	2.65	2.61	2.81[**]
How often disagree 3rd discussant	2.60	2.79	2.84	0.70

[*] $p < 0.10$; [**] $p < 0.01$; [***] $p < 0.001$ (one-tailed test).

characteristics of each effects grouping's pattern of political discussion. The first is the regularity with which its members see the first, second and third persons with whom they regularly discuss politics; their answer is on a four-point scale ranging from less than once a month to almost every day so that the higher the score the more frequent the political discussion.[22] The second is the percentage of first, second and third discussion partners who are of the same partisanship, Conservative or Labour. Finally, they are asked how frequently they disagree in their political discussions – never, rarely, sometimes and often. Taken overall, the table suggests that low leader effects among the least frequent and least politically attentive television viewers are some function of their relatively infrequent and consensual pattern of political discussion, as well as of their probably related lack of political interest and involvement. That is, while this low effects grouping is no less likely than the others to restrict its political discussion to conversations with fellow partisans, it is different in that it engages in political discussion substantially less often and the discussions it does engage in involve considerably less disagreement.

By way of summary, the evidence suggests that, especially among the medium and high effects groupings in Tables 4.9 and 4.10, the relative merits of the Conservative and Labour party leaders would seem to have been a matter of sufficient disagreement and debate among relatively interested and involved identifiers to have persuaded some of them to defect to the opposition at the election. Those among whom both political discussion and disagreement were less common were less likely to fall under the sway of the party leaders; their political environment away from the television set would appear to have challenged their party loyalties less because it did not raise the party leaders as a divisive issue with the potential to prise identifiers away from their party at the polls.

Television would seem to prime best, then, under four conditions. The first is when viewers are more politically interested and involved, and feel more integrated into the political mainstream. The second is when they sit before the television set without their partisan defences raised, as in the case of impartial (in a partisan sense) news programmes as opposed to PEBs and leader interviews. The third is when they are infrequent viewers of newscasts but are still moderately or highly attentive to their political content. The fourth, and perhaps this is the reason why they do not watch the television news that often despite being relatively attentive to its political content, is when they regularly talk and disagree about politics even though their discussion partners are mostly fellow partisans. The findings in Tables 4.9 and 4.10 suggest that some of this disagreement revolves around the party leaders and perceptions of their relative merits and demerits can encourage partisans to defect to the other major party at the polls.

The medium of television, in short, is not an autonomous political force. The type of message it communicates, the socioeconomic and political characteristics of message recipients and the interpersonal context in which the messages are processed all play an important part in determining the influence it has, if any, on viewers' short-term political attitudes and behaviour.

Conclusion

This chapter represents an initial effort to specify the nature of the linkage between two recent developments in British electoral politics, the greater electoral impact now enjoyed by the prime minister and leader of the opposition, and especially the former, and the increased attention paid to the Conservative and Labour party leaders the printed press and on television. As such, it is part of the growing literature rejecting the conventional wisdom that the media reinforce political attitudes and behaviour in parliamentary elections, but do not change them (see also Gunther and Mughan 2000; Miller et al.

1991; Mughan 1996; Norris et al. 1999). In the manner of a simple stimulus-response model, this minimal effects thesis was based an overly narrow and demanding notion of what constitutes a media effect. Its basic requirement is conversion; the media have to determine the party choice of voters or define the issues they see as significant before they can be said to have had an effect. US studies, by contrast, point to an important and consequential media effect being, more modestly, to influence the relative weights of the various considerations voters bring to bear on their evaluation of issues, politicians and parties. This process is known as priming and the key argument of this chapter is that that the increasingly leader-centred character of British politics in general and the greater television attention to the party leaders during campaigns have primed a presidential response from the voter by making the personalities of these same leaders (and the way they are presented in the news) a weightier contributor to her voting decision.

Not all media are equal, however. Nor is the same medium equal under all circumstances. Rather, this study of the presidentialization of electoral impact in recent British general elections shows quite clearly that complexity is the defining characteristic of media effects. For a start, newspapers are found to play little or no systematic role in priming message recipients and enhancing the leaders' electoral impact. It was investigation of this medium which gave rise to the minimal effects thesis in the 1940s and 1950s and the evidence of this study is that it continues to apply, at least to the highly partisan British press of today. They may pay more attention to the party leaders, but there is no evidence that this greater attention has contributed to the presidentialization of electoral outcomes. Television is a different story; its effects are neither simple nor straightforward in that they vary with type of political programme, with the frequency of watching the news and degree of attentiveness to its political content, and with the socioeconomic and political characteristics of viewers.

We shall consider type of political programme first. Televised interviews with the party leaders do not encourage leader-based defection from the vote no matter how often they are seen during a campaign. Partisan defences when watching this type of programme would just seem to be too high. There is some evidence that PEBs might be different insofar as they appear to have some success in priming voters exposed to a small number of them. It seems, however, that this particular instance of influence reflects less a generic characteristic of PEBs and more the success of a single PEB centred around the Conservative leader in the 1992 campaign. More generally, though, the intriguing possibility is raised that the 'diminishing importance attached to party broadcasts' (Butler 1989: 99) is fundamentally misguided on the part of the Conservative and Labour parties since, in the absence of paid political advertising, leader-centred PEBs may come as close as is possible under British electoral law to the unregulated, highly personalized and successful political advertisements aired on commercial television in US presidential election campaigns. The truth may be in fact that party strategists have shown greater acuity than academic election analysts on this matter so that it is no coincidence that there has been a leader-centred PEB in each of the last three campaigns.

Television news broadcasts are undoubtedly the most potent of the three types of political broadcast through which British party strategists can seek to project their leader and influence public opinion in election campaigns. Ample evidence has been provided that they prime voters and promote leader-based voting defection among Conservative and Labour partisans. Put simply, in lavishing more attention on the Conservative and Labour leaders in the 1980s and 1990s, television newscasts seem to have encouraged interested and involved voters in particular to discuss and disagree over them, treating their relative merits as an issue in the campaign. Their potential to stimulate defection among supporters of the other party has been thereby enhanced and parliamentary elections in Britain have become more presidential in both style and outcome.

But what are the larger implications of presidentialization? How long term a change is it? Does it alter the terms of the debate about the power of the prime minister over his cabinet and parliamentary colleagues? Does it have implications for how we view the rationality of the personality-based vote? These are some of the questions addressed in the next two chapters.

5
Scale and Durability of Leader Effects

Using Britain as a test case, the analysis to this point has confirmed the need to reconceptualize our understanding of modern parliamentary elections to take account of the personalities of the party leaders being substantial influences on their outcomes. Political parties' growing dependence on television as their campaigning vehicle of preference has obliged them more than in the not-too-recent past to project themselves and shape their popular image through their principal spokesperson, their leader and de facto prime ministerial candidate. By simultaneously encouraging and taking their cues from this more personalized style of campaigning, the print and electronic media in turn have come to lavish more attention on the party leaders and, in so doing, have helped to make them more salient and powerful electoral stimuli for the voting public. The evidence presented in the previous three chapters of this book makes for a persuasive case that British general elections have, in terms of both presentation and impact, become more presidential. To make this argument, however, does not exhaust all there is to be said about this change since it neglects two related, if distinct, facets of the personalization of election campaigns – namely, its scale and durability. That is, not addressed to this point are the questions of, first, how influential the party leaders are relative to each other and to other short-term determinants of the vote and, second, how permanent a change to the dynamics of parliamentary election contests is presidentialism likely to represent. These questions are the focus of this chapter.

When examining change, a sense of balance and perspective must always be maintained. Recent British elections may indeed have presidentialized, but this might mean no more than that the Conservative and Labour party leaders have gone from the utterly inconsequential to the marginally consequential. Relatedly, the presidentialization that has taken place might be dismissed as an epiphenomenon that is liable to be reversed in future elections as political parties return to more tried-and-tested ways of running for office. To this point the analysis in this book has been one-sided insofar as it has neglected both these possibilities, a neglect that risks distorting our understanding of the dynamics of election outcomes because it focuses on only part of the bigger picture. Uncertainty consequently remains about just where the party leaders fit into this bigger picture. More specifically, if party leaders have become more important for British election outcomes, just how important is important? In particular, what is their impact relative to that of a much more widely investigated influence on the vote, campaign issues? Similarly, since uncertainty is inherent in a trend extrapolated in good part from the experiences of only three elections (1987, 1992 and 1997), is presidentialization better interpreted as a transitory blip in a fundamentally stable order of things or a structural change in the determinants of the way individuals vote and elections turn out?

These questions beg answers and this chapter tries to provide them. It does not seek to present a comprehensive account of stability and change in the pattern of recent election outcomes in Britain or elsewhere. Rather, the two goals it sets for itself are more limited. The first is to establish that party leaders can be a non-trivial influence on election outcomes, their importance in this regard being established in two ways – by showing that a party's prime ministerial candidate can make the difference between defeat and victory for his party in a closely fought contest and by showing that leaders are generally more influential than issues in determining the way people vote. The second goal is to make the argument that the conduct of 1987, 1992 and 1997 election campaigns, and particularly the role of television in them, represents the way of the future so that the presidentialization that has taken place, while its magnitude may vary with the personalities of the party leaders and the specific circumstances of future contests, is hardly likely to go into reverse.

Scale: the party leaders compared

Leader effects do not necessarily translate into election loss or victory for one party or another. Rather, prime ministerial candidates can win or lose votes for their parties without the gains and losses accruing to them personally making any net difference to the final distribution of the vote between the parties. Such an outcome transpires when the two leaders cancel each other out; each of them has the same impact so that their respective parties gain no net advantage from their individual presidential appeal. Thus, the true measure of the worth of a leader is not whether she can win votes that would otherwise not have gone to her party, but whether she represents a comparative advantage for her party. Is her personality a net asset for the party in terms of popular support at the polls?

It is possible to make a tentative estimate of the net impact of an individual leader's personality traits by simulating how the election would have turned out had the Conservative and Labour parties each been under different leadership. More specifically, it can be estimated how different the distribution of the vote would have been had the Conservative leader been at the helm of the Labour party and the Labour leader at the helm of the Conservatives?[1] The starting point of this simulation is the observation that the personalies of the leaders, as reflected in the traits popularly ascribed to them, has two dimensions, both of which must be taken into account when assessing their overall impact on the election. The first of them involves the strength of the impact of these traits on the vote. Do, for example, some traits have an impact, and others not. Relatedly, do negative traits have a stronger impact than positive ones? Personality's second dimension of importance relates to the distribution of these traits. If it is found that certain traits are influential, then it follows that the larger the number of voters who see these traits in a particular leader, the greater will be that leader's overall impact not only on the party that they choose, but also on the way the election turns out. Regression analysis is a statistical technique that allows us to take account of both dimensions of the importance of personality traits. On the one hand, it generates a coefficient, b, for each variable included in the equation and this coefficient is an estimate of that variable's impact on the dependent variable. More precisely, this unstandardized coefficient is an estimate of the amount of change, negative or positive, in the dependent variable associated with a one-unit change in the independent variable. On the other hand, regression analysis is also able to take the distribution of an independent variable into account by multiplying its mean value by the matching regression coefficient to arrive at an overall estimate of that variable's contribution to the value of the dependent variable.

Using the same summed trait variables as in previous chapters, Table 5.1 summarizes just such a regression analysis.[2] The first column for each year presents the mean scores for all Conservative and Labour identifiers and voters on the party identification and positive and negative trait

Table 5.1 Distribution and Impact of Summed Positive and Negative Trait Variables in 1987 and 1992

	1987			1992		
	$\bar{X}$	b	$\bar{X}^*b$	$\bar{X}$	b	$\bar{X}^*b$
Party Identification	0.57	0.759^{***}	0.433	0.57	0.835^{***}	0.476
PM Positive	1.70	0.025^{*}	0.043	2.11	0.054^{***}	0.114
PM Negative	1.17	-0.037^{***}	-0.043	0.77	0.014	0.011
OL Positive	1.52	-0.005	-0.008	1.43	-0.006	-0.009
OL Negative	1.25	0.026^{***}	0.033	1.38	0.021^{**}	0.029
R^2	0.869				0.894	

$^*p < 0.05$; $^{**}p < 0.01$; $^{***}p < 0.001$ (one-tailed test).

variables for the prime minister (Thatcher in 1987 and Major in 1992) and opposition leader (Kinnock in both elections). The second column contains the partial regression coefficient estimating each independent variable's impact on the likelihood of voting for the Conservative party in 1987 and 1992 respectively. Positive evaluations of the prime minister and negative ones of the opposition leader can be expected to boost the Conservative vote, while negative evaluations of the prime minister and positive ones of the opposition leader should depress it. Column 3 is the product of the figures in the first two columns and represents an estimate, net of other variables in the equation, of the percentage added to or subtracted from the Conservative vote by positive or negative perceptions of the leaders (see note 2 for the full specification of this equation). In 1987, for example, the results suggest that, net of party identification and the other variables in the table, perceptions of the positive in Prime Minister Thatcher were worth an extra 4.3 per cent of the two-party vote to the Tories. At the same time, however, negative perceptions of her depressed the party's vote share by the same amount, meaning that on balance she was neither an asset nor a liability for her party in that election. The Labour leader, in contrast, cost his party more votes than he brought to it with the result that he was a clear liability to it.

These results make it clear that neither party leader contributed decisively to the 1987 election outcome. With a greater than 11 percentage point advantage over Labour in vote share and a 102-seat majority, the Conservative party would have won even had Kinnock been the same neutral influence on his party's fortunes that Thatcher was on her's. The 1992 election, though, is an altogether different story. To be sure, the Tories won for the fourth consecutive time, but with a majority that dropped sharply to 21 seats. Indeed, the margin of victory was narrower than even a parliamentary majority of this size might suggest. An analysis of the constituency results concludes: '(T)he picture is quite dramatic. The Conservatives' overall majority would disappear if there were just a 0.5% swing from Conservative to Labour' (Butler and Kavanagh 1992: 351). From a leader effects perspective, the crucial difference in 1992 is that Thatcher's successor, John Major, was the pivotal element in the party's winning a parliamentary majority at all. His centrality to the narrow Tory victory can be demonstrated by asking whether the Tories would have done the same, better or worse under different leadership. More specifically, what would have been its vote share had Margaret Thatcher, with the same trait profile as in 1987, still been Tory leader in 1992? In the same vein, what would have been the Tory vote share had Mr Kinnock enjoyed the same trait profile in 1992 that Mr Major did?

It is possible to highlight Major's crucial 1992 role by simulating these two scenarios with the information presented in Table 5.1.[3] Take the Thatcher one first. The mean trait values in the table show that she was viewed both less positively and more negatively in 1987 than Major was in 1992 and, in point of fact, either distributional difference is sufficient on its own to have cost the Conservative party its parliamentary majority in 1992. The starting point in substantiating this claim is to ask the question: what would have happened to the Tory vote in 1992 if Major had been viewed no more positively than Thatcher had been some five years earlier? A tentative answer is provided by subtracting the mean of the 1987 summed positive traits for Thatcher from the same figure for Major in 1992; the difference is 0.41 in the latter's favour. When this figure is then multiplied by the matching regression coefficient in the 1992 equation, 0.054, the product is 0.022, or 2.2 per cent. This figure is an initial estimate of the amount by which the Conservative vote would have dropped in 1992 had the Thatcher of 1987 still been its leader in that contest.[4] Repeating this exercise for the negative traits of the two Conservative leaders results in an estimated vote increase for the party as a result of having Major at its helm in 1992 of 0.006 (0.40×0.014), or 0.6 per cent. The key point is that both estimates exceed the 0.5 per cent swing that it would have taken to deprive the Tories of the small parliamentary majority they actually won. It would seem, therefore, that the fears of the Conservative backbenchers who forced Mrs Thatcher to resign as leader in November 1990 for fear that she would cause them to lose the next election may not have been altogether unfounded (Young 1991: 579–91).

The fact that John Major attracted relatively few negative evaluations from voters is at the root of his comparative advantage over the leader of the Labour opposition as well. A notable feature of Table 5.1 is that in neither election do positive evaluations of the Labour leader have a significant impact on his party's vote share. By contrast, those for both Thatcher and Major, and especially the latter, do. One interpretation, popular at the time, is that Tories thought Kinnock ultimately not of prime ministerial calibre and so could not bring themselves to vote for his party regardless of their goodwill towards him personally. This relative inability to translate goodwill into votes notwithstanding, however, Kinnock might still have deprived the Conservatives of their parliamentary majority had only he been viewed no less negatively than John Major in 1992. This conclusion is suggested by taking the amount by which the Labour leader's mean negative trait score exceeds the prime minister's (0.61) and multiplying it by Kinnock's regression coefficient on this variable (0.021). The product of this exercise is an estimate of the percentage figure by which the Labour vote would have increased had all else remained the same except for Kinnock being viewed no more negatively than Major. That the value of this figure is 1.28 per cent (0.061×0.021) indicates that had the sitting prime minister's public image been as negative as the Labour leader's, the Tories would, other things being equal, likely have lost enough votes to have deprived them of the small parliamentary majority they did manage to win in 1992. This would not necessarily have meant victory for Labour, however. Rather, given its poor performance in the election, a hung Parliament would probably have ensued.[5]

At this point, a word of caution is in order. Simulated estimates in the region of 1 or 2 per cent are not great, but, in one sense, their small magnitude enhances their plausibility since large leader effects are hardly to be expected in parliamentary elections where party is still a key driving force and issues also play some role in shaping the popular vote (Franklin 1985; Heath et al. 1991; Rose and McAllister 1986). It is also the case, of course, that these estimates are subject to error, a problem common to all sample survey measures. Such error as there may be, however, could just as easily underestimate leader effects as overestimate them. Especially telling about Table 5.1, though, is that the results all point in the direction of a pivotal effect for John Major (see also Brown 1993; Jones and Hudson 1996). Popular goodwill towards him may not have been sufficient to allow his party to maintain the triple-digit majorities that it had won in 1983 and 1987, but the cumulative evidence is that he was the difference between the formation of a majority Conservative government and a hung Parliament in 1992. Moreover, if elections are more competitive and seats more easily swung by small changes in the vote in an effectively multi-party system like the current British one, then parties cannot afford to ignore the difference, even if only at the margins, that their leaders can make in a television age. Modern parliamentary parties ignore the potential presidential appeal, or lack of it, of their leaders at their own peril.

Scale: issues vs leaders

It is the case, then, that the greater appeal of one party's leader relative to another's can make a difference to the way individuals vote as well as to the distribution of the vote. The possibility remains, however, that the appeal of the leaders is epiphenomenal, being itself a function of that much more widely investigated short-term influence on the vote, campaign issues. These are policy matters that divide both parties and voters. Some are ephemeral, such as economic recession or involvement in an overseas conflict, whereas others are perennial because they have traditionally been an integral part of the ideologies that divide the country's governing Conservative and Labour parties – these might include public ownership, welfare spending, nuclear disarmament, the redistribution of wealth, and so on. Normally, issue preferences, like leader evaluations, are to some degree a function of party identification; the stance that individuals take on an issue coincides with that of their party and reinforces their vote for that party. Issue voting takes place, however, when voters cast their ballot on the basis of their policy preferences rather than their partisanship.[6] Thus, along with candidates for the position of chief executive, issues have generally been seen as the principal short-term force making for defection from partisanship in democratic elections (Butler and Stokes 1974; Campbell et al. 1960; 1966).

In the context of parliamentary elections, at least, issues have received far more attention from analysts than have prime ministerial candidates (see, for example, Budge and Farlie 1983; Crewe and Denver 1985; Dalton et al. 1984; and Franklin et al. 1992). The explanation of this preferential treatment is both normative and empirical. Normatively speaking, issues, and not partisanship or party leaders, have generally been seen as the touchstone of voter rationality and democratic accountability. Voters are generally seen to be rational to the extent that they vote on the basis of their issue preferences and analysts have long been concerned to determine whether voters actually are as immune to the influence of issues in their voting choice as early voting studies had concluded. These painted a picture of an electorate moved by long-standing social group or political party identifications and almost totally oblivious to the issues raised and debated during the campaign (see, for example, Berelson et al. 1954; Blondel 1963; Campbell et al. 1960 and Milne and Mackenzie 1958). The argument has been made that erosion of these identifications in the 1960s and 1970s was accompanied by indications that voters, at least in Britain, were 'better informed about political issues than…twenty years ago' (Franklin 1985: 128). Under these circumstances, attention turned quite naturally to a re-examination of the role of issues in shaping individual voting choice and election outcomes, with the big question lurking in the background being whether voters have become more rational and governments thereby more accountable for their actions or inactions in office.

This question has not been answered to everybody's satisfaction and part of the reason is disagreement over how issue voting should be measured. On the one hand, there are those who argue that it is sufficient simply to gauge whether voters place themselves to the left or the right on an issue and then to assess the influence of their self-placement on the way they vote. Under this methodology, no attention is paid to the voters' perceptions of where the parties stand on the issue in question. It is simply assumed that if the voter is to the right in her partisanship but to the left on the issue at hand and she then votes for the party of the left then she has engaged in issue voting (see, for example, Heath et al. 1991: 32–51). On the other hand, there are those who argue that correlation does not mean causation. Their position is that if an issue is to be claimed to have been truly instrumental in shaping party choice, then it is not enough simply for the voter to have a preference, whether to the left or right, on that issue. In addition, this argument continues, the parties have to take up opposing stances on the issue and the voter has to be able to identify correctly where each party stands on it. Only when the voter has synchronized her preference on the issue and the party reflecting that preference can she be said to have voted on the basis of that issue (Butler and Stokes 1974; Franklin 1985). No attempt will be made here to adjudicate between these competing definitions of issue voting. Rather, both will be examined to make for a more complete analysis of the relative electoral impact of issues and leaders.

The measurement of popular evaluations, negative and positive, of the party leaders has already been described and it involves the summation of perceived negative and positive personality traits (see note 10 in Chapter 3). For the sake of comparability, issues are measured following the same simple summation logic. The 1987 and 1992 BES cross-section surveys have in common four issue questions on which respondents are asked to state their own preference, as well as their perception of where each of the Conservative and Labour parties stand on each of them. Thus, two types of issue preference can be calculated. The first of them taps just individuals' own issue positions. In response to a request to say where they stand, voters place themselves either to the left or to the right on each issue separately. They cannot be both left and right so that if they give a pro-Labour response on a particular issue, their Conservative score on it is automatically 0.[7] Two variables can then be created by summing each respondent's number of pro-Labour preferences and, separately, his number of pro-Conservative preferences on the four issues. Each of these measures therefore ranges between 0 and 4 in value.

The second measure follows the same summation logic, but it is a little different in content because it is designed to combine personal issue preferences with the accurate perception of where the Tory and Labour parties place themselves on the issues. In other words, just as individuals are asked to say where they stand on an issue and are coded as being to the left or right, so too are they asked to place each major party on that issue so that it too is coded as having a left or right stance on it. Two new variables are thereby created, one a position imputed to Labour on each issue and the other a position imputed to the Conservatives on the same issue. The next step is to multiply ideological self-placement (left or right) first by Labour and then by Conservative party issue placement. Thus, a leftist voter (with a score of 1) on an issue who also accurately identifies Labour as being to the left (with a score of 1) on the same issue will score 1, while respondents with a score of 0 on either or both of self-placement or party placement will score 0. In the same way, rightist voters correct in their perception of the Tories as occupying the same ideological position as themselves on an issue will score 1 and 0 otherwise. The result is two measures of respondent–party issue agreement, one Conservative the other Labour and both ranging in value between 0 and 4.

Thus, conceptually speaking, for each party two different issue preference measures have been generated, one focusing on the individual's self-placement to the left or right on the issues and the other on the degree to which self-placement and correct party placement overlap. Despite their different underlying assumptions about the conditions

Table 5.2   Mean Issue and Issue–Party Scores by Year and Partisanship

	1987		1992	
	Con. Id.	*Lab. Id.*	*Con. Id.*	*Lab. Id.*
Con. issue preferences	1.55	0.34	0.67	0.16
Con. Issuez–party preferences	1.37	0.22	0.58	0.09
Lab. Issue preferences	1.43	3.00	0.91	1.53
Lab. Issue–party preferences	1.12	2.79	0.69	1.41

under which issues can be said to have affected the vote, however, it turns out, empirically speaking, that the two measures of issue preference are very similar to each other for both parties. In 1987, the simple correlation for between being on the right on the one hand and being on the right *and* correctly placing the Tory party on the right on the other is 0.93, while the matching correlation for leftists is 0.90. The same figures in 1992 are 0.94 and 0.93 respectively. Moreover, it might be noted that the relationship between voters' personal left or right issue preferences is not zero-sum in the sense of the one being the mirror image of the other. If it were, the correlation between them would be negative and complete at -1.0. As it happens, however, they are correlated at no more than -0.69 in 1987 and at 0.02 in 1992, while the matching figures for the combined individual-party preference measures are -0.62 and -0.01 respectively. It can be seen, in other words, that their relationship is actually positive, albeit only just, in one instance in 1992 and the reason, as Table 5.2 shows, is that even Tory partisans preferred Labour on the issues in this election.

As well as being of interest in itself, the fact that both Conservative and Labour partisans prefer the opposition on some issues is important because it leaves plenty of room for defection should partisanship and issue preferences overlap insufficiently. Thus, just like party leaders, issues are, at least in principle, capable of generating voting defection from partisanship. Looking at the role of issues from 1979 to 1992, the discussion in Chapter 2 showed that issue effects were present in all four elections and were more unchanging in their impact than leader effects (see Table 2.3). However, the question addressed here concerns not their pattern over time, but their relative magnitude. Which of these competing short-term forces is stronger in any given election? Once again, regression analysis can answer this question, although this time the coefficients presented in Table 5.3 are standardized, which

Table 5.3 Issues, Leaders and the Conservative Vote, 1987 and 1992

	1987		1992	
	β	β	β	β
Conservative Identification	0.77***	0.75***	0.84***	0.84***
Middle Class	0.02*	0.02*	0.01	0.01
Home Owner	0.02**	0.02**	0.01	0.01
Female	−0.02*	−0.02*	−0.00	−0.00
PM Positive	0.05**	0.05**	0.11***	0.11***
PM Negative	−0.06**	−0.05**	0.03	0.03
OL Positive	−0.01	−0.01	−0.02	−0.02
OL Negative	0.06***	0.06***	0.04*	0.04*
Con. Issue Preference	0.02*	—	0.01*	—
Lab. Issue Preference	−0.04***	—	−0.03***	—
Con. Issue–Party Preference	—	0.02*	—	0.01
Lab. Issue–Party Preference	—	−0.06***	—	−0.03***
R^2	0.87	0.87	0.89	0.89

*$p < 0.05$; **$p < 0.01$; ***$p < 0.001$.

means that the value any variable enjoys can be directly compared with that of any other variable in the same equation to determine their relative impact on the vote. That is, if variable A has a value of 0.05 and variable β has one of 0.10, then it can be concluded that β is twice as influential as A. An important limitation, though, is that, unlike in the case of the unstandardised coefficients in Table 2.3, the values of the same variable cannot be compared from one equation to the other. Nonetheless, the advantage of unstandardized coefficients, or beta weights (β), for present purposes is that they allow us to determine which is the more forceful influence on the individual voting decision in any one election, issues or leaders.

A second caveat before turning attention to Table 5.3 is that this comparison of the relative influence of issues and leaders does not have the same goal as the simulation exercise as in Table 5.1. Instead of asking what would have happened to the Tory share of the 1992 vote if, say, Neil Kinnock had been viewed no more negatively by voters than John Major, Table 5.3 takes no account of the distributions of leader and issue preferences, asking instead the more conventional question of which of them has the stronger impact on the party for which individuals vote.[8] In this regard, a number of interesting and pertinent conclusions are suggested by the table. Starting with the narrower ones, it is very noticeable that the way issue preferences are measured in fact has few implications for conclusions about the effect of issues on party choice; empirically speaking at least, the two measures are all but indistinguishable in their electoral impact. Second, two key conclusions of earlier chapters are confirmed. Leader effects are higher relative to party identification in 1987 than 1992 and, combined, the negative traits of the party leaders are the more influential in 1987 and the positive in 1992. Third, just as the nature of leader effects varies, so too does that of issue effects. The table shows, for example, that Conservative issue preferences were similar to positive prime ministerial evaluations in their impact on the 1987 vote (0.02 compared to 0.05), but in 1992 the gap between them widened to 11 to 1 in favour of evaluations of the prime minister (0.11 compared to 0.01).

This decline in the relative importance of issues is probably the result of two developments that converged to eliminate the Tory advantage on matters of concern to a good part of the electorate. The first is that the party's own legislative initiatives in office reduced the political salience of certain issues, nationalization and trade union power in particular, that had previously brought the Conservative party bonus votes. The second is that both parties moved towards the centre between 1987 and 1992. The efforts of the Conservative party to moderate its harsh and uncaring Thatcherite image have already been described. The Labour party too saw a need for change. In the aftermath of its third successive defeat in 1987, it undertook a wide-ranging review of its policy commitments in the hope of broadening its electoral appeal. The result was 'in part, a restoration of the party's past social democratic traditions and in part a radical shift towards a future that involved an embrace of the market and a rejection of trade union legal immunities' (Seyd 1993: 85).

The most important feature of the table, however, concerns what it tells us about the relative impact of issues and leaders, and here a number of observations follow. First, as in Table 2.3, the two forces, in one manifestation or another, are influential in both elections. Second, their relative impact is variable, changing with the circumstances of specific elections. Leader and issue effects, for example, are more comparable in the magnitude of their impact in 1987 than in 1992 when John Major proved to be such an asset to his party. Finally, variation notwithstanding, leader effects are almost always substantially stronger in relative terms (see also Miller et al. 1990: 253).[9] The explanation of this gap is not apparent from the table, but it may lie in voters' well-documented ability to distort their perception of campaign issues in a way that 'maximizes agreement with (their) own side and maximizes disagreement with the opposition' (Berelson et al. 1954: 231). This kind of psychological accommodation to reduce dissonance may not be available to voters in their reactions to personalities whom they regularly see with their own eyes and listen to with their own ears, and especially during the campaign. Put differently, the more intimate and less abstract character of this interaction may make it more difficult for voters to discount their more positive reaction to the leader of the opposing party.

With partisan dealignment at its highest level since at least the early 1960s (see Table 3.3), elections have become more open contests than they were in the past. Moreover, Table 5.3 would indicate that issues and leaders are dynamic in their short-term electoral impact and one reason for this dynamism is that they are manipulable to some degree. That is, parties in their efforts to secure victory can, and do, have some choice in their selection of issues or leaders and they can try to present both in such a way as to make them more appealing to voters. Importantly, though, the two short-term forces are not equally manipulable. Moreover, nor will they necessarily have equal pay-offs. Manipulation in the sense of presenting a favourable face to the electorate involves principally mass communication through the media and two observations are in order with regard to issues. First, the available evidence indicates that television coverage of the campaigns that parties try to orchestrate has at best limited power to change voters' issue agendas (see Chapter 4). Second, and relatedly, even if issue agendas were open to change as the result of television coverage, Table 5.3 suggests that the electoral pay-offs for parties will be greater to the extent that voters can be persuaded of the virtues of their leaders rather than their issue positions. In this regard, John Major's apparently key role in the Conservative party's unexpected outright victory in 1992 may speak volumes for the efficacy of the party's meticulously orchestrated 'caring and competence' campaign in helping to shape such an asymmetrically positive image for a leader who by common acclaim appeared remarkably dull and ordinary ('grey' was the epithet often used to describe him) after the highly opinionated, aggressive and divisive Margaret Thatcher.

In addition, if leaders are indeed a stronger and more manipulable short-term electoral force than issues, Conservative and Labour strategists are unlikely to roll back their investment in television-based, personality-centred election campaigning. This being so, the relatively high levels of presidentialism characteristic of recent election contests would seem to represent more of a structural change than a blip on the horizon. This conclusion becomes all the more compelling when changes in party organization – that is, the ability to fight more traditional, locally oriented and labour-intensive campaigns, are also taken into account.

Durability: Party organization

The central question to be asked in any assessment of the durability of the presidentialism characteristic of recent election contests is whether the parties in fact have plausible alternatives to this new television-based and more leader-centred electioneering style. There are at least two reasons for arguing forcefully that they do not. The first involves the British public's ever greater exposure to, and informational dependence on, television and the second the parties' own reluctance to move away from style of campaigning that enables them at the same time to overcome their weakened organization at the local level and to centralize power and control in party headquarters, thereby running a more controlled, efficient and effective campaign.

It is no more than a truism to observe that political parties have to adapt to the prevailing mode of communication in society if their messages are to reach the mass public, mobilize their own loyalists and, hopefully, convert waverers to their cause. Here, the plain fact of the matter is that, as with other political parties in democracies worldwide, the Tories, Labour and other UK parties are increasingly thrown back onto television to get their messages across. Not the least reason is that the British public spends more and more of its leisure time in front of the television set. Figures from the BBC Broadcasting Research Department indicate that, net of other activities like working, eating, sleeping and playing, adults spent an average 13 hours and 42 minutes per week watching television in 1960.[10] By 1970, this figure had crept up to 15 hours and 33 minutes and by 1980 it had risen to 18 hours and nine minutes. The BBC then changed its measurement system in 1981, which resulted in the reported hourly average being 22 hours and nine minutes. In 1992, and under the same measurement system, the reported average had increased yet again, to 26 hours and 22 minutes.

Moreover, television's communicational pre-eminence has been achieved at the expense of other media through which parties made their play for popular support in the past. The decline of newspaper readership has been documented in the last chapter. Similarly despite the proliferation of local and national radio stations in the final decades of the twentieth century BBC figures show that radio listening did no better than remain stable at between eight and nine hours a week.[11] Thus, to the extent that television is the public's favourite communications medium, as well as the one that it finds most informative, credible and trustworthy, political parties would risk political suicide to ignore its potential in the daily course of building, consolidating and expanding their support base. Today, election campaign politics in particular are inconceivable without television. As Harrop (1987: 46) has strongly put it: 'Communication has always been central to politics; the mass media are now central to political communication. In elections especially, the media do not cover the campaign; they are the campaign.'

But while the contemporary political importance of the mass media of communication cannot be gainsaid, Harrop's argument is overstated if it is interpreted in such a way as to underestimate the reciprocal and mutually constraining nature of the relationship between political parties and the media. To be sure, the vast majority of voters keep up with the campaign through the mass media, and television in particular, but it remains the case that the media's ability to set the campaign agenda is far from unlimited since they are in a position unilaterally to determine neither the course of the campaign nor the content or context of the messages they convey to voters. This is more the preserve of the party strategists who decide on the kind of campaign they want to run, stage it and then strive mightily to ensure that broadcast television, constrained by law to be impartial and balanced in its political coverage, reports the campaign as they want it to be seen in the regular news bulletins that attract millions of viewers. These efforts to shape the reporting of the campaign are one reason that broadcasters complain about being used by the parties. To go back to the 'stopwatching' example, tired of being manipulated by the parties into covering staged campaign events of little or no political significance or importance, '[s]ome months before the 1992 campaign, ITN announced that they would no longer 'stopwatch' (that is, give news coverage to the parties in proportion to their PEB allocation) the coverage and that news value would be the sole criterion for inclusion in the bulletin' (Semetko et al. 1994: 26).

Constraint works both ways, though. The autonomy of party strategists in their relations with the media is also limited in one very important respect. They may try to manipulate the political content of media messages by unveiling poster after poster, staging walkabouts, photo opportunities, and the like, but they are not in a strong position to dictate it. This is because they need television and, in the absence of being able to command it through purchasing advertising time, legislative diktat, or the like, are generally in the position only of being able to persuade journalists and producers to cover the campaign in a manner advantageous to their party. Moreover, they cannot afford to shun this task in favour of some other method of getting their message across, partly because television is the informational medium of choice for most voters and, perhaps more importantly, partly because the Conservative and Labour parties' organizational deterioration over the past three decades or so has weakened their ability to communicate with voters and mobilize their support through more traditional, labour-intensive means centred around campaign activity at the local level. To put it simply, parties have become more dependent on the media, and especially television, first to get their message out to voters and second to get their voters out to the polls.

The need for persuasion stems both from an inability to command and from there virtually always being a greater number of worthwhile stories than the media have time to report. Except when extended during election campaigns, news bulletins are rarely more than 30 minutes long and party politics is never the only game in town. Even at the height of election campaigns, there is competition for air time from overseas stories, human interest stories, sports, and so on. Therefore, even though they might be constrained by obligations of impartiality and balance, broadcasters still exercise considerable discretion and choice in deciding what makes a story newsworthy; they perform a gatekeeping function that is beyond legal regulation and party strategists have no option but to take account of this reality if they want the free, widespread and, for them, necessary exposure that comes with being featured in news broadcasts. Their tasks, in other words, include not only ensuring that news coverage is sympathetic, but that they win coverage for their party in the first place.

A great deal has been said and written on the subject of 'what is news?' What makes one story worthy of coverage and another not? In discussions of this question, widespread agreement has emerged that personality is an important ingredient of newsworthiness. For example, when discussing newspapers and television, Alistair Hetherington, a practitioner as former editor of the *Guardian* newspaper, nominated as his top criterion of newsworthiness the social, political, economic and human 'significance' of events. His secondary criteria were:

- Drama – excitement, action, etc. in the event;
- Surprise – the unexpected, the fresh;
- Personalities – royalty, show business, political actors, etc.;
- Sex – scandal, crime, etc.;

  – Numbers – numbers affected, etc.

(Quoted in Negrine 1989: 141; see also Gans 1979)

Thus, to the extent that parties are compelled to give television what it wants to win free news coverage and publicity, a focus on the 'top person', the leader of the political party, the captain or leading goal scorer of the football team, or whatever, would seem to be unavoidable. This is not to say that a leadership focus will be the only criterion for newsworthiness, or even the most important one. It does mean, however, that broadcasters are unlikely to neglect personality for long. As long as politics is pervasive in news broadcasts, the party leaders will be in demand in their role as the authoritative political spokespersons on matters of party, national and international policy. Moreover, an advantage of this situation for party strategists is that the leader is a party resource that, in contrast to other characteristics of newsworthy stories like 'significance', 'drama' and 'surprise', has an identity and image that is somewhat manipulable and therefore always has the potential to be constructed, reconstructed and made more appealing to voters. Witness the PEBs on Kinnock in 1987, Major in 1992 and Blair in 1997, as well as the consciously wrought changes to Margaret Thatcher's dress, hairstyle and speaking voice between 1983 and 1987 (see more generally Bruce 1992).

The upshot would seem to be that the presidentialism characteristic of recent British election campaigns is here to stay. It suits the self-promotional needs of the parties campaigning for national office, as well as the presentational demands of the dominant medium of political communication in contemporary democratic society, television. A further, and no less important, reason is that the parties really have little choice but to play the television card. Their only realistic alternative at the beginning of the new millennium is to turn back the clock and reinstate traditional methods of campaigning with their emphasis on the local conduct of campaigns with party agents and constituency candidates enjoying some substantial autonomy in shaping the public perception of both party policy and party image, with national party leaders descending occasionally to address the party faithful in local church halls, and with the mobilization of support through voluntary activity, and especially intensive canvassing, at the constituency level.

The truth is that the ability of virtually all parties to electioneer effectively in this traditional way has eroded. The Conservative and Labour parties for certain have allowed their structures at the constitutency level to weaken as they have centralized in London responsibility for

Table 5.4 Numbers of Conservative and Labour Agents and Individual Party Members by Election Year

	Full-Time Agents[a]		*Members (000s)*[b]	
	Con.	*Lab.*	*Con.*	*Lab.*
1964	520	200	2800	830
1966	499	204	n.a.	776
1970	386	141	n.a.	680
1974	375	125	1500	692
1979	n.a.	70	n.a.	666
1983	320	52	1200	295
1987	300	68	1000	289
1992	n.a.	n.a.	500	280
1997	309	n.a.	400	405[c]

Sources:
[a] Nuffield Election Studies.
[b] Webb (1994:113). The Labour figures exclude corporate member.
[c] The 1997 membership figures were provided by Paul Webb in private correspondence.

the planning and conduct of campaigns that have become increasingly national in content and direction (Webb 1994). Two indicators of this lessened ability to contest elections constituency by constituency are the lower numbers of both Conservative and Labour professional agents and dues-paying party members available for mobilizational activity at the constituency level. Data on both these indicators are presented for selected years in Table 5.4. The immediately striking conclusion is one of substantial decline on both counts. At best, organizational deterioration bottomed out in the 1990s; there is no sign of reversal. In 1992, for example, Labour had 100 professional organizers 'in the field', but as well as full-time constituency agents this figure includes regional staff appointed to assist lay agents (Butler and Kavanagh 1992: 232; see also Rosenbaum 1997: 223–53). It is small wonder that the national campaign now enjoys unquestioned pre-eminence over the local one (Denver and Hands 1997: 3–29).

Another important consideration is that the leadership of Britain's largest parties are unlikely to want to revert to a more traditional, locally based campaigning style. Television has helped parties to nationalize the dissemination of political information and to put their leaders in direct contact with unprecedented numbers of actual and potential supporters: 'British party leaders can now talk to more people in a few minutes than did Gladstone and Disraeli together throughout their entire careers' (Denver and Hands 1997: 26). It has also helped to centralize control of the campaign. Daily press conferences, regular television appearances and the strategic timing of policy speeches give party headquarters greater control in shaping the public image of the party, as well as in defining the policies associated with it in the public eye. They can also use their ready media access to adapt policy and image to changes in the public mood revealed by daily opinion polling. Quite deliberately, the casualty of greater control at the centre has been internal party democracy in the form of local autonomy. Local activists are still valued and encouraged, but now for their mobilizational efforts at election time rather than for any contribution they may aspire to make to the formulation of party policy. This is nowhere more evident than in the successful efforts of Neil Kinnock and Tony Blair to reverse the tide of declining Labour party membership (see Table 5.4). The result of their efforts has not been more vibrant internal party debate and democracy. Rather,

> (t)he Labour Party itself has become a prop rather than an engine of Blairism. The party is mainly a campaigning organization under his centralized control. The *Partnership in Power* proposals likely to be approved today mean that this is the last conference where big unions and fractious constituency activists can pass hastily cobbled together motions challenging a Labour Government.
>
> (Riddell 1997)[12]

The point is that the centralized control made possible by, among other things, television-based campaigning is accorded high priority because it allows the party to avoid public displays of disunity and to be seen to be speaking with one voice, both of which are commonly thought to be conducive, if not essential, to victory at the polls in parliamentary elections.

Conclusion

With the reality of electoral presidentialism taken as a given, this chapter has spoken to the twin issues of its scale and its durability. The basic conclusion is that it scores high on both.

Take scale first. As long as they do not neutralize each other's electoral impact, party leaders can have a substantial and occasionally perhaps even a decisive influence on the outcome of an election. If neither main party enjoys a clear advantage with the electorate, the leader may turn out to be the difference between success and failure for his party;

witness John Major's performance in the 1992 election. Nor should such circumstances be thought necessarily rare. Despite the lopsided majorities characteristic of the 1980s and 1990s, close contests have in fact been reasonably common in post-war Britain. Of the 15 general elections since 1945, one (February 1974) produced a short-lived minority government, three (1950, 1964 and October 1974) returned governments with majorities of five or fewer seats and two (1951 and 1992) led to governments with small majorities of 17 and 21 seats respectively. In short, six of the 15 can reasonably be described as close contests. Moreover, at least for recent general elections, the indications are that party leaders have generally been more influential than issues in shaping the inter-party distribution of the vote. As such, leaders are an electoral asset or liability that cannot be ignored by victory-seeking political parties and their campaign strategists.[13]

The second conclusion to be drawn from this chapter concerns the durability of the presidentialism apparent in recent election contests. The basic message to emerge is that it is a change that is here to stay, at least as long as communications technologies and political parties' usage of them are not revolutionized in the near future through, for example, the spread of internet campaigning. Under current technological conditions, there is absolutely no reason to believe that the pattern of party campaign activity seen in recent elections, with its emphasis on television and the personalization of politics, is a passing fad foisted on reluctant political parties through some kind of technological determinism. The key consideration is that, as things stand at the moment, the party hierarchs are wedded to a presidential strategy that they themselves have cultivated for their own purposes and in which they have already invested so much. Developments in society, developments in communications technology and developments in their own extra-parliamentary organizations leave them little choice. Electoral presidentialism may not enjoy a long lineage in British general elections, but the absence of a past does not mean the absence of a future. Even more than the study of issues, a better understanding of the party leaders, their personal appeal and their television-mediated effect on voters would seem to be a sine qua non of a full understanding of the dynamics of electoral stability and change in Britain, as well as numerous other parliamentary democracies.

6
Conclusion

The main purpose of this book has been to put to the empirical test the thesis that British general elections have presidentialized in the sense that party leaders have come to play a more prominent role than they used to in structuring both media coverage of the campaign and the party people choose at the polls. It needs to be reiterated here that the book makes no claims to being a comprehensive analysis of the role of prime ministerial candidates in parliamentary electoral politics. Rather, it is an analysis of their direct effects on individual voting choice and on election outcomes. Their indirect effects are not considered herein. These may take the form, for example, of the leaders shifting their party's ideological centre of gravity to enhance its electoral appeal or of their shaping the party's image in the public eye through the projection on to the party of personal characteristics like competence, probity and caringness that the public perceives in him (Webb 2000: ch. 5). Also ignored are minor party leaders. The decision was taken to exclude them so as to make the test of the presidentialization thesis especially rigorous. Specifically, the supporters of the traditionally class-based Conservative and Labour parties are notable for being firmer in their loyalty at the polls than their third-party (Liberal/ Liberal-Social Democratic Alliance/Liberal Democratic) counterparts. In addition, disillusioned major party supporters are more likely to stop at the 'halfway house' that the Liberals represent than to switch to the other class party at the opposite end of the ideological spectrum (Butler and Stokes 1974). The upshot is that the aggregate electoral importance of the party leaders is in all likelihood understated in this book. Its major party focus ignores the potential for the Conservative and Labour leaders to siphon off support from smaller parties, as well as for the possibility of minor party leaders attracting the vote of supporters of the two major parties. Such caveats notwithstanding, this study of electoral presidentialization has produced three clear and important conclusions.

First, the cumulation of evidence confirms that recent British general elections have indeed presidentialized in terms of both presentation and impact. From the mid-1980s onwards, the Conservative and Labour party leaders have figured more prominently than previously in media coverage of the campaign as well as in voters' choice of party. Second, this development is not trivial in terms of either magnitude or potential practical significance. The indications are that prime ministerial candidates are generally a more substantial influence on the vote than campaign issues and that having the right leader can mean the difference between victory and defeat for a party in closely fought contests, including the 1992 British general election. Third, and more speculatively, presidentialism would appear to be a characteristic of modern parliamentary elections that is unlikely to go away, largely because political parties have become more dependent in their communications with voters on the essentially visual and personality-based medium of television. For parties, television is their principal means of reaching voters and for voters it is their principal and most trusted source of political information. The relationship is thus one of mutual dependence. Moreover, since political parties have chosen to build their campaign strategies around this pervasive and flourishing medium, their leaders have become more clearly their public face and, at the same time, a more important determinant of the image the public holds of them.

The bulk of this book has been spent establishing the actuality, nature and extent of leader effects. But this was never intended to be its sole purpose. Precisely because presidentialization is part and parcel of a number of important debates in the study of the politics of advanced industrial democracies, it is a phenomenon of broader interest. An appropriate way of concluding, therefore, is to ask how the growth of presidentialism might affect the terms of these debates.

Three such debates can be identified and are foreshadowed in Chapters 1 and 2. The first of them concerns the tension between the institutionalist claim that parliamentarism and presidentialism are, and remain, very different forms of government and the contrary claim that parliamentary and presidential forms of government are converging on each other sin some respects. The second debate relates to the implications of electoral presidentialism for the distribution of power in government in parliamentary systems. Does personal popularity and electoral impact enhance the personal political influence and power of prime ministers and make for the erosion of the collective ethos and practise of cabinet government? The final debate raises the question of the normative implications of presidentialism for what might be termed the 'quality of democracy'. More specifically, does the increased importance of prime ministerial candidates as voting cues leave the electorate open to cynical manipulation by professional image makers, thereby trivializing its choice at the polls and weakening the democratic accountability of governments?

The discussions that follow shows how electoral presidentialization adds interesting new twists to these established and complex debates. Possibilities are raised and questions asked but, with the study of the personalization of parliamentary politics still in its infancy, closure is not sought.

Institutional convergence

This book is an effort to adjudicate the divergent opinions on the reality of a theoretically and practically important development in parliamentary systems of government, namely electoral presidentialization. On the one hand, attention has been drawn to the numerous, largely journalistic and impressionistic observations from parliamentary democracies worldwide that their elections were presidentializing as campaign strategies and appeals centred more and more around the personalities of the prime ministerial candidates. On the other hand, the traditional institutionalist view has been shown still to hold sway in some quarters. In this view, parliamentary party and leader cannot be separated in the public eye because prime ministers are not directly elected by the public (Wilson 1976; Hart 1991). Moreover, the emergence in the 1990s of a literature arguing that parliamentary and presidential systems of government had very different implications for political outcomes like public policy outputs and democratic stability only added to the credibility of this traditionalist view (see, for example, Weaver and Rockman 1993; Linz and Valenzuela 1994; and von Mettenheim 1997).

The message of this book, however, is that a strict institutionalist perspective can easily overstate the impact of the institutional environment on the dynamics of election campaigns, individual voting choice and electoral outcomes. This danger is evident in the still-common neglect of the increased, and at times critical, importance of the Conservative and Labour prime ministerial candidates for the outcome of parliamentary elections whose outcomes have tended to be viewed as being dictated by organization at the level of the party and loyalty at the level of the individual. The lesson here is that institutional differences are bridgeable. Importantly, though, this is not the same as saying that they do not matter; nothing could be further from the truth. An example is a comparison of leader effects in the 1987 Australian parliamentary and 1984 US congressional elections. The leaders of the victorious parties, Labor in Australia and the Republicans in the US, were about equally popular. Bob Hawke, the Labor prime minister, scored an average 6.2 on a ten-point thermometer scale, while Republican president Ronald Reagan scored 6.4. Moreover, both had an independent electoral impact. But despite their similar levels of popularity, the US leader still generated a substantially larger electoral bonus for his party than the Australian leader did for his (Mughan 1995). In other words, the parliamentary system of government may not preclude the possibility of an electoral impact for a popular party leader, but it does seem to allow such popularity to translate into party advantage as readily as it does in a presidential system where everybody has the right to vote in the election of the chief executive, thereby encouraging their mobilized reaction to him to affect their separate vote for his party.

Institutions, then, undoubtedly shape political outcomes, but to overemphasize the differences between parliamentary and presidential systems of government risks overlooking theoretically interesting and practically consequential similarities between them at both the elite and mass levels of politics. An example is that the US Congress and the French National Assembly show similarities despite operating in different constitutional frameworks. Thus, a study of French governments' resort to the restrictive legislative procedures of the package vote and the 'guillotine' concludes:

> Specifically, the data suggest that restrictive legislative procedures are used on the same types of issues in the French National Assembly and in Congress. Future studies of parliamentary systems could therefore reap benefits by ... study(ing) the types of issues that divide parties, and to explore how institutional arrangements are designed to permit competing parties to make and to preserve policy agreements.
>
> (Huber 1992: 685)

Similarly, at the mass level, the very fact of electoral presidentialization suggests that the crucial question is no longer whether institutional structure prevents the outcome of such elections from becoming personalized, but rather what are the conditions under which they do so. In particular, is electoral presidentialism the product of forces – such as television-based election campaigning – common to parliamentary regimes generally or is it a function of certain institutional characteristics not shared by all of them? Given, for example, that single-party governments offer voters a more hierarchical authority structure, a sharper focus of accountability and a clearly identifiable and highly visible head of government, then they might reasonably be expected to be more prone to presidentialism than multi-party coalitions counting several prominent party leaders in their ranks. In point of fact, however, the evidence points in the opposite direction; the party of the prime minister in coalition governments is more likely to be held accountable at the polls for national economic performance than it is in single-party governments (Royed et al. 2000). But are popular prime ministers more or less equally able to mitigate the swing against their party in both types of government when times are hard? If the answer is yes, then a reasonable conclusion would be that there is a personalized response from voters that is strong enough to transcend the institutional differences separating single-party from coalition governments. If the answer is no, a research agenda needs to be developed that seeks to disaggregate voters' electoral reactions to economic performance and to separate personal from institutional effects.

The bottom line is that exogenous forces, like television-based election campaigning, appear capable of bringing presidential and parliamentary systems of government to look more like each other in some of the ways that they operate. Moreover, an institutional perspective does not necessarily preclude recognition of this kind of convergence. Rather, it should highlight that neither presidential nor parliamentary regimes are institutionally homogeneous so that their capacity for shaping political relationships and outcomes is variable and remains very much a matter for further study and refinement. In particular, if we start from the premise that the personalization of electoral politics is a function of change in the political role of television and that this change is common to democracies worldwide, attention needs to be paid to identifying the characteristics of parliamentary government that enhance or retard the translation of presidentialization of presentation into presidentialization of impact. It may be, for example, that coalition governments are less of an impediment in this translation process than single-party governments, but is this true of all forms of coalition government? Does the number of parties in the coalition make a difference? Alternatively, does it matter how long the coalition has been in office or whether the prime minister is the leader of the largest party in the coalition and therefore perhaps more reasonably held to account for the performance of the government as a whole?

Prime ministerial power

Two central features of the constitutional theory of British parliamentarism are, first, that the political executive is selected from the parliament and is directly answerable to it and, second, that this executive, otherwise called the cabinet, comprises a series of departmental ministers who enjoy the same standing in cabinet as its titular head and chair, the prime minister. The latter, in other words, is no more than 'first among equals'. In at least the post-Second World War period, both these sets of relationships have changed in the direction of the prime minister becoming a more autonomous and independently influential figure in British politics. In short, the prime minister has become less the creature of the parliament and the cabinet and, like the US president, more an independent and autonomous figure seeking to shape them to his policy ends. Take the relationship between cabinets and prime ministers first.

Prime ministers and their cabinets

The relations of influence and power between prime ministers and their cabinets have always been variable, depending very much on personality and circumstance. War, for example, has often served to propel prime ministers into a position of unusual ascendancy and personalized leadership (Mackintosh 1968). In the 1960s, however, the argument was made that these relations had undergone a qualitative transformation in the sense that prime ministerial ascendancy over cabinet had become entrenched; prime ministerial government had replaced cabinet government. The changed circumstances underpinning this change were held to be that the modern prime minister was at the 'apex not only of a highly centralised political machine, but also of an equally centralised and vastly more powerful administrative machine' (Crossman 1963: 51). The same author, a high-ranking figure in the Labour party, went on to conclude: 'If we mean by presidential government, government by an elective first magistrate then we in England have a president as truly as the Americans' (Crossman 1963: 22–3; see also Mackintosh 1968: 627).

This diagnosis of the new distribution of power and authority in British government aroused a flurry of protest and criticism. Among its fiercest critics has been George W. Jones (1965: 178), who immediately countered it with the argument that 'the prime minister's power had been exaggerated and that the restraints on his ascendancy were as strong as ever, and in some ways even stronger'. The debate that ensued, however, has proven frustratingly inconclusive, largely because the secrecy surrounding the conduct of government in Britain discourages hard evidence and promotes speculation based on anecdote and personal conviction and preference (an excellent summary of this debate is Foley 1993: 1–23).[1] For every 'insider' or academic assertion that prime ministerial government has arrived in Britain, it is possible to find the counter-assertion that cabinet government remains the order of the day. Take the premiership of the imperious Margaret Thatcher as an example. Reg Prentice served first as a Labour minister and then as a Conservative one under Thatcher. Noting her 'presidential style', he goes on to observe that 'the British constitution has been changing … over the time I've been in politics. The old idea that the Prime Minister was the first among equals has given way, step by step, towards a more presidential situation' (quoted in Young and Sloman 1986: 45–6). In sharp contrast, Fry (1988: 90) is of the clear opinion that 'there is no substantial evidence that the Thatcher years have witnessed the displacement of Cabinet government by Prime Ministerial government'.

In point of fact, there are two related reasons to argue that prime ministers have become more like presidents in their relations with their cabinet colleagues. The first concerns their enhanced electoral role and the second their consequent greater autonomy in the appointment and dismissal of cabinet ministers. Take the electoral perspective first. A key plank in the argument against the prime ministerial government thesis was the argument, based on the findings of voting studies of the 1950s and 1960s, that prime ministers cannot be institutionally pre-eminent in cabinet because they do not enjoy the independent authority afforded by a personal electoral power base. 'The leader is as much the prisoner of the image of his party as the other candidates. Although much of the propaganda of the parties concentrates on the leaders, there is no evidence that it is effective … If the leader is not the individual whom the electors vote for, then there is no mandate on the MPs to support their leaders' (Jones 1965: 174–5). The same author reiterates this same argument a quarter of a century later, but this time basing it on a measure of electoral presidentialism that has already been dismissed as unrealistically demanding in Chapter 1 of this book because it requires the leader to win the election for her party rather than simply to have some positive impact on its share of the vote. 'Elections have not become presidential, despite the concentration of party publicity on the leader. If they were, then Prime Ministers would not have lost in 1970, 1974 and 1979 when they were personally more popular in opinion surveys than the leaders of the winning opposition parties' (Jones 1990: 5).[2]

But, as this book has shown, party leaders can now affect the share of the vote won by their parties and, perhaps more significantly, are recognized as having the potential to do so by their party colleagues in the House of Commons. Moreover, television and the personalization of politics are recognized as being significant power resources for prime ministers by students of parliamentary regimes in general. Noting that 'modern prime ministers and their cabinets are becoming more like presidents and their cabinets in presidential regimes', Linz (1994: 31–2), for example, holds:

> Certain trends, however, are likely to lead to a degree of convergence between (parliamentary and presidential) systems that are in principle different. I am thinking of parliamentary systems with highly disciplined parties and a prime minister with an absolute majority or those that follow the *Kanzlerdemokratie*, in which the prime minister is free to select his cabinet without parliamentary approval. All this together with the tendency to personalize power in modern politics (particularly thanks to television) has reduced the sense of collective responsibility and the collegial nature of cabinet government.

The second area of convergence between prime ministers and presidents involves their freedom of choice when selecting cabinet members. The conventional thinking is that British prime ministers are relatively constrained in their choice of cabinet personnel because of their need to balance ideological tendencies or factions so that the cabinet is a microcosm of the larger parliamentary party. This 'ideological arithmetic' is held to be essential to the maintenance of party unity and discipline in the legislature (James 1992: 101). Elected separately from his party, the US president is not subject to the same constraints. He is in fact at liberty to appoint whoever he wishes and his usual practise is to surround himself with loyal supporters who will protect his political interests and further his policy goals. Discussing presidential strategies of cabinet-building, for example, Polsby (1983: 90–1) observes:

> It is possible to see in Richard Nixon's cabinet appointments a mirror of his emerging view of the role of the President vis-à-vis the rest of the government. After beginning with a group of cabinet appointees

that was both politically diverse and reasonably visible, Mr. Nixon increasingly appointed people with no independent public standing and no constituencies of their own. In this shift we can read a distinctive change in the fundamental political goals and strategies of the Nixon administration from early concerns with constituency building to a later preoccupation, once Mr. Nixon's reelection was assured, with centralizing power in the White House.

A similar concern to centralize power in 10 Downing Street can be detected in British politics and it coincides more or less with the era of greater presidentialism in election outcomes. From the 1980s onwards, shows of prime ministerial strength have almost inevitably been associated with the striving for pliant cabinets that accede to the prime minister's wishes. Two examples in particular stand out and both involve the purging of ideological dissent. The first followed Thatcher's winning of a huge 144-seat majority in the 1983 election. She interpreted this success as a popular mandate for both herself and the often controversial policies that she championed and she took advantage of it to remove from her cabinet virtually all the 'wets' who had resisted her radicalism during her first term as prime minister between 1979 and 1983. In their place, she put her own men, showing little regard for balancing the ideological diversity that still characterized the parliamentary Conservative party. Perhaps the most surprising victim of her purge was the foreign secretary, Francis Pym.

> There was a time when his power would have saved him. But the politics of interest, of faction, of groupings and collaborations within the party, which a leader might ignore at her peril, had entirely vanished. Now it was every man for himself. Francis Pym became the unlamented centrepiece of a reconstruction which brought new men to the top, who owed their place to this leader and to her alone.
>
> (Young 1991: 332–3)

The second example involves Thatcher's successor, John Major. In mid-1995, he voluntarily resigned as party leader and put himself up for re-election as way of gaining a personal vote of confidence after a protracted and highly divisive struggle over European policy with a highly vocal minority of 'Eurosceptics' in his own parliamentary party. This was an unprecedented gamble for a Tory leader and there was considerable uncertainty about the wisdom of his decision right up until the leadership election results were announced on 4 July. He was re-elected on the first ballot and immediately reshuffled his cabinet to diminish its Eurosceptic representation and to appoint new members apparently rewarded for being loyal to him personally. *The Economist* (8–14 July 1995: 53) commented:

> His reshuffle was widely reported as a shift to the left... But, other than over Europe, left and right are boxes into which the modern Conservative Party refuses to fit. Most Tory MPs are neither... The real gainers from the reshuffle are not left or right... None is publicly left or publicly right. None has a power base. All are his reliable allies.

Nor is the desire for a loyal and quiescent cabinet restricted to Tory leaders. Tony Blair's behaviour after Labour's huge victory in 1997 gave no indication that he intended to depart from the Thatcher/Major model of cabinet-building. In both his initial appointments and his subsequent leadership style, he too showed a predilection for an acquiescent cabinet rather than a collective decision-making body where difficult issues could be discussed, disagreements thrashed out and policy determined. Thus, the Labour government installed in the wake of the 1997 election victory was characterized by a leading political columnist as being 'in thrall to its own disproportionate triumph on May 1, and to the leader who produced it... The cabinet itself has taken further giant strides into the desert of irrelevance towards which Mrs Thatcher propelled it.' Moreover, this same columnist felt confident in view of past experience that the asymmetry of power and influence would only get worse as the party stayed in government. 'There will be a clean-out of the old sweats who are there on sufferance, whose opinions, though seldom uttered, do not enjoy the leader's respect. They will be replaced by new men and women whom the leader does respect because they can be relied on, down at the wire, to agree with him' (Young 1997).[3]

Looked at from both an international and a domestic perspective, then, there is good reason to argue that the presidentialization of electoral politics in parliamentary systems of government has helped to reshape power and authority relations at the very highest levels of the political process. Inevitably, this argument will remain contentious in the absence of reliable evidence documenting on the one hand the relationship between prime ministers and their cabinets and linking the alleged increase in prime ministerial power to electoral presidentialization on the other. At the very least, however, its plausibility is strengthened by a key plank of the 'cabinet government regardless' thesis being no longer valid. Prime ministers can have an independent electoral base and, just like presidents of the United States, they can deploy it as a power resource when they seek to bend their backbench and frontbench party colleagues to their will. Thus, the characterization of the prime minister as a president, with all that this entails about our understanding of how British government actually works, becomes harder to dismiss on the grounds that it is unrealistic and at odds with the theory and practice of modern parliamentary government.

The need to reassess the role of modern prime ministers is more pressing in the case of their relationship with their parliamentary party. Here, the evidence of structural change and increased autonomy for 'presidential' prime ministers is compelling.

Prime ministers and their parliamentary party

Traditionally, government in Britain has been seen as party government (Rose 1974). Members of the same parliamentary party comprise a cohesive, undifferentiated unit that runs for office as a team and is seen by the electorate as being collectively accountable for its (in)actions in office. The prime minister and senior party leaders are not elected separately from other members of the parliamentary party, but they are directly responsible to them for their stewardship of the executive branch of government. Thus, voters draw no meaningful or consequential distinction between the prime minister and other members of her party; they cast their ballot for a party and then hold that party collectively accountable for what it does or does not do in office.

In reality, however, the very fact of electoral presidentialization means that the party basis of government is eroding, at least in the eyes of the mass public. A key reason for the emergence of a distinct electoral identity for prime ministers, however, may well be that they, as chief executives, have been distancing themselves from their party in parliamentary for some time. Arguing that the prime minister's active participation in parliamentary proceedings is a key mechanism for ensuring the accountability of the executive, Dunleavy et al. (1993) chart prime ministerial participation in four kinds of Commons activities: answering parliamentary questions; making ministerial statements; making formal speeches; and intervening in various inpromptu ways in debates. Their 'results establish unequivocally that the *direct* (emphasis in original) parliamentary accountability of the prime minister has fallen sharply over the whole period since 1868, and that this change has accelerated in the last decade and a half' (Dunleavy et al. 1993: 290). In other words, 'Thatcher's record is the longest and most consistently below average set of (activity) scores for any prime minister' (Dunleavy et al. 1993: 287).

It could well be that Thatcher's unprecedented estrangement from Commons activity played some role in the apparent erosion in the 1980s and 1990s of the deference that Tory MPs have traditionally shown to their party leader. This erosion, rooted apparently in the parliamentary party's heightened sensitivity to the public standing of its leader, is evident in its treatment of its three most recent prime ministers, Edward Heath, Margaret Thatcher and John Major.

Edward Heath was the head of the Conservative party from 1965 to 1975, and he retained his position despite leading his party to defeat in three of four general election contests. But perhaps more to the point, his leadership was only challenged in the wake of the final contest and third defeat. When the challenge did come after the October 1974 loss, he was unexpectedly turned out of the leadership to be replaced by the relatively unknown Margaret Thatcher. His two successors, in contrast, have been treated far less gently by their parliamentary party colleagues when unpopular. Unlike in the case of Heath, Thatcher and Major were not given the opportunity to lead the party to defeat in even one election before a serious challenge to their leadership was mounted. Take Thatcher first. Her story prior to 1990 was one of unmitigated electoral success. She won all three general elections that she fought at the head of the Conservative party in 1979, 1983 and 1987, the last two with majorities of more than 100 seats. Nonetheless, the failure of Tory MPs to confirm her position on the first ballot of the 1990 leadership contest obliged her most reluctantly to resign as party leader and, hence, prime minister. Her basic problem was that her ratings at the time of the successful challenge to her leadership were the lowest since opinion polling had begun and this, fuelling a fear that she would lead the party to defeat in the next general election, was the crucial factor in many Conservative backbenchers denying her the support she would have needed to win reelection to the party leadership on the second ballot (Young 1991: 589–91).

A somewhat similar fate befell John Major in mid-1995, about three years after he had gloried in leading his party to an unexpected victory in the 1992 election and had himself been the difference between its victory and a hung Parliament (see Chapter 5). Subsequently, divisions in the parliamentary party, principally over Europe, fragmented its unity, even leading to the withdrawal of the whip from eight rebels. Under these circumstances, both Major and the Conservative party became very unpopular in the opinion polls when compared to the

Labour opposition and its new leader, Tony Blair. To re-establish his authority within the parliamentary party, Major resigned the leadership in June 1995, precipitated an election, presented himself as a candidate in it and won on the first ballot. The outcome was not a clear vote of confidence in his leadership, however and he had no illusions about his victory. 'In the event, more than 100 MPs did fail to back him. There is some evidence that Major had to be persuaded by colleagues to stay' (Norton 1998: 102). But what is important about this episode from the point of view of electoral presidentialization is that at least some of the opposition to his continuation as leader appears to have come from the same fear that brought Thatcher down before him, that he and his pro-European policies were so unpopular in the country at large that he could only be a liability for his party in a general election due within two years at the latest. This message is clearly implied in the campaign slogan of his 1995 challenger for the leadership, John Redwood: 'No change, no chance.'

It might be countered that these two episodes in the 1990s should not be overinterpreted; two cases do not add up to a law. Nothing really changed in the relationship between Conservative leaders and their parliamentary party, this interpretation of events continues, since it was entirely fortuitous that Heath did not go earlier. To be sure, he lost heavily in 1966, but he then consolidated his leadership position by winning unexpectedly in 1970. Moreover, it is not altogether clear that the February 1974 defeat was really a defeat since the Tories won a larger number of votes than a Labour party that subsequently formed a minority government. His fate was sealed only when he led his party to defeat for the third time in an October 1974 election that returned a Labour government with a bare majority of three seats.

Ultimately, however, and as in the case of the prime ministerial government thesis, disagreement cannot be resolved by speculation and anecdote alone. More decisive is whether speculation can be given some firm foundation in the shape of systematic evidence that prime ministers' control over their parliamentary party is greater to the extent that they are popular with the mass public. While, to the best of my knowledge, this relationship has not been established empirically, several separate studies can be pieced together to provide indirect evidence that it does indeed characterize parliamentary relations. In the first place, we know that prime ministerial approval helps to shape government approval (Clark and Stewart 1995) and that this approval in turn strongly determines how governments perform in by-elections (Mughan 1986). In the second place, we know that, among governing party MPs at least, dissenting voting in the House of Commons is negatively related to their party's by-election performance; the bigger the swing against the governing party in by-elections, the higher the level of dissension (Mughan 1990). Much as with US presidents, in other words, a prime minister's popularity would seem to have an influence, albeit an indirect one, on his ability to carry a reluctant parliamentary party with him. In this sense, the prime minister is not just an equal member of his parliamentary party in the public eye, but is an important influence on its unity in the Commons and on its electoral prospects. Put differently, his role in the legislative process is more like that of the US president than conventional thinking might lead us to believe. Thus, the phenomenon of presidentialization can profitably be seen in future thinking and research on the nature of politics in parliamentary systems of government as encompassing not only the study of political parties and elections, but that of some aspects of government and parliament as well. Even the quality of democracy itself is argued to have been affected, many would say adversely, by the personalization of parliamentary politics.

Quality of democracy

There is a pervasive view that the personalization inherent in the presidentialization of parliamentary politics is harmful to democracy. Chapter 2 of this book, for example, has shown that this aversion to the politics of personality permeated the editorial pages of *The Times* in the 1960s and 1970s especially. During the 1970 campaign and in the aftermath of the publication of McGinniss's *The Selling of the President*, the newspaper's editor noted that the

> most chilling aspect of modern elections is their impersonal quality. The elector is invited to vote not for a Member of Parliament, but for a Party; not for a Party but for its Leader; and not for its Leader but for a pre-packaged television presentation of what Market Research suggests the Leader should be.
>
> (*The Times*, 2 June 1970)

The next step in this line of reasoning is the conclusion that this development is to be deplored because it represents a diminution of the intellectual content of campaigns and this serves to dilute the rationality of voters and thereby the accountability of elected politicians.

The basis of this argument is a notion of representative democracy that assumes policy agreement to be the only legitimate basis of linkage between voters and political parties. According to this view, elections are events in which parties commit themselves to competing policy, or issue, promises in order to win over voters and their performance in government is subsequently judged in terms of their success or failure in turning these promises into public policy. Put differently, democratic politics are mandate-driven; governments are elected prospectively on the basis of the promises they make to voters and are returned to office by a vigilant and informed electorate, voting retrospectively, if they keep those promises. If they do not, they will be held to account and thrown out of office in the next election (Pomper with Lederman 1980). Rooted in this means–ends calculation, issue-based choice energizes democracy. Personality-based choice, by contrast, leaves the door open to voter manipulation by skilled image-builders and risks the public making its voting decision on the basis of characteristics of the candidates for the position of chief executive that are irrelevant to the business of governing. It is thus deemed not to be the product of the same kind of rational calculation and, as a result, is held to weaken the democratic link tying governors and governed. But is it the case that leader-based choice is the prerogative of the politically uninvolved and unthinking couch potato? Does personality-based choice really trivialize the voting decision and amount to voter irrationality? In parliamentary elections at least, the answer to this question differs somewhat according to whether voting is seen as a retrospective or prospective decision. I shall now explain why.

Candidate personality and voter rationality

In what might be called classical democratic theory, for voters to act rationally means essentially that they vote instrumentally; they weigh the policy promises and/or performance in office of the different parties and choose on the basis of the satisfaction of their own interests and goals. In the case of retrospective voting, the choice involved in the vote is whether or not to vote for the party or parties in government given their performance since elected to office. In its extreme form, retrospective rationality would involve voters remembering what the party in government had promised in its last election campaign and holding it accountable for keeping those promises in the intervening period. To expect this degree of memory and calculation is unrealistic, however. The large majority of voters simply do not have, and are not interested in exercising, that kind of long-term political memory. Governments are not always attracted to it either, often preferring instead to muddy the waters of voter recall by emphasizing their policy successes and ignoring their failures. Indeed, they can even dissemble occasionally to avoid electoral recrimination for not performing as promised or expected. The Thatcher governments, for example, altered the official definition of unemployment more than a dozen times in an effort to keep down the publicly announced numbers of workers on the dole.

For such reasons, the usual definition of retrospective rationality is relatively minimal, involving voters having general policy preferences, an opinion on the government's performance, and being moved to vote for or against it on these bases. The classic statement is V.O. Key's study of retrospective voting in US presidential elections. He argues:

> The perverse and unorthodox argument of this little book is that voters are not fools... [I]n the large the electorate behaves about as rationally and responsibly as we should expect, given the clarity of the alternatives presented to it and the character of the information available to it... [T]he portrait of the American electorate that develops from the data is not one of an electorate straitjacketed by social determinants or moved by subconscious urges triggered by devilishly skillful propagandists. It is rather one of an electorate moved by concern about central and relevant questions of public policy, of governmental performance, and of executive personality.
>
> (Key 1966: 7–8)

The problem is that to vote retrospectively on the basis of 'executive personality' may make good sense in a presidential system, but it does not always do so in a parliamentary system. To be sure, voting for presidents or prime ministers is rational if their governments have performed well in office and delivered on their promises, but it is sometimes rational and sometimes irrational if their performance is judged to have been poor. In this latter situation, personality-based voting can still be thought rational in a system of separated powers if voters blame presidential failure on a recalcitrant and obstructionist legislature. A similar situation under the fused powers of parliamentary government is where the leader of a coalition government is held hostage by parties in the coalition other than her own. Assuming that her stalemated government stays in power long enough to face the electorate a second time, it would be perfectly rational for voters to cast their vote for her party on the grounds that the obstructionism of others had denied her the opportunity to deliver on her promises and that a larger presence in the coalition for her party would allow her to do so. Under British-style majoritarian parliamentary government, however, rational voters would find it very difficult to place the blame for failure on other political actors than the prime minister since he is supposed to be the principal player in the team that is collectively responsible for government decision-making. In this situation, personality-based retrospective voting that benefited the prime minister's party could hardly be judged to be rational since it would have to be a function of factors, perhaps the chief executive's gender, physical appearance, class or ethnic origins, unrelated to performance in office on policy issues of concern to voters.

In sum, personality-based retrospective voting under conditions of poor governmental performance may be rational under some circumstances in parliamentary elections, but irrational under others. In sharp contrast, no such conditionality afflicts the rationality of personality-based prospective voting. This type of voting is different from its retrospective counterpart in that the choice that voters make is based on their assessment of the future, and not the past, on the promise of government, and not its performance. Prospective rationality means basically that people weigh the policy promises of the different parties and choose the package that, in their judgment, will best satisfy their own interests and goals. There seem to be two logics underpinning the often implicit assumption that personality-based voting is incompatible with prospective rationality. The first is that voting of this kind is the preserve of gullible voters whose perceptions are easily shaped and reshaped by television and the uses to which it is put by the professional image-makers who are part and parcel of modern-day election campaigns. The second is that policy, or issue, promises are superior to personalities in democratic decision-making. Each of these logics will now be examined in some detail.

At least in Britain, real concern about personality as the criterion of voting choice seems to have crystallized in the 1960s around a number of developments. The first of them, as detailed in Chapter 2, was the rapid growth of political television after its hesitant, almost apologetic emergence in the 1959 election campaign. The second was Harold Wilson's adeptness with this new medium combined with a highly personalized leadership style that was evident from the time he was elected Labour leader in 1963. Finally, there was the often unspoken fear that gullible, 'couch potato' voters addicted to television and inordinately influenced by it were unable to resist the broadcast messages of manipulative, professional image-makers. The ultimate fear was that the party choice of such voters would be determined not by the match between their own and their party's issue promises, but by such trivial, television-induced criteria as liking the look of one or other leader's face or preferring one or the other's lifestyle and family.

In point of fact, the fear that those moved in their vote by leader personality would be gullible and easily manipulated is clearly unfounded. As Chapter 4 has shown, the voters most susceptible to leader effects are not in fact the least politically interested and involved, but are the most qualified, as reflected in the possession of characteristics like being politically knowledgeable, caring which party won the election and reading election literature (see Table 4.9). Moreover, the aspects of the leaders' characters that influence the vote are related to ability to perform well in the job rather than politically irrelevant considerations, like whether they are likeable. As Bean and Mughan (1989: 1176) observe:

> Nor is there much reason to believe that it is the trivial in leaders that appeals to voters. If it were, we would expect the highly personal quality of likability to have had a strong – if not the strongest – effect on voters. As it turns out, however, it is of little importance overall. Instead, perceived effectiveness dominates how voters respond to leaders, and few would deny that this is a key ingredient of successful political leadership ... [4]

The crucial point that needs to be made here is that issue promises depend for their delivery to some extent on the character of the prime minister as government leader so that it is rational for voters to be influenced by their perception of his competence, probity and trustworthiness, as well as by the policy promises he makes. Thus, insofar as the politically interested and involved are most susceptible to leader effects *and* the presidentialism of their electoral response is based on performance-related character traits, their decision to choose a party on the basis of which leader they prefer would seem to be perfectly compatible with a voting calculus that does not trivialize the democratic process, but strengthens it.

Indeed, the stronger democratic credentials of those especially prone to leader effects raise the question of whether choice on the basis of issue promises is indeed a more suitable criterion of voter rationality than choice on the basis of the personalities of the prime ministerial candidates. And, on reflection, the argument that it is proves to be underwhelming in its persuasiveness. Its key assumption is that these promises, having been clearly stated in election manifestos, are fixed reference points against which voters can choose and subsequently judge governmental performance, whereas television allows images of party leaders to be created and recreated in the public mind so that individual voters can be manipulated to make their party choice on the basis of trivial criteria devoid of policy content or assessment of potential performance in office. Party strategists and marketing experts, in other words, can manufacture and 'sell' a misleading image of party leaders through the skilful use of mass communications technology, much as totalitarian leaders, like Hitler, are presumed to have succeeded in doing (Neuman 1991: 23–31).

In this view, the power of television is conceptualized in terms of a simple stimulus–response model; a particular message is broadcast and viewers absorb it slavishly. Almost needless to say, however, this conceptualization vastly underestimates the complexity of political communications in modern democratic societies (Gunther and Mughan 2000). In them, the communications media are characterized by high levels of pluralism and competition so that for every attempt to use one party leader's personal appeal to persuade voters to support his party at the polls, there are countervailing attempts by rival leaders to have them vote differently. For every attempt by strategists to paint their party's leader as competent or caring, the strategists of rival parties counter with claims of her having neither of these qualities or even of being incompetent and uncaring. Voters, in other words, have available to them a huge volume of information about the prime ministerial candidates, some of it laudatory but much of it critical, some of it consistent with their own partisan preferences but much of it not, and some of it direct from the party leaders, but much of it through interpretative 'middlemen' like other politicians, political journalists, family, friends and co-workers.

The point is that voters seem perfectly able to sift this wealth of diverse information and make a choice on the basis of reasoning, means–end criteria.[5] All parties, of course, seek to present their leaders in the best possible light. In the words of a popular song, they 'accentuate the positive, eliminate the negative…'. Competence, trustworthiness, likeability, and caringness are among the desirable qualities that parties strive to have seen in their leaders. As Chapter 3 has demonstrated, however, voters are far from always persuaded. They detect such qualities in the personalities of some leaders, but not others. They can even be sensitive to political context and attribute them to a particular leader in one election campaign, but not another. Recall the very different numbers of voters who perceived Margaret Thatcher to be caring in 1987 compared to 1983. Moreover, and perhaps most importantly, even when seen in the party leader, all positive qualities are not equally important for the behaviour of voters. Effectiveness matters if they are to defect from their partisanship, likeability does not (Bean and Mughan 1989; Jones and Hudson 1996). It should as well. Competence is an important indicator of whether the party leader will make a good prime minister, whether she will be able to run the government and deliver on her promises. Her likeability or otherwise, by contrast, does not have the same direct implications for job performance.

This underestimation of the voter is one important weakness of the 'personalization as voter irrationality' thesis. Perhaps still more damaging to its credibility is its unquestioned assumption that compared to policy, it is somehow irrational and harmful to democracy for voters to be influenced by their evaluations of the party leaders. Personality is presented as a bill of goods 'sold' to a gullible electorate, whereas issues are a fixed set of promises that the same electorate can readily and objectively determine to have been kept or not.

Two points cry out to be made here. First, to the extent that issues are influential, they are not specific election promises independently retrieved from memory by voters who have carefully studied the parties' manifestos. Rather, the topics to which political elites draw attention are generally the issues to which voters respond. In Zaller's (1992: 36) words: '(T)he flow of information in elite discourse determines which considerations are salient (for voters).' In this regard, 'selling' is precisely what parties generally do, and have always done, with issues. Local party activists, party conferences and opinion polls are used to find out which issues exercise the electorate and the parties then craft and recraft their policy promises to maximize their vote by appealing as broadly as possible on these same issues.[6] In so doing, they commonly make promises that they must at least doubt their ability to keep before the next election. Modern examples are a promise of a generous welfare state and low taxes, of low inflation and full employment, and of reduced taxes and a balanced budget. It is not at all clear why unrealistic position-taking of this kind is any less harmful to democracy than appealing on the basis of 'manufactured' leader images. Contrived issue promises can deceive and end up in thwarted expectations for voters, just as contrived leader images can and both are equally good reasons for voting against the sitting government the next time around.

Second, and more pragmatically, if the essence of democracy is that governments seek election on the basis of a set of policy promises, then there has never been much evidence that individual voters base their party choice on these promises. The fact, shown repeatedly, is that few citizens have the political information, memory or even inclination to be able to do so. Indeed, the majority of them have consistently been shown to make their political decisions on the basis of low information and limited involvement and awareness of government and politics. 'Voters have a limited amount of information about politics, a limited knowledge of how government works, and a limited understanding of how governmental actions are connected to consequences of immediate concern to them' (Popkin 1991: 8). But what these same voters do have in abundance is experience in making important decisions on the basis of their judgment of other people. Again, to quote Popkin (1991: 65),

> How do we choose a new baby-sitter for our young children when we must make an emergency trip? How do we choose a nurse for a critically ailing parent who lives at the other end of the continent. We want to hire competent people, but without the time or resources to evaluate their past performance, we must make a judgment based largely on clues to personal character, from a conversation, or from what our friends tell us; will this person do what we would like done? Delegation in such situations involves emotions and values and bonds between people. It involves evaluating empathy and understanding, deciding who shares one's own concerns.

Why, especially for the large majority who are not issue sophisticates, should this calculus be any different in the political realm? Why is it somehow irrational to make a decision in an area of peripheral interest and concern using tried and tested means based on personality assessment, especially when parliamentary political parties encourage this behaviour by making themselves more and more leader-centred in their appeal?

Seen in this light, television can hardly be argued to weaken representative democracy by undermining an issue agreement between party and voter that has never had a strong grounding in reality. Indeed, the reverse argument might well be made – television strengthens democracy. If voters choose to be guided by the party leaders, television is a medium that can enhance the informational base and rationality of their eventual party choice by providing voters with multiple and diverse low-cost opportunities to get to know them, the people with whom they associate and the policies for which they stand. To be sure, some of these opportunities are highly staged for the television cameras, largely under the control of the parties and designed to convey a certain image. Examples are sympathetic PEBs, speeches before friendly audiences, policy pronouncements in appropriate settings on the campaign trail and walkabouts. But others present the prime minsterial candidates in less controlled situations where they have to deal with questions from an audience that is anything but deferential. These questions may arise at a press conference, in interviews with various experienced and sometimes inquisitorial political journalists or even in phone-in shows from members of the public. Under an unrelenting public eye, even seasoned politicians can lose their composure and self-control and show sides of their personalities they might prefer the voting public not to see for fear of adverse effects on its evaluation of them.

The point being made here is that television is a highly complex and pluralistic medium of communication in democratic societies. An important virtue is that it ties leader and party in the public eye and, giving plentiful coverage to the party leaders, ensures that they are seen by viewers from a wide variety of angles and in a wide variety of situations. In so doing, it provides a diversity of relevant information to people accustomed to making judgments about organizations, like schools, banks and political parties, on the basis of personal reaction to their authoritative representatives. This is not to argue, of course, that personality is somehow superior or preferable to policy as a means for people to choose who governs them. It is simply to say that given the way people make important decisions on a day-to-day basis, the personality of the party leaders is not an unreasonable or irrational cue for them when it comes to making a political decision they may not think of as being centrally important to their daily lives.

In sum, even though there may be occasions when voters are influenced in their party choice by politically irrelevant characteristics of party leaders, presidentialism is not by and large synonomous with gullible voters being taken for a ride by unscrupulous politicians and image-makers and a consequent enfeeblement of democratic choice. It is no less rational a way of behaving than voting on the basis of issues and, for better or worse, the personality of the party leaders has become a somewhat more important cue for voters as a whole in recent elections. In the 1980s and 1990s, personality appears to have become an 'information shortcut' (Popkin 1991: ch. 2) that is particularly influential for a British electorate that is not by and large comprised of issue sophisticates, that is unprecedentedly weak in its partisan attachments, and that is increasingly exposed to, and dependent for its political cues on, television.

More generally, this exploration of electoral presidentialization's implications for the rationality of the voting decision, and hence the quality of democracy, is a suitable point at which to end this discussion of the bearing of personalization on some larger issues in the study of parliamentary government and the character of parliamentary democracy. Let it be said one last time that the cumulation of evidence shows that the personalities of the prime ministerial candidates have been a real force, in 1992 a decisive one, in recent British general elections. There is also no reason to believe that electoral presidentialization is a transient phenomenon. It seems to be deeply rooted in a shift in the way political parties choose to communicate with voters in modern democratic election campaigns, presidential or parliamentary. As long as the technology of communication does not change profoundly, there is no reason why prime ministerial candidates should not remain the same important means by which the political parties project themselves to the electorate in an effort to shape its political perceptions and behaviour. The task now facing political analysts is not to establish that this relationship exists or instinctively to lament and condemn its existence. Rather, it is to forge a better understanding of, first, its nature, second, how, and with what effects, it is mediated and, third, its consequences for parliamentary and governmental politics on the one hand and the character of parliamentary democracy in Britain and elsewhere on the other.

Notes

1 The Presidentialization Debate

1. While it may be its central characteristic, the construction and conduct of the election campaign around the party leaders is only one aspect of a syndrome that might be called the 'new' campaigning in modern elections. Other aspects of this syndrome are: (i) campaigns are increasingly centralized and national in scope, with battle lines being drawn between the contending party leaders; (ii) professional advisors or consultants are increasingly used to provide advice in specialist areas like marketing and the leader's presentation of self; (iii) professionals in other areas have adapted their skills and talents to suit the electoral market. This is especially apparent in the area of opinion poll research. In the past, campaign strategists would have relied on volunteer party workers, party spokesmen, and the like to provide them with feedback on how the campaign was progressing. Increasingly, this feedback is being provided by scientific opinion polls (see, for example, Bowler and Farrell 1992).
2. It is worth noting that for the first time ever there was serious consideration of staging debates between the leaders of the British Conservative and Labour parties during the 1997 election campaign (Butler and Kavanagh 1997: 85–9).
3. Similar sentiments are evident in a book written by the former Labour prime minister, Harold Wilson. He simply refuses to entertain the possibility of convergence between the parliamentary and presidential forms of government (Wilson 1976: 169–90).
4. Much of the presidentialization debate is frustrating because the participants in it, starting with dissimilar definitional frameworks, talk past each other. Foley (1993: 119) observes astutely of opponents of the presidential analogy: 'They can overstate their case by denying (it) in one respect, or even in several respects, solely on the ground that it is not a valid comparison in all possible respects.'
5. It is an empirical statement to say that parliamentary elections are contests between parties. Individuals and non-party collectivities can perfectly legally contest elections as long as they satisfy the minimum requirements of the electoral law. The truth of the matter, though, is that political parties have emerged as by far the most important vehicle for aggregating voters' demands and interests on the one hand and organizing governments on the other. Democracy, at least as we know it, is inconceivable without political parties. 'While the study of politics may be approached through other processes besides political parties, notably the judicial or the administrative, the growth and evolution of democracy and rule by public opinion has been uniquely connected with the rise of party government since the seventeenth century' (Leiserson 1967: 34).
6. In his thoughtful essay on the concept of party government, Katz (1986: 55) confirms party government's close links with parliamentarism. 'Party

government is more likely in parliamentary systems because party is more useful to leaders in such systems... Party is a device by means of which stable majorities may be achieved... Presidential government, on the other hand, both makes personalism more likely and entails two rival arenas for decision-making.'

7. The term presidential is also often used in a static, constitutional sense to imply institutionalized dissimilarity that does not admit of the possibility of convergence. Thus, a number of parliamentary regimes are presidential in the straightforward sense that they have a president rather than a constitutional monarch as head of state. See Riggs (1988: 248).

8. A still more subtle and dynamic balance between presidentialism and parliamentarism is struck in the 'semi-presidential' constitution of the Fifth French Republic. Constitutional ambiguity and political circumstance have allowed the president to hold the upper hand over the prime minister and cabinet (council of ministers) for most of the republic's existence, but parliamentary supremacy has reasserted itself on occasion (Elgie and Machin 1991). As in the German case, this kind of transition from parliamentary to presidential supremacy is constitutional presidentialization and the circumstances making for it may be of interest to students of this phenomenon. Nonetheless, it is a fundamentally different process of change from, say, the British case because the Fifth Republic's constitution creates a president vested with his own independent powers. 'Pure' parliamentary constitutions, in contrast, do not make provision for a political executive independent of the government so that any increase in the power of party leaders in them is informal.

9. This is not an iron law, however. Political circumstance and individual personality sometimes combined to produce strong, decisive prime ministers even under conditions of factionalism and/or multipartism. Recent examples are Craxi in Italy and Nakasone in Japan.

10. Especially when they have been successful in winning elections, the Conservative party has traditionally been more deferential to its leaders than the Labour party (Beer 1965: 79–102). But, as discussed more fully in Chapter 6, this deference would appear to be eroding. Mrs Thatcher was ejected from the Conservative party leadership in November 1990 despite having a record three consecutive election victories under her belt and a serious challenge was mounted to Mr Major's leadership in July 1995 despite his having steered the party to an unexpected outright election victory some three years earlier. A key element in both these challenges was the fear among backbenchers that the sitting prime minister had become so unpopular as to be likely to lead the party to defeat in the next general election.

11. This line of argument can be criticized for being speculative when it is in principle amenable to empirical testing. The problem is that what is possible in principle is not always feasible in practice. The insuperable barrier to any kind of comparative analysis of presidentialization in parliamentary democracies is the lack of relevant, comparable data collected over time. While cross-sectional studies of leader effects are sometimes possible (see, for example, Graetz and McAllister 1987), to the best that I have been able to determine, no other parliamentary democracy has survey data that allow

a longitudinal study of leader effects comparable to what is possible for Britain. As will become apparent as the analysis in this book proceeds, this is far from saying that the data available for Britain are perfect. Nonetheless, they do afford some systematic insights into stability and change in the role of party leaders in elections in that country over the last three decades.

12. This contrast makes the general point that British heads of government have on average enjoyed long stays in the premiership. There is, of course, great individual variation. The position has in fact been dominated by four individuals since 1945. These are Attlee (75 months in the office), Macmillan (81 months), Wilson (92 months) and Thatcher (129 months). In other words, four of ten prime ministers held the position for just over 60 per cent of the 1945–97 period. This variation is repeated in other countries, like Canada and West Germany, whose premiers have also enjoyed long tenure in the job on average. See Strom (1990: 246–69) for details of prime ministerial turnover in a number of western democracies.

2 Presidentialization of Presentation and Impact

1. This conclusion is the more persuasive for being shared by a number of voting studies conducted in the 1950s in other parliamentary democracies sharing the Westminster model of government. For Australia and New Zealand, see respectively Rawson and Holtzinger (1958) and Mitchell (1962).

2. Something like the same exercise could have been carried out using the Nuffield general election studies since their inception in 1945. This is the usual 'bible' for accounts like this one. From the perspective of this analysis, however, a shortcoming of this series is that it reports events without commenting normatively on them, whereas an important concern of the presidentialization thesis is the normative reaction to the emergence of the politics of personality in general elections. The editorial pages of a leading newspaper, like *The Times*, provide a more suitable mix of interpretative journalism and normative reaction.

3. These figures were provided by the Broadcasting Research Department of the British Broadcasting Corporation in private correspondence. I am most grateful to Robin McGregor for his cooperation.

4. Unlike television coverage, the strict rules governing campaign financing have barely changed over the post-war period. A more complete account of these and other facets of post-war broadcasting is Seymour-Ure (1991).

5. For example, while not figuring prominently in Conservative party political broadcasts, Mr Macmillan's considerable skill at manipulating television to create just the right effect did shine through in other ways. In an interview with me in April 1990, a former Tory cabinet minister who first entered Parliament in 1959 recalled two contrived television images intended to persuade voters of Macmillan's status as a leading world statesman. The first was a broadcast in the company of the US president, Eisenhower, and the second was one of Macmillan standing beside a globe and 'patting [it] affectionately'.

6. I am grateful to Dominic Wring for pointing out to me that the 'talking head' format was the norm, but there were deviations from it. In its single

1951 party election broadcast, for example, Labour had sought to engage viewers by having a dialogue between Hartley Shawcross and Christopher Mayhew. More generally, see Cockerell (1988: 1–95).

7. There is also, of course, radio. This medium is ignored in this analysis for two reasons. First, few British voters use it for political information. Dunleavy and Husbands (1985: 111), for example, found that only 4 per cent of their respondents named it as their most important information source. The matching figures for television and newspapers are 63 and 29 per cent respectively. Second, the surveys used in Chapters 2, 3 and 4 rarely ask questions about radio exposure.

8. Traditionally, 21 days have separated the dissolution of Parliament and polling day. This period was lengthened to 23 days after the October 1974 election, but I have retained the 21-day definition for the sake of continuity. Equally, only the final 21 days of the unusually long 1997 campaign are used in the tables.

9. Matching correlation coefficients for *The Guardian* are 0.29 and −0.07 for the prime minister and opposition leader respectively.

10. The (shadow) cabinet mentions include references to the cabinet collectively and to individual members of it.

11. With a correlation coefficient of 0.29, *The Guardian* also attests to the greater attention paid to prime ministers relative to their parties. There is no similar evidence for the opposition leaders, whose matching correlation is non-existent at −0.07.

12. More explicitly, the data for Figure 2.3 come from Butler and Rose (1965: 170); Butler and King (1967: 130); Butler and Pinto-Duschinsky (1971: 208); and Butler and Kavanagh (1974: 341), (1975: 142), (1980: 209), (1984: 160), (1988: 145), (1993: 169), (1997: 144).

13. A similar trend is apparent in a shorter time series looking at news stories about the party leaders. With the leaders being treated as package, the average number of news stories about them in 1983 was 4.7, a figure that jumped to 9.3 in 1987 and then fell back somewhat to 6.9 in 1992 (Semetko 1991: 177; Semetko et al. 1994: 33). It fell a little further again in 1997 (Norris et al. 1999: 73).

14. Crewe and King admit that their conclusions need to be interpreted 'with a little caution' because of sharp discontinuities in question format and wording in their key party leader measures. Even so, they probably understate the gravity of their methodological problems. Even under the best of conditions leader effects in Britain are weak relative to more enduring influences like partisanship. This weakness makes the estimation of the magnitude of their effects particularly prone to differences in how voter reaction to the party leaders is measured. Crewe and King resort to open-ended leader 'like–dislike' questions for the 1964 and 1970 elections, to leader 'thermometer' questions for the February 1974 and 1979 elections and the summed responses to a number of discrete character trait questions for the 1987 election.

The inescapable problem with such eclecticism is that responses to open-ended and closed-ended questions are not directly comparable. A simple example illustrates their incomparability. The February 1974, October 1974 and 1979 British Election Studies fortunately contain both types of question.

Unlike their 1964–87 predecessors, they do not include open-ended questions targeted at the individual party leaders. They do, however, include an open-ended question for each party and its leader is one of the categories of response. These three surveys also have closed-ended thermometer questions tapping affect for the party leaders. When separate regression equations are run for each type of party leader measure (plus party identification and a range of common issue questions), the open-ended questions produce no significant leader effects, whereas the closed-ended questions yield highly significant coefficients.

15. The data are merged files of individual Gallup quota surveys collected at several points during each campaign and weighted to reflect the party distribution of the vote in each election. The numbers of respondents are 5790 in 1964, 9634 in 1970, 10 517 in February 1974, 9444 in October 1974, 11 334 in 1979, 7708 in 1983 and 10 204 in 1987. Gallup then radically changed the content of its campaign questionnaire in 1992, eliminating a number of the questions I use. The questions were all asked, however, in a survey of 1880 respondents that went into the field immediately after the election and this post-election survey is my data base for that election. This post-election survey was then abandoned in 1997. Other work using one or more of these Gallup surveys includes Franklin and Mughan (1978) and Rose and McAllister (1986; 1990).

16. The exact questions asked in these surveys are: 'Which party has the best policies?'; 'Which party can best handle the most important problems facing the country?'; 'Which party has the best leaders?'; and 'Who would make the best prime minister?'.

17. The correlation between the independent variables in Table 2.4 range between 0.6 and 0.9. Careful examination of the estimates and their standard errors as each was entered sequentially into the regression equation indicated that multicollinearity was not a serious problem. The value of the standard errors did not jump about wildly with the addition of new predictor variables and there was always a significant increase in the equation's R^2 value when the prime ministerial preference variable was forced to enter the equation last.

18. Ordinary least squares regression estimates are presented because they are more easily interpreted than probit or logical regression coefficients and are thus more appropriate for a general audience.

19. To reiterate, in order to put the presidentialization thesis to the stiffest possible test only respondents giving Conservative or Labour responses to the party identification, prime ministerial preference and voting variables are included in the analysis.

20. The precise issues identified in the survey varied somewhat from election to election since not all the same issues were salient in every campaign. Figuring in all four surveys were unemployment, taxation, strikes and law and order. Race relations was covered in 1979, nuclear arms in 1983, inflation and EEC membership in 1979 and 1983, Scottish and Welsh special interests in 1979, 1983 and 1987, international peace in 1983 and 1987 and the National Health Service in 1983, 1997 and 1992.

21. Other such variables can be found in one or more of the surveys, but not all four of them. These include principally level of educational attainment and

home ownership. Including them in the estimation of the equations for the years for which they are available does nothing to alter the conclusions reached in the text on the basis of the more limited range of predictors presented in Table 2.3.

3 Explaining Leader Effects

1. Agenda-setting is not the full extent of the advances in media theory. Priming and framing are variations on the theme of indirect, but still potent, media effects. See Iyengar and Kinder (1987) and Iyengar (1991).
2. The decline of party is more multi-faceted than partisan dealignment alone would indicate. More comprehensive discussions can be found in Finer (1980). My discussion in this chapter, for example, excludes significant organizational changes like declining membership and the drop in the number of full-time agents in the employ of both major parties. See Chapter 5, however, for a brief consideration of Conservative and Labour organizational decline for the pattern of election politics in Britain.
3. Besides movement in and out of abstention, issues are the most widely touted, and investigated, source of short-term fluctuation in the inter-party distribution of the vote. As with party leaders, however, there is disagreement over whether they have become more influential with dealignment. Compare the positive answer of Franklin (1985) with the negative one of Heath et al. (1991: 32–51).
4. The numbers of respondents is 15 424 in the combined 1964–70 grouping, 39 000 in the 1974–83 grouping and 12 081 in the 1987–92 one. As in the previous analysis, the vote distribution is weighted by election to reflect the actual outcome of that particular contest.
5. It may also be that, as an American heavily involved in the articulation of the Michigan social psychology-based model of voting choice, Stokes brought a fresh perspective to understanding the dynamics of electoral choice in Great Britain.
6. The source of the two sets of popularity measures are given in the discussion of Figure 2.4 and Table 2.2 respectively in the last chapter.
7. It is also to be noted that the wording of the trait questions changed after the 1983 election. In 1983, respondents were simply asked whether they thought, say, Mrs Thatcher to be effective, caring, or whatever. Those replying affirmatively were coded '1' and all other respondents in the survey were coded '0'. In 1987, 1992 and 1997, the format of the question was changed so that respondents were now asked whether a particular party leader was 'caring', 'uncaring', or 'neither or both'. For the sake of continuity with the 1983 format, I coded those replying 'caring' and 'good at getting things done' '1' in 1987, 1992 and 1997 and all other respondents '0'.
8. From 1983 to 1992 inclusive, the character traits questions used in the construction of Tables 3.6 and 3.7 were asked in the cross-section survey. In 1997, responses to the 'caring' question in these tables were taken from the final wave of the 1996–97 panel study. This switch was made necessary by the fact that the trait questions were only asked of the leader of the victorious party in the election, Tony Blair, in the 1997 cross-section.

9. Making use of limited data, this analysis cannot claim to be definitive. Additional aspects of the leaders' personalities are likely to have electoral implications as well. Bean and Mughan (1989), for example, find an explanatory role also for those of 'listening to reason' and 'sticking to principles' as well as the 'caring' and 'effective' traits. But these trait questions were simply not asked in the 1987, 1992 and 1997 BES surveys used in the constructions of Tables 3.6 and 3.7. Given the centrality commonly accorded to leaders being effective (read competent in some studies) and caring, though, there is little reason to doubt that this examination of their effect on the vote over several elections will yield generalizable insights into the dynamics of leader effects in recent British elections.

10. The best source for these opinion poll data is Butler and Butler (1994).

11. Note 7 describes the coding of the positive responses to the trait questions for use in Tables 3.5 and 3.6. For continuity, the procedure established there is continued here. Each trait question is recoded to make two separate variables, with respondents seeing a particular party leader as, say, 'moderate' being coded '1' and all others '0' and, in a separate variable, those seeing her as 'extreme' coded as '1' and all others '0'. This procedure was repeated for the questions asking whether individual party leaders were capable or incapable of strong leadership and looked after one class or all classes.

    In the analysis to follow and in line with the apparent spirit of the surveys, positive character traits are seen to be 'moderate', 'capable of strong leadership' and 'looks after all classes'. Negative traits are 'extreme', 'incapable of strong leadership' and 'looks after one class'. The positive and negative traits are summed separately to create two composite leader evaluation measures, each of which ranges from 0 to 3 in value. The 1987 and 1992 data come from the BES cross-sectional surveys and the 1997 data from the final wave of the 1992–97 BES panel study. The 1987 and 1992 surveys also contain the 'caring/uncaring' item reported in Table 3.6, but its absence for 1997 means that it had to be excluded from the composite evaluation measures for the three elections.

12. The results of this exercise are not included in Table 3.8 because differences in question format make the two sets of findings not directly comparable. To reproduce them in the text could easily be taken to imply otherwise. The complication is that the 1987, 1992 and 1997 mean figures in the table are based on responses to specific closed-ended trait questions, whereas the 1964, 1966 and 1970 figures are based on respondent likes and dislikes that commonly go beyond the personality of the party leader. They include as well, for example, references to his party and its domestic and foreign policy.

    But while direct comparison of responses to the two types of question may be problematic, comparison of the relative incidence of the positive and negative within each type is not. Thus, if the argument is that the negative always predominates in popular perceptions of leaders, it can be expected to do so in the pattern of responses to the open-ended 1964, 1966 and 1970 questions as well as that in the closed-ended 1987, 1992 and 1997 ones.

13. Based on the summation of the first four likes and dislikes of the party leaders, the mean positive score for the sitting prime minister (Alec Douglas-Home) in 1964 is 0.72 and for the opposition leader (Harold Wilson) it is 1.27. The matching negative scores are 0.90 and 0.42 respectively. In 1966 and 1970

the prime minister was Wilson and the leader of the opposition Heath. Their 1966 positive scores are 1.50 and 0.70 respectively and the negative ones 0.59 and 0.90 respectively. By 1970, however, Heath had become slightly more popular than unpopular, with a positive score of 0.81 and a negative one of 0.75. Wilson's fortunes, in contrast, had travelled in the opposite direction in the sense that his negative score (0.69) had closed the gap on his positive score (1.07).

14. It may have been noticed that Table 3.9 is unique in this and the last chapter for not indicating a clear drop in the magnitude of leader effects in 1992 relative to 1987. The essential reason for this anomaly is that the summed traits do not include the caring character trait since it was not available in the 1997 panel wave that is the source of the other trait responses in the table. It was asked in the 1987 and 1992 cross-section surveys used in Table 3.9, however, and when included in the summed traits, the drop in leader effects in 1992 is more obvious. The PRE coefficients for the positive traits in 1987 are 0.16 and 0.09 for the prime minister and opposition leader respectively. The matching figures for 1992 are 0.11 and 0.05 respectively. The same pattern characterizes the summed negative traits. In 1987, the PRE coefficients are 0.18 for the prime minister and 0.07 for the opposition leader. The matching figures in 1992 are 0.10 and 0.04 respectively.

15. The same conclusion follows from entering the four sets of summed leader evaluations into a multiple regression equation along with party identification. In 1987, the two top-ranked predictors among these evaluations by some margin are negative responses to Kinnock and Thatcher. In 1992, by contrast, the two top-ranked predictors are positive responses to Major and Kinnock respectively.

16. Again, the 1964, 1966 and 1970 figures are not included in the table in the text because they are not directly comparable with the figures in the table. For information, though, the bivariate R^2 relationship in 1964 is 0.90. Controlling for positive evaluations of both party leaders reduces this figure to 0.85 and for negative evaluations to 0.87. The same figures for 1966 are 0.91, 0.85 and 0.86 respectively. For 1970, they are 0.88, 0.80 and 0.84.

    Albeit with caution, it is also worth noting that a comparison of these 1964–70 figures with those in Table 3.9 in the text validates the larger argument of this book to the effect that party leaders are a more substantial electoral force in 1987 and 1992 than they were previously. The mean PRE value for positive evaluations is 0.05 for the aligned elections of the 1960s and 1970, whereas it is substantially higher at 0.09 for the three most recent elections in Table 3.9. With a value of 0.04 for the first group of elections and of 0.08 for the second group, the matching figures for negative evaluations point to a gap of similar magnitude.

17. Confirmation of this interpretation of the contrasting images of the Conservative and Labour leaders in the 1987 and 1992 contests is the changing behaviour of the individual caring/uncaring, looks after one/all classes, extreme/moderate and capable/incapable of strong leadership trait variables that are presented collectively in Table 3.11. When the individual negative and positive traits are entered into a regression equation with party identification, the strongest predictor of the vote in 1987 was the perception of Thatcher as uncaring. Kinnock's inability to provide strong

leadership was not far behind. In 1992, the two leading predictors were the perception of Major as looking after all classes and being moderate.

4 Media and Leader Effects

1. ITN announced prior to the 1992 campaign that it would no longer 'stop-watch' and that the future criterion for inclusion in its newscasts would be the newsworthiness of the story. In practice, however, the air time given to the parties in both 1992 and 1997 closely reflected the distribution of party election broadcasts between them. See Norris et al. (1999: 30–1).
2. There are alternative perspectives and methodologies, of course. See, for example, Dunleavy and Husbands 1985; Newton 1992, who argue for an independent electoral effect for newspaper readership.
3. The analysis in this book focuses on short-term leader effects because establishing and explaining them is its central concern. I recognize, however, that the story could be somewhat different for long-term effects. The same newspaper study, for example, found evidence that 'newspapers did have a little influence over their readers' when change is examined not over the period of the campaign, but between 1987 and 1992 (Curtice and Semetko 1994: 56; see also Harrop 1987).
4. Newspapers appear to be no more successful than television in setting voters' issue agendas (Curtice et al. 1994: 19–22).
5. The scope and rigour of the empirical analysis to come are limited by the paucity of pertinent data, especially in regard to television. The hegemony enjoyed by the minimal effects thesis means that information over time on voters' media exposure, and especially in regard to television, is difficult, even impossible, to come by. Negrine (1989: 207), for example, has lamented generally that '(t)he absence of empirical evidence makes it difficult to substantiate the belief that the media are important influences on voting behaviour'.
6. As in Chapter 3, the figures in Table 4.1 are respectively the summed positive and negative responses to three character traits questions relating to Mr Major's being seen as 'moderate/extreme', 'looking after all classes one class' and his being 'capable/incapable of strong leadership'. It is worth reiterating here that it is not possible to extend this analysis back beyond 1987 since comparable leader evaluation measures are not available before that date. See notes 7 and 10 in Chapter 3.
7. An intriguing hypothesis is that the *Sun* is actually responsible for electoral presidentialization insofar as the pattern of leader effects among this newspaper's readers peak in 1987 and dip in 1992. It is impossible, however, to estimate their magnitude in 1997 since comparison with the previous two elections throws the analyst back on data from the 1992–97 panel study and the small number of *Sun* readers, 95 to be precise, in the 1997 wave all vote according to their party identification. The 1997 cross-section unfortunately does not contain the same character trait questions that its 1987 and 1992 counterparts do.
8. It might be pointed out that the same essential inconclusiveness emerges when voters are broken down into readers and non-readers of newspapers.

In 1987 and 1992, there is little to choose between the two groups in terms of leader effects, although their magnitude is a little higher among reader in both elections. In 1997, the situation reverses and leader effects are clearly greater among non-readers. The precise figures are available from the author on request.

9. The figure for each year comprises respondents who answered 'Yes' one or more times to the question asked separately for each of the three parties. The great majority were influenced by one broadcast only, but a minority (1.1 per cent of all respondents in 1979, 0.7 per cent in 1983 and 1.6 per cent in 1987) claimed to have been influenced by two.

10. The 1992 British Election Study was a particularly rich source of information on television, assessing respondents' exposure to PEBs and party leader interviews, as well to newscasts. In 1997, the cross-section survey dropped the PEB and leader interview questions, changed the wording and format of the newscast questions and asked the trait questions of only the victorious party leader, Labour's Tony Blair. For these reasons, television's implications for the leaders' presidential impact can be investigated at no more than one time point, 1992.

11. These partisan defence mechanisms are usually described in terms of the psychological mechanisms of selective exposure, selective perception and selective retention. They lie at the basis of the explanation of why the media reinforce rather than change opinions and behaviour. See Klapper (1960).

12. Respondents were asked how often they had seen PEBs – never, once, twice or more than twice. Similarly, they were asked how often they had seen Major, Kinnock or Ashdown interviewed on television – never, once, twice or more than twice.

13. On a three-point identification scale where 1 is 'not very strong', 2 is 'fairly strong' and 3 is 'very strong' and following the ordering of the categories in Table 4.3, the mean strength figures are 1.93, 1.89, 2.08 and 2.12 for PEBs and 1.97, 1.91, 2.05 and 2.12 for leader interviews. A one-way analysis of variance showed the differences between the means for each programme to be statistically significant at the 0.01 level.

14. The reader should bear in mind that caringness is not one of the qualities included in the summed measures of leader evaluations used in Tables 4.3 and 4.4.

15. The importance of perceived caringness for Major's electoral impact is also evident when we look at how he fares relative to Kinnock on terrain more favourable, at least in terms of campaign image-building, to the opposition leader, that is, on the 'capable of strong leadership' character trait. Table 4.4 shows the difference between leader effects for the prime minister and opposition leader on the caringness variable to be 0.03, 0.06, 0.09 and 0.03 respectively for non-viewers of no, one, two or more than two PEBs. However, this advantage for the prime minister erodes considerably in the case of the strong leadership variable when the matching differences, still in his favour, are 0.02, 0.03, 0.02 and 0.01 respectively.

16. Applying to viewers and non-viewers of PEBs, the dependent variable in this analysis is coded '0,' '1', '2' and '3'. The question identifications in the 1992 BES cross-section study are: IDSTRNG (Strength of partisanship), V915B (Sex), V915C (Age), HEDQUAL (Education), RRGCLASS (Social class),

V2A (Newspaper reader), V1 (Care which party won), V212 (Talk about politics), V201B (Read election leaflet), V201A (Candidate meeting), POLQUIZ (Political knowledge), V220B (No say in government) and V220C (Government doesn't care). Missing data are deleted pairwise.

17. Cable news broadcasts are ignored because of their small audiences in 1992, which was their first election campaign. The main such broadcaster, Sky, attracted no more than 1.7 per cent of the news audience in the 2.4 million homes that had access to it (Butler and Kavanagh 1992: ch. 8).

18. In 1992 television news programmes, the election was pervasive in news broadcasts, but did not monopolize them. '(T)he election swamped almost everything else for the entire month, absorbing 65 percent of the main bulletins on BBC1 and 59 percent on ITV (against 60 percent and 52 percent respectively in 1987) and 80 percent on Channel 4 (72.5 percent)' (Butler and Kavanagh 1992: 158).

19. The exposure question asked respondents how often they had watched, say, the BBC1 *9 O'Clock News*, the response options being 'never,' 'once a week or less,' '2–3 days a week,' and '4+ days a week'. The attentiveness question (V208) asked respondents how much attention they had paid to the items on politics and the election campaign in the television news. The response options are 'a great deal', 'quite a bit', 'some', 'a little' and 'none'. With regard to the exposure question, the analysis in this chapter focuses on those respondents who watched the single most popular evening news broadcast, the BBC1 *9 O'Clock News*.

20. Those who never watch the 9 o'clock television news are, by definition, excluded from this table since they cannot give an answer to the political attentiveness question. If they were not excluded, there would be empty cells in Table 4.8.

21. This means that 129 respondents are contained in the low effects group, 1150 in the moderate effects one and 187 in the final, high effects category. It was decided to place the respondents falling in the 0.17 cell in Table 4.8 in the medium effects category when an argument can be made just as easily to place them in the high effects grouping. Their precise placement, however, is not of great consequence since it has no implications for the substantive conclusions drawn from Tables 4.9 and 4.10.

22. In response to a 'Yes/no' answer to the question of whether she talks regularly about politics, the respondent is asked how often she sees the first, second and third person whom she talks to about politics. The responses are 'almost every day', 'more than once a week', 'more than once a month' and 'less often'.

5 Scale and Durability of Leader Effects

1. The simulation exercise to follow could envisage any change of leadership. Instead of simply swapping the Conservative and Labour leaders, for example, it could be asked what would have happened if the deputy leader of one or other party had been at the helm. The range of possible simulations is constrained, however, by the fact that the personality trait questions have been asked only of the individuals leading the Conservative, Labour and Liberal parties at the time of the general election.

2. A similar simulation exercise for the 1983 election can be found in Bean and Mughan (1989). None is carried out for 1997 because the election outcome was so one-sided that the results of a simulation would have looked very like those for 1987 presented in the text. For simplicity of presentation and ease of interpretation, the results summarized in Table 5.1 in the text are in fact an abbreviated version of a fuller regression equation controlling on other variables that might potentially influence the party, Conservative or Labour, for which people vote. The full equations are:

	1987	*1992*
	b	*b*
Party Identification	0.76***	0.83***
PM Positive	0.02*	0.04***
PM Negative	−0.04***	0.01
OL Positive	−0.01	−0.01
OL Negative	0.03***	0.02**
Conservative Issues	0.01***	0.00
Labour Issues	−0.01***	−0.01**
Social Class	0.02***	0.00
Home Ownership	0.03**	0.01
Female	−0.02**	−0.00
R^2	0.87	0.89

*$p < 0.05$; **$p < 0.01$; ***$p < 0.001$ (one-tailed test).

The construction of the issue variables in the above table is described in note 3 below. Other social background variables experimented with but not included in the final table include age, education, share ownership and trade union membership.

3. The full table from which the values in Table 5.1 are derived is presented in note 2 above. It contains a number of control variables that may have implications for the magnitude of leader effects, but that, for simplicity, are not presented in the discussion in the text. Prominent among these control variables is respondents' pro-Conservative or pro-Labour issue stance. For the sake of compatibility with recent work, I use the same issue variables as Heath et al. (1991: 32–51) – nationalization/privatization, trade union power, big business power, government spending on welfare, government spending of defence, nuclear weapons policy, race and the Common Market. The matching variables from the 1992 BES cross-section study are: V27 (Common Market membership); V31B (defence spending); V32 (nuclear weapons policy); V45A (nationalization/privatization); V50A (welfare spending); V50E (racial equality); V51A (trade union power); and V51B (big business power). To make the issue variables as alike as possible to the summed character traits of the party leaders, I simply identify the Conservative position on each issue and score those subscribing to it '1'. Others are scored '0'. This exercise is then repeated exactly for the Labour position on each issue. Each respondent thus has two

separate scores of '0' or '1' on each of the eight issues. These scores are then added to give separate summary measures, ranging from 0 to 8, for each party.

4. This exercise, of course, ignores differences between the two elections in the strength of matching regression coefficients. It is unwise to engage in the same kind of simulation exercise using them rather than the distribution of character traits, however. The reason is that these coefficients capture perhaps unique aspects of character that cannot be assumed transferable. Taking the positive traits for Thatcher and Major as an example, the reason why the coefficient is much higher in the case of Major is probably that voters found him a gentler and kinder human being than Thatcher and, in consequence, one by whom it was relatively easy to be persuaded to vote Conservative. Thus, while it seems reasonable to speculate about what would have happened had Major been burdened with Thatcher's negative image, it stretches belief more to ask what would have happened had he been of her gender and had her manner, style, demeanour, character, and so on.

5. It should be noted here that the estimates arrived at here are the product of an estimation procedure with its own implicit assumptions. Other estimation procedures, with different underlying assumptions, will likely produce estimates of different magnitude. An example is Jones and Hudson (1996). What is important to recognize, however, is that these different estimation procedures do not produce contrasting conclusions about the electoral importance of prime ministerial candidates. In another study focusing, on John Major, for example, Jones and Hudson (1996: 243) conclude similarly: '(I)t would appear that some (though not all) of the perceived personality traits of a prime minister exert a relatively important impact on voting intentions.' Jones and Hudson are not able to comment on Major's contribution to the outcome of either the 1992 or 1997 general election because they use opinion poll data collected by Gallup between the two elections.

6. This is a narrow definition of issue voting, of course. Such voting can also take place when issue preferences reinforce partisanship and thereby discourage the voting defection that would have otherwise taken place.

7. I was unable to use the issues enumerated in note 3 above because there were rarely questions asking for both individual and party placement on them in either the 1987 or 1992 survey. The four issues that do have the appropriate questions and that do figure in both surveys are phrased in trade-off terms and they involve unemployment vs inflation, taxing vs spending, nationalization of industry vs privatization, and greater or lesser effort to equalize incomes. For each issue, respondents are presented with an 11-point scale and asked to place themselves, the Conservative party and the Labour party on it. I collapsed these answers into a series of dummy variables, with 1 to 5 categorized as pro-Labour answers and 7 to 11 as pro-Conservative. In the case of a respondent giving a pro-Labour answer, points 6 through 11 on the scale were scored 0 and when the answer was pro-Conservative points 1 through 6 were scored 0. Because of the indeterminacy of their responses, voters placing themselves or the parties at the midpoint of the scale, that is, at point 6 on the scales, were always placed in the 0 category. The issue questions are numbered, V28, V29, V34 and V35 in the 1987 BES cross-section and VA35, VA36, VA37 and VA38 in its 1992 counterpart.

These four issue questions also figure in the 1997 BES cross-section survey, but the leader traits questions are asked only of Tony Blair, and not the Conservative leader, John Major. This absence of leader trait questions meant that the analysis in Table 5.3 could not be replicated for the 1997 contest.

8. It is perfectly possible, of course, to modify Table 5.3 to take the form of a simulation exercise asking how the two parties' share of the vote would have changed had they enjoyed different patterns of advantage and disadvantage on the distribution of both leader evaluations and issue preferences. This is not the purpose of this exercise, however. Rather, in keeping with conventional discussions of short-term influences on the vote, it is designed to answer the simple question of whether it is issues or candidates that have the stronger direct impact.

9. The picture would appear to be different in the 1960s in that a PRE analysis produces R^2 reduction coefficients of 0.05 for positive leader evaluations, 0.03 for negative ones and 0.04 for issues. The matching figures in 1966 are 0.06, 0.05 and 0.04 respectively. This smaller difference between issue and leader effects in the earlier period constitutes yet further evidence of presidential change in the 1980s and 1990s. It also suggests that issues today might be no more important than they were two or three decades ago (see also Heath et al. 1991: 32–51).

10. These figures were made available to me in private correspondence from the BBC's Broadcasting Research Department. I am grateful to Robin McGregor for his help.

11. Television offerings as well, of course, are becoming more plentiful and diverse. Channel 5 has been introduced since 1992 and Britain is on the edge of a boom in cable and satellite broadcasting. Indeed, *The Economist* (6–12 May 1995: 56) predicted that cable and satellite will claim some 15 per cent of the total television audience by 2003 and Channel 5 about 6 per cent. The political ramifications of these developments are not altogether clear at this point. The political importance and effect of television could be intensified. Alternatively, however, it could be moderated as viewers take the opportunity increasingly available to them to meander from channel to channel avoiding political programmes in favour of less demanding fare like quiz shows, soap operas, films, and the like. Sky television certainly offered a more entertainment-based form of political programming in its debut 1992 campaign. Not only did the campaign feature less often in its news broadcasts than those of the other channels, but also even when the campaign was featured substantially more attention was paid to the spectacle of the race than to substantive issues (Stanyer and Nossiter 1993; but see Goddard et al. 1998 for the 1997 campaign on television).

12. In a similar vein, a Labour MP, Peter Hain, opposed Blair's efforts to modernize the Labour party in the mid-1990s because he saw it as 'destroying the activist base and creating an "empty shell of a party"' Quoted in Sopel (1995: 278–9). Five years later, Mr Hain is a prominent minister in the Foreign Office.

13. While it does not loom large in academic accounts of the electoral process, other political observers seem not to doubt the importance of a leader's image for voters. Commenting on John Major some two years after his 1992

election success, *The Economist* (9 April 1994: 64) observed: 'Across the nation, people seem bored by his tuneless voice and mundane appearance. Such superficial considerations should not, of course, matter. But they do. Looks and lilt can kill.' Politicians are no less sensitive to the importance of appearance for the top job. In the same *Economist* article, mention is also made of Robin Cook, 'the cleverest Labour performer in parliament, (who) has touchingly confessed that he is "too ugly" ever to be prime minister. Indeed, it cannot help if you look like an angry garden gnome with a beard – and red hair'. Mr Cook became British Foreign Secretary after Labour's victory in 1997.

6 Conclusion

1. This indeterminacy is probably an important reason why the prime ministerial power debate has been described as 'one of the most sterile of controversies of the last decade' (Walkland 1978: 241).
2. Another example of this neglect of the prime minister's public standing is James' (1992) recent text entitled *British Cabinet Government*, which does not even entertain the possibility that the mass public may be significant for power relations at the highest level of British government. Notably absent from the index are entries like 'general elections', 'personal popularity' and 'public opinion polls'.
3. Young's prescience soon became obvious for all to see. Discussing the resignation of cabinet minister Jack Cunningham in October 1999, Watt (1999) comments:

   > Jack Cunningham knew he would have to leave the cabinet before the general election, but Tony Blair's speed in ending his ministerial career caught the veteran Labour fixer by surprise … [Cunningham's] departure from government means that Mr Blair has moved one step further in severing New Labour's links with the last Labour government. Margaret Beckett, the leader of the Commons, is the only Callaghan minister left in cabinet.

4. The conclusions of Bean and Mughan (1989) relate to Michael Foot and Margaret Thatcher as, respectively, Conservative and Labour party leaders in the 1980s. For more or less the same conclusions using a different methodology and looking at Mrs Thatcher's Conservative party successor in the 1990s, John Major, see Jones and Hudson (1996).
5. My conception of the rational voter is heavily influenced by Popkin's book *The Reasoning Voter* (1991). He rejects the notion that voters are ignorant of politics. Rather, they

   > actually do reason about parties, candidates and issues. They have premises, and they use those premises to make inferences from their observations of the world around them. They think about who and what political parties stand for; they think about the meaning of political endorsements; they think about what government can and should do. And the performance of government, parties, and candidates affects their assessments and preferences. (p. 7)

6. This is normal practice, but exceptions do happen, usually for reasons of internal party politics. The Labour party's swing to the left in the late 1970s and early 1980s, for example, resulted in a very radical 1983 election manifesto. One senior Labour party politician described it as 'the longest suicide note in history'.

Bibliography

Barker, Geoffrey. 1984. 'The Future of Democracy', *Melbourne Age*. 20 October.

Bartels, Larry. 1993. 'Messages Received: The Political Impact of Media Exposure', *American Political Science Review*, 87: 267–85.

Bean, Clive. 1993. 'The Electoral Influence of Party Leader Images in Australia and New Zealand', *Comparative Political Studies*, 26: 111–32.

Bean, Clive and Anthony Mughan. 1989. 'Leadership Effects in Parliamentary Elections in Australia and Britain', *American Political Science Review*, 83: 1165–80.

Beer, Samuel H. 1965. *Modern British Politics*. London: Faber.

Benney, Mark, A.P. Gray and R.H. Pear. 1956. *How People Vote*. London: Routledge & Kegan Paul.

Berelson, Bernard R., Paul F. Lazarsfeld and William N. McPhee. 1954. *Voting: a Study of Opinion Formation in a Presidential Campaign*. Chicago: University of Chicago Press.

Blake, Lord. 1975. *The Office of Prime Minister*. Oxford: Oxford University Press.

Blondel, Jean. 1963. *Voters, Parties and Leaders*. Harmondsworth: Penguin.

Boulton, Adam. 1998. 'Television and the 1997 Election Campaign: a View from Sky News', in Ivor Crewe, Brian Gosschalk and John Bartle (eds), *Political Communications: Why Labour Won the General Election of 1997*. London: Frank Cass.

Bowler, Shaun and David Farrell (eds). 1992. *Electoral Strategies and Political Marketing*. London: Macmillan.

Brown, J.A. 1993. 'The Major Effect: Changes in Party Leadership and Party Popularity', *Parliamentary Affairs*, 46: 549–64.

Bruce, Brendan. 1992. *Images of Power: How the Image Makers Shape Our Leaders*. London: Kogan Page.

Budge, Ian and Denis Farlie. 1983. *Explaining and Predicting Elections*. London: Allen & Unwin.

Butler, David. 1952. *The British General Election of 1951*. London: Macmillan.

Butler, David. 1988. 'The 1987 General Election in Historical Perspective', in Robert Skidelsky (ed.), *Thatcherism*, Oxford: Blackwell.

Butler, David. 1989. *British General Elections since 1945*. Oxford: Blackwell.

Butler, David and Gareth Butler. 1994. *British Political Facts, 1900–1994*. London: Macmillan.

Butler, David and Anthony King. 1965. *The British General Election of 1964*. London: Macmillan.

Butler, David and Anthony King. 1967. *The British General Election of 1966*. London: Macmillan.

Butler, David and Dennis Kavanagh. 1974. *The British General Election of February 1974*. London: Macmillan.

Butler, David and Dennis Kavanagh. 1975. *The British General Election of October 1974*. London: Macmillan.

Butler, David and Dennis Kavanagh. 1980. *The British General Election of 1979*. London: Macmillan.

Butler, David and Dennis Kavanagh. 1984. *The British General Election of 1983*. London: Macmillan.

Butler, David and Dennis Kavanagh. 1988. *The British General Election of 1987*. London: Macmillan.

Butler, David and Dennis Kavanagh. 1993. *The British General Election of 1992*. London: Macmillan.

Butler, David and Dennis Kavanagh. 1997. *The British General Election of 1997*. London: Macmillan.

Butler, David and Michael Pinto-Duschinsky. 1971. *The British General Election of 1970*. London: Macmillan.

Butler, David and Austin Ranney (eds). 1992. *Electioneering: a Comparative Study of Continuity and Change*. Oxford: Oxford University Press.

Butler, David and Donald Stokes. 1974. *Political Change in Britain*. 2nd edn. London: Macmillan.

Campbell, Angus, Philip E. Converse, Warren E. Miller and Donald E. Stokes. 1960. *The American Voter*. New York: Wiley.

Campbell, Angus, Philip E. Converse, Warren E. Miller and Donald E. Stokes. 1966. *Elections and the Political Order*. New York: Wiley.

Campbell, Colin. 1980. 'Political Leadership in Canada: Pierre Elliott Trudeau and the Ottawa Model', in Richard Rose and Ezra N. Suleiman (eds), *Presidents and Prime Ministers*. Washington DC: American Enterprise Institute.

Clarke, Harold D. and Marianne C. Stewart. 1995. 'Economic Evaluations, Prime Ministerial Approval and Governing Party Support: Rival Models Reconsidered', *British Journal of Political Science*, 25: 145–70.

Cleveland, Les. 1980. 'The Mass Media', in Howard R. Penniman (ed.), *New Zealand at the Polls: the General Election of 1978*. Washington DC: American Enterprise Institute.

Cockerell, Michael. 1988. *Live From Number 10: the Inside Story of Prime Ministers and Television*. London: Faber & Faber.

Cohan, Alvin, Robert D. McKinlay and Anthony Mughan. 1975. 'The Used Vote and Electoral Outcomes: The Irish General Election of 1973', *British Journal of Political Science*, 5: 363–83.

Cohen, Bernard C. 1963. *The Press and Foreign Policy*. Princeton: Princeton University Press.

Crewe, Ivor. 1984. 'The Electorate: Partisan Dealignment Ten Years On', in Hugh Berrington (ed.), *Change in British Politics*. London: Frank Cass.

Crewe, Ivor and David Denver (eds). 1985. *Electoral Change in Western Democracies*. London: Croom Helm.

Crewe, Ivor and Martin Harrop. 1989. 'Preface', in Ivor Crewe and Martin Harrop (eds), *Political Communications: the General Election Campaign of 1987*. Cambridge: Cambridge University Press.

Crewe, Ivor and Anthony King. 1993. 'Are British Elections Becoming More "Presidential"?', in M. Kent Jennings and Thomas Mann (eds), *Elections at Home and Abroad: Essays in Honor of Warren E. Miller*. Ann Arbor: University of Michigan Press.

Crossman, Richard. 1963. 'Introduction', in Walter Bagehot. *The English Constitution*. London: Fontana.

Curtice, John and Holli Semetko. 1994. 'Does It Matter What the Papers Say?', in Anthony Heath, Roger Jowell and John Curtice with Bridget Taylor (eds), *Labour's Last Chance: The 1992 Election and Beyond*. Aldershot: Dartmouth.

Curtice, John, Anthony Heath and Roger Jowell. 1994. 'Media Influence in Britain'. Paper prepared for delivery at the 1994 Annual Meeting of the American Political Science Association, New York.

Dalton, Russell J. 1996. *Citizen Politics in Western Democracies*. 2nd edn. Chatham, NJ: Chatham House.

Dalton, Russell J., Scott C. Flanagan and Paul Allen Beck (eds). 1984. *Electoral Change in Advanced Industrial Democracies*. Princeton: Princeton University Press.

Day, Barry. 1982. 'The Politics of Communication, Or The Communication of Politics', in Robert M. Worcester and Martin Harrop (eds), *Political Communications' The General Election Campaign of 1979*. London: Allen & Unwin.

Denver, David T. 1989. *Elections and Voting Behaviour in Britain*. London: Philip Alan.

Denver, David T. 1998. 'The Government That Could Do No Right', in Anthony King (ed.), *New Labour Triumphs: Britain at the Polls*. Chatham: Chatham House.

Denver, David T. and Gordon Hands. 1997. *Modern Constituency Electioneering: Local Campaigning in the 1992 General Election*. London: Frank Cass.

Dunleavy, Patrick and Christopher T. Husbands. 1985. *British Democracy at the Crossroads: Voting and Party Competition in the 1980s*. London: George Allen & Unwin.

Dunleavy, Patrick and G.W. Jones, with Jane Burnham, Robert Elgie and Peter Fysh. 1993. 'Leaders, Politics and Institutional Change: The Decline of Prime Ministerial Accountability to the House of Commons, 1868–1990', *British Journal of Political Science*, 23: 267–98.

Eckstein, Harry. 1992. *Regarding Politics: Essays on Theory, Stability, and Change*. Berkeley: University of California Press.

Edwards, George C. III. 1989. *At the Margins: Presidential Leadership of Congress*. New Haven: Yale University Press.

Elgie, Robert and Howard Machin. 1991. 'France: The limits to Prime Ministerial Government in a Semi-presidential System', in George W. Jones (ed.), *Western European Prime Ministers*. London: Frank Cass.

Epstein, Leon D. 1968. 'Parliamentary Government', in *International Encyclopaedia of the Social Sciences*, vol. 11. New York: Macmillan and Free Press.

Finer, Samuel E. 1980. *The Changing British Party System*. Washington DC: American Enterprise Institute.

Foley, Michael. 1993. *The Rise of the British Presidency*. Manchester: University of Manchester Press.

Franklin, Bob. 1994. *Packaging Politics: Political Communications in Britain's Media Democracy*. London: Arnold.

Franklin, Mark. 1985. *The Decline of Class Voting in Britain*. Oxford: Clarendon Press.

Franklin, Mark N., Thomas T. Mackie and Henry Valen (eds). 1992. *Electoral Change: Responses to Evolving Social and Attitudinal Structures in Western Countries*. Cambridge: Cambridge University Press.

Franklin, Mark N. and Anthony Mughan. 1978. 'The Decline of Class Voting in Britain: Problems of Analysis and Interpretation', *American Political Science Review*, 72: 523–34.

Fry, Geoffrey K. 1988. 'Inside Whitehall', in Patrick Dunleavy, Andrew Gamble and Gillian Peele (eds), *Developments in British Politics 2*. rev. edn. London: Macmillan.

Gamble, Andrew. 1994. *Britain in Decline: Economic Policy, Political Strategy and the British State*, 4th edn. New York: St Martin's Press.

Gans, Herbert. 1979. *Deciding What's News: a Study of CBS Evening News, NBC Nightly News, Newsweek, and Time*. New York: Pantheon Books.

Gilmour, Ian. 1969. *The Body Politic*. London: Hutchinson.

Goddard, Peter, Margaret Scammell and Holli A. Semetko. 1998. 'Too Much of a Good Thing? Television in the 1997 Election Campaign', in Ivor Crewe, Brian Gosschalk and John Bartle (eds), *Political Communications: Why Labour Won the General Election of 1997*. London: Frank Cass.

Graetz, Brian and Ian McAllister. 1987. 'Popular Evaluations of Party Leaders in the Anglo-American Democracies', in Harold D. Clarke and Moshe Czudnowski (eds), *Political Elites in Anglo-American Democracies*. DeKalb: Northern Illinois University Press.

Gunter, Barrie and Carmel McLaughlin. 1992. *Television: the Public View*. London: John Libbey.

Gunther, Richard and Anthony Mughan. 1993. 'Political Institutions and Cleavage Management', in R. Kent Weaver and Bert A. Rockman (eds), *Do Institutions Matter?* Washington DC: Brookings.

Gunther, Richard and Anthony Mughan (eds). 2000. *Democracy and the Media: a Comparative Perspective*. New York: Cambridge University Press.

Harrop, Martin. 1987. 'Voters', in Jean Seaton and Ben Pimlott (eds), *The Media in British Politics*. Aldershot: Avebury.

Hart, John. 1991. 'President and Prime Minister: Convergence or Divergence', *Parliamentary Affairs*, 44: 208–25.

Heath, Anthony, Roger Jowell, John Curtice, Geoff Evans, Julia Field and Sharon Witherspoon. 1991. *Understanding Political Change: The British Voter 1964–1987*. Oxford: Pergamon.

Heffernan, Richard. 2000. 'Presidentialization in the United Kingdom: Prime Ministerial Power and Parliamentary Democracy'. Paper prepared for delivery at the 28th Joint Sessions of Workshops of the European Consortium of Political Research, Copenhagen, 14–19 April.

Hine, David and Renato Finocchi. 1991. 'The Italian Prime Minister', in George W. Jones (ed.), *Western European Prime Ministers*. London: Frank Cass.

Hoffmann, Stanley. 1992. 'Heroic Leadership: the Case of Modern France', in Anthony Mughan and Samuel C. Patterson (eds), *Political Leadership in Democratic Societies*. Chicago: Nelson-Hall.

Holme, Richard. 1988. 'Selling the PM', *Contemporary Record*, 1: 23–5.

Huber, John. 1992. 'Restrictive Legislative Procedures in France and the United States', *American Political Science Review*, 86: 675–87.

Iyengar, Shanto. 1991. *Is Anyone Responsible? How Television Frames Political Issues*. Chicago: University of Chicago Press.

Iyengar, Shanto and Donald Kinder. 1987. *News that Matters*. Chicago: University of Chicago Press.

James, Simon. 1992. *British Cabinet Government*. London: Routledge.

Johnson, Nevil. 1983. *State and Government in the Federal Republic of Germany*. 2nd edn. Oxford: Pergamon Press.

Johnston, Richard, André Blais, Henry E. Brady and Jean Crête. 1992. *Letting the People Decide: Dynamics of a Canadian Election*. Stanford: Stanford University Press.

Jones, George W. 1965. 'The Prime Minister's Power', *Parliamentary Affairs*, 18: 167–85.

Jones, George W. 1990. 'Mrs Thatcher and the Power of the PM', *Contemporary Record*, 3: 2–6.

Jones, Philip and John Hudson. 1996. 'The Quality of Political Leadership: a Case Study of John Major', *British Journal of Political Science*, 26: 229–44.

Kaase, Max. 1994. 'Is There Personalization in Politics? Candidates and Voting Behavior in Germany', *International Political Science Review*, 15: 211–30.

Kaid, Lynda Lee and Christina Holtz-Bacha (eds). 1995. *Political Advertising in Western Democracies: Parties and Candidates on Television*. London: Sage.

Katz, Richard S. 1986. 'Party Government: a Rationalistic Conception', in Francis G. Castles and Rudolf Wildenmann (eds), *The Future of Party Government, Volume 1: Visions and Realities of Party Government*. Berlin: de Gruyter.

Kavanagh, Dennis. 1995. *Election Campaigning: the New Marketing of Politics*. Oxford: Blackwell.

Kernell, Samuel. 1977. 'Presidential Popularity and Negative Voting: an Alternative Explanation of the Midterm Congressional Decline of the President's Party', *American Political Science Review*, 71: 44–66.

Key, V.O. 1966. *The Responsible Electorate: Rationality in Presidential Voting, 1936–1960*. New York: Vintage Books.

Kinder, Donald R., Mark D. Peters, Robert P. Abelson and Susan T. Fiske. 1980. 'Presidential Prototypes', *Political Behavior*, 2: 315–37.

King, Anthony (ed.). 1985. *The British Prime Minister*. 2nd edn. London: Macmillan.

Kircheimer, Otto. 1966. 'The Transformation of the Western European Party Systems', in Joseph LaPalombara and Myron Weiner (eds), *Political Parties and Political Development*. Princeton: Princeton University Press.

Klapper, Joseph. 1960. *The Effects of Mass Communications*. New York: Free Press.

Krauss, Ellis S. 2000. 'Japan: News and Politics in a Media-Saturated Democracy', in Richard Gunther and Anthony Mughan (eds), *Democracy and the Media: a Comparative Perspective*. New York: Cambridge University Press.

Krosnick, Jon A. and Laura A. Brannon. 1993. 'The Impact of the Gulf War on the Ingredients of Presidential Evaluations: Multidimensional Effects of Political Involvement', *American Political Science Review*, 87: 963–75.

Lazin, Fred A. 1997. 'Transforming Israeli Democracy Under Stress', in Metin Heper, Ali Kazancigil and Bert A. Rockman (eds), *Institutions and Democratic Statecraft*. Boulder: Westview.

LeDuc, Larry, Richard Niemi and Pippa Norris (eds). 1996. *Comparing Democracies: Elections and Voting in Global Perspective*. London: Sage.

Leiserson, Avery. 1967. 'The Place of Parties in the Study of Politics', in Roy C. Macridis (ed.), *Political Parties: Contemporary Trends and Ideas*. New York: Harper & Row.

Lijphart, Arend. 1984. *Democracies: Patterns of Majoritarian and Consensus Government in Twenty-One Democracies*. New Haven: Yale University Press.

Lijphart, Arend. 1994. 'Presidentialism and Majoritarian Democracy: Theoretical Observations', in Juan J. Linz and Arturo Valenzuela (eds), *The Failure of Presidential Democracy*. Baltimore: Johns Hopkins University Press.

Lijphart, Arend (ed.). 1992. *Parliamentary Versus Presidential Government*. Oxford: Oxford University Press.

Linz, Juan J. 1994. 'Presidential or Parliamentary Democracy: Does it Make a Difference?', in Juan J. Linz and Arturo Valenzuela (eds), *The Failure of Presidential Democracy*. Baltimore: Johns Hopkins University Press.

Linz, Juan J. and Arturo Valenzuela (eds). 1994. *The Failure of Presidential Democracy*. Baltimore: Johns Hopkins University Press.

Lipset, Seymour Martin and Stein Rokkan. 1967. *Party Systems and Voter Alignments*. New York: Free Press.

McGinniss, Joe. 1988. *The Selling of the President*. New York: Viking Penguin.

Mackintosh, John P. 1968. *The British Cabinet*, 2nd edn. London: Methuen.

March, James G. and Johan P. Olsen. 1989. *Rediscovering Institutions: the Organizational Basis of Politics*. New York: Free Press.

Marletti, Carlo and Franca Roncarolo. 2000. 'Media Influence in the Italian Transition From a Consensual to a Majoritarian Democracy', in Richard Gunther and Anthony Mughan (eds), *Democracy and the Media: a Comparative Perspective*. New York: Cambridge University Press.

Massari, Oreste. 1996. 'Italy: a Postwar Transition in Contemporary Perspective', in Geoffrey Pridham and Paul G. Lewis (eds), *Stabilising Fragile Democracies*. London: Routledge.

May, Annabelle and Kathryn Rowan. 1982. *Inside Information: British Government and the Media*. London: Constable.

Von Mettenheim, Kurt. 1997. *Presidential Institutions and Democratic Politics: Comparing Regional and National Contexts*. Baltimore: Johns Hopkins University Press.

Miller, Arthur H., Martin P. Wattenberg and Oksana Malanchuk. 1986. 'Schematic Assessments of Presidential Politics', *American Political Science Review*, 80: 521–40.

Miller, William L. 1991. *Media and Voters*. Oxford: Clarendon Press.

Miller, William L., Harold D. Clarke, Martin Harrop, Lawrence LeDuc and Paul F. Whiteley. 1990. *How Voters Change*. Oxford: Clarendon Press.

Milne, R.S. and H.C. Mackenzie. 1958. *Marginal Seat 1955*. London: Hansard Society for Parliamentary Government.

Mitchell, Austin V. 1962. 'The Voter and the Election: Dunedin Central', in Robert M. Chapman, William K. Jackson and Austin V. Mitchell (eds), *New Zealand Politics in Action: the 1960 General Election*. Oxford: Oxford University Press.

Mughan, Anthony. 1978. 'Electoral Change in Britain: the Campaign Reassessed', *British Journal of Political Science*, 8: 245–53.

Mughan, Anthony. 1986. 'Toward a Political Explanation of Government Vote Losses in Midterm By-Elections', *American Political Science Review*, 80: 761–75.

Mughan, Anthony. 1990. 'Midterm Popularity and Governing Party Dissension in the House of Commons, 1959–79', *Legislative Studies Quarterly*, 15: 341–56.

Mughan, Anthony. 1993. 'Party Leaders and Presidentialism in the 1992 Election: a Post-War Perspective', in David Denver, Pippa Norris, David

Broughton and Colin Rallings (eds), *British Elections and Parties Yearbook 1993*. London: Harvester Wheatsheaf.

Mughan, Anthony. 1995. 'Television and Presidentialism: Australian and U.S. Legislative Elections Compared', *Political Communication*, 12: 327–42.

Mughan, Anthony. 1996. 'Television Can Matter: Bias in the 1992 General Election', in David M. Farrell, David Broughton, David Denver and Justin Fisher (eds), *British Elections and Parties Yearbook 1996*. London: Frank Cass.

Mughan, Anthony and Richard Gunther. 2000. 'The Media in Democratic and Nondemocratic Regimes: a Multilevel Perspective', in Richard Gunther and Anthony Mughan (eds), *Democracy and the Media: a Comparative Perspective*. New York: Cambridge University Press.

Negrine, Ralph. 1989. *Politics and the Mass Media in Britain*. London: Routledge.

Neuman, W. Russell. 1991. *The Future of Mass Audience*. Cambridge: Cambridge University Press.

Newton, Kenneth. 1992. 'Do People Read Everything They Believe in the Papers?: Newspapers and Voters in the 1983 and 1987 Elections', in Ivor Crewe, Pippa Norris, David Denver and David Broughton (eds), *British Elections and Parties Yearbook 1991*. Hemel Hempstead: Harvester Wheatsheaf.

Newton, Kenneth. 1993. 'Caring and Competence: the Long, Long Campaign', in Anthony King (ed.), *Britain at the Polls 1992*. Chatham: Chatham House.

Norris, Pippa, John Curtice, David Sanders, Margaret Scammell and Holli A. Semetko. 1999. *On Message: Communicating the Campaign*. London: Sage.

Norton, Philip. 1998. 'The Conservative Party: "In Office but Not in Power" ', in Anthony King (ed.), *New Labour Triumphs: Britain at the Polls*. Chatham: Chatham House.

O'Shaughnessy, Nicholas. 1990. *The Phenomenon of Political Marketing*. London: Macmillan.

Patterson, Samuel C. and Anthony Mughan (eds). 1999. *Senates: Bicameralism in the Contemporary World*. Columbus: The Ohio State University Press.

Polsby, Nelson W. 1983. *Consequences of Party Reform*. New York: Oxford University Press.

Pomper, Gerald M., with Susan S. Lederman. 1980. *Elections in America: Control and Influence in Democratic Politics*. New York: Longmans.

Popkin, Samuel L. 1991. *The Reasoning Voter: Communication and Persuasion in Presidential Campaigns*. Chicago: University of Chicago Press.

Pryce, Sue. 1997. *Presidentializing the Premiership*. New York: St Martin's Press.

Pulzer, Peter G.J. 1967. *Political Representation and Elections: Parties and Voting in Britain*. London: Allen & Unwin.

Ranney, Austin. 1983. *Channels of Power: the Impact of Television on American Politics*. New York: Basic Books.

Rawson, Donald W. and Susan M. Holtzinger. 1958. *Politics in Eden-Monaro*. Sydney: Heinemann.

Richardson, Bradley and Scott Flanagan. 1984. *Politics in Japan*. Boston: Little Brown.

Riddell, Peter. 1997. 'This Is All Too Good To Last', *The Times*, 29 September.

Riggs, Fred W. 1988. 'The Survival of Presidentialism in America: Para-constitutional Practices', *International Political Science Review*, 9: 247–78.

Rose, Richard. 1974. *The Problem of Party Government*. London: Macmillan.

Rose, Richard. 1980. 'British Government: The Job at the Top', in Richard Rose and Ezra N. Suleiman (eds), *Presidents and Prime Ministers*. Washington DC: American Enterprise Institute.

Rose, Richard. 1988. *The Postmodern President*. Chatham: Chatham House.

Rose, Richard and Ian McAllister. 1986. *Voters Begin to Choose*. London: Sage.

Rose, Richard and Ian McAllister. 1990. *The Loyalties of Voters*. London: Sage.

Rosenbaum, Martin. 1997. *From Soapbox to Soundbite: Party Political Campaigning in Britain Since 1945*. London: Macmillan.

Royed, Terry J., Kevin M. Leyden and Stephen A. Borrelli. 2000. 'Is "Clarity of Responsibility" Important for Economic Voting? Revising Powell and Whitten's Hypothesis', *British Journal of Political Science*, 30.

Sanders, David. 1993. 'Why the Conservative Party Won – Again', in Anthony King (eds), *Britain at the Polls 1992*. Chatham: Chatham House.

Sanders, David and Pippa Norris. 1998. 'Does Negative News Matter? The Effect of Television News on Party Images in the 1997 British General Election', in David Denver, Justin Fisher, Phillip Cowley and Chareles Pattie (eds), *British Elections and Parties Review*. London: Frank Cass.

Särlvik, Bo and Ivor Crewe. 1983. *Decade of Dealignment*. Cambridge: Cambridge University Press.

Scammell, Margaret. 1995. *Designer Politics: How Elections Are Won*. London: Macmillan.

Semetko, Holli. 1991. 'Parties, Leaders and Issues: Images of Britain's Changing Party System in Television News Coverage of the 1983 and 1987 General Election Campaigns', *Political Communication and Persuasion*, 8: 163–81.

Semetko, Holli A., Jay G. Blumler, Micheal Gurevitch, David H. Weaver, with Steve Barkin and G. Cleveland Wilhoit. 1991. *The Formation of Campaign Agendas*. Hillside, NJ: Lawrence Erlbaum.

Semetko, Holli, Margaret Scammell and Tom Nossiter. 1994. 'The Media's Coverage of the Campaign', in Anthony Heath, Roger Jowell and John Curtice (eds), *Labour's Last Chance: The 1992 Election and Beyond*. Aldershot: Dartmouth.

Seyd, Patrick. 1993. 'Labour: The Great Transformation', in Anthony King (ed.), *Britain at the Polls 1992*. Chatham: Chatham House.

Seymour-Ure, Colin. 1991. *The British Press and Broadcasting since 1945*. Oxford: Blackwell.

Seymour-Ure, Colin. 1997. 'Editorial Opinion in the National Press', in Pippa Norris and Neil Gavin (eds), *Britain Votes 1997*. Oxford: Oxford University Press.

Smith, Anthony. 1981. 'Mass Communications', in David Butler, Howard R. Penniman and Austin Ranney (eds), *Democracy at the Polls*. Washington DC: American Enterprise Institute.

Sopkl, Jon. 1995. *Tony Blair: the Modernizer*. London: Michael Joseph.

Stanyer, James and Tom Nossiter. 1993. 'The 1992 British General Election on Satellite Television News', Department of Government, London School of Economics. Unpublished paper.

Stewart, Marianne C. and Harold D. Clarke. 1992. 'The (Un)Importance of Party Leaders: Leader Images and Party Choice in the 1987 British Election', *Journal of Politics*, 54: 447–70.

Strom, Kaare. 1990. *Minority Government and Majority Rule*. Cambridge: Cambridge University Press.

Swanson, David L. and Paolo Mancini (eds). 1996. *Politics, Media and Modern Democracy*. Westport: Praeger.

Trenaman, Joseph and Dennis McQuail. 1961. *Television and the Political Image*. London: Methuen.

Tyler, Rodney. 1987. *Campaign! The Selling of the Prime Minister*. London: Grafton Books.

Verney, Douglas V. 1959. *The Analysis of Political Systems*. London: Routledge & Kegan Paul.

Walkland, S.A. 1978. Review of John Mackintosh's *The British Cabinet*, 3rd edn., in *West European Politics*, 1: 271.

Watt, Nicholas. 1999. 'Cunningham: Fixer Caught in a Fix', *The Guardian*, 12 October.

Wattenberg, Martin P. 1991. *The Rise of Candidate-Centered Politics: Presidential Elections of the 1980's*. Cambridge: Harvard University Press.

Waxman, Chaim I. (ed.). 1969. *The End of Ideology Debate*. New York: Simon & Schuster.

Weaver, R. Kent and Bert A. Rockman (eds). 1993. *Do Institutions Matter?* Washington DC: Brookings.

Webb, Paul. D 1994. 'Party Organizational Change in Britain: the Iron Law of Centralization?', in Richard Katz and Peter Mair (eds), *How Parties Organize*. London: Sage.

Webb, Paul D. 2000. *The Modern British Party System*. London: Sage.

Weller, Patrick. 1985. *First Among Equals: Prime Ministers in Westminster Systems*. London: Allen & Unwin.

Whiteley, Paul. 1997. 'The Conservative Campaign', in Pippa Norris and Neil T. Gavin (eds), *Britain Votes 1997*. Oxford: Oxford University Press.

Wilson, Harold. 1976. *The Governance of Britain*. London: Weidenfeld & Nicolson.

Wober, Mallory. 1989. 'Party Political and Election Broadcasts, 1985–87: Their Perceived Attributes and Impact Upon Viewers', in Ivor Crewe and Martin Harrop (eds), *Political Communications: the General Election Campaign of 1987*. Cambridge: Cambridge University Press.

Wring, Dominic. 1996. 'From Mass Propaganda to Political Marketing: the Transformation of Labour Party Election Campaigning', in Collin Rallings, David Farrell, David Denver and David Broughton (eds), *British Elections and Parties Yearbook 1995*. London: Wheatsheaf.

Young, Hugo. 1991. *One of Us: a Biography of Margaret Thatcher*. London: Macmillan.

Young, Hugo. 1997. 'Amazingly Good So Far', *The Guardian*, 30 December.

Young, Hugo and Ann Sloman. 1986. *The Thatcher Phenomenon*. London: BBC.

Zaller, John R. 1992. *The Nature and Origins of Mass Opinion*. Cambridge: Cambridge University Press.

Index